POST OFFICE CLERK-CARRIER

THE COMPLETE STUDY GUIDE FOR SCORING HIGH

POST OFFICE
Clerk–Carrier

UNITED STATES POSTAL SERVICE

BY DAVID R. TURNER, M.S. in Ed.

arco 219 Park Avenue South
New York, N.Y. 10003

Thirteenth Edition (B-3716)
Ninth Printing, 1981

Published by Arco Publishing, Inc.
219 Park Avenue South, New York, N.Y.   10003

Library of Congress Cataloging in Publication Data
Turner, David Reuben, 1915-
   Post office clerk carrier, United States Postal
Service

   1. Postal service--United States--Employees.
2. Postal service--United States--Letter-carriers.
3. Civil service--United States--Examinations.
I. Arco Publishing, New York.   II. Title.

HE6499.T788   1979   383'.145'076   78-23985

IBSN 0-668-04846-8 (Paper Edition)

Printed in the United States of America

CONTENTS

HOW TO USE THIS INDEX
Slightly bend the right-hand edge of the book. This will expose the corresponding Parts which match the index, below.

PART ONE
APPLYING AND STUDYING
FOR YOUR EXAM

PART

1

2

3

4

5

6

...continued on next page

CONTENTS continued

PART

1

2

3

4

5

6

PART TWO
THREE MODEL EXAMS
TO DIRECT YOUR STUDY

CONTENTS

HOW TO USE THIS INDEX
Slightly bend the right-hand edge
of the book. This will expose
the corresponding Parts
which match the index, below.

PART

PART THREE
PRACTICE WITH EXAM SUBJECTS

1

An often-met type of question presented as a series of one page tests. Answer sheets and correct answers appearing with each test help you gauge your ability. Before you begin, to insure understanding, study our analysis of two typical questions.

2

Valuable instruction in training your memory and useful hints for dealing with this special type of exam question. A series of exam-type quizzes gives the practice so essential to doing well with memory questions. Correct answers appear after each test.

3

PART FOUR
PRACTICE WITH SUBJECTS
FROM PREVIOUS EXAMS

4

5

Valuable suggestions for building word power. Basic Letter Combinations: prefixes, suffixes and stems, with illustrative examples. Shows how etymology can improve your vocabulary. A series of exam-type quizzes for self-testing. Each quiz is followed by correct answers.

6

Some helpful hints followed by steps to take and some traps to avoid in developing your ability to comprehend what you read. Reading passages, followed by questions to test your ability. Correct answers.

Reading passages from official sources, similar to those you're likely to get. Carefully selected to probe your ability to read instructions and interpret their meaning.

This challenging type of question tests your ability to see the relationship between elements of a series. Step-by-step analysis of sample questions teaches how to determine the rule that binds the elements together. Test-type quizzes, many with answers explained for further instruction, give practice in selecting the answer that follows the rule.

...continued on next page

CONTENTS continued

PART

1

2

3

4

5

6

PART FIVE
POSTAL INFORMATION

Brief descriptions of the types of work you will be doing. Jobs include culling, batching mail, facing, postmarking, and tying bundles.

How to do the job. Incoming mail & parcel post. Delivery of 'special service' mail. Precancelled stamps on returned parcels. "Mounted" collections and delivery. Operating trucks.

PART SIX
FINAL EXAM

An examination specially constructed to give you a comprehensive and authoritative view of the actual test. An opportunity to employ all you've learned. A situation that closely simulates the real thing.

You'll want to consult this list of Arco publications to order other invaluable career books related to your field. The list also suggests job opportunities and promotions that you might want to go after with an Arco self-tutor.

WHAT THIS BOOK WILL DO FOR YOU

ARCO Publishing, Inc. has followed testing trends and methods ever since the firm was founded in 1937. We specialize in books that prepare people for tests. Based on this experience, we have prepared the best possible book to help *you* score high.

To write this book we carefully analyzed every detail surrounding the forthcoming examination . . .
- the job itself
- official and unofficial announcements concerning the examination
- all the previous examinations, many not available to the public
- related examinations
- technical literature that explains and forecasts the examination

CAN YOU PREPARE YOURSELF FOR YOUR TEST?

You want to pass this test. That's why you bought this book. Used correctly, your "self-tutor" will show you what to expect and will give you a speedy brush-up on the subjects tested in your exam. Some of these are subjects not taught in schools at all. Even if your study time is very limited, you should:

- Become familiar with the type of examination you will have.
- Improve your general examination-taking skill.
- Improve your skill in analyzing and answering questions involving reasoning, judgment, comparison, and evaluation.

- Improve your speed and skill in reading and understanding what you read—an important part of your ability to learn and an important part of most tests.

This book will tell you exactly what to study by presenting in full every type of question you will get on the actual test.

This book will help you find your weaknesses. Once you know what subjects you're weak in you can get right to work and concentrate on those areas. This kind of selective study yields maximum test results.

This book will give you the *feel* of the exam. Almost all our sample and practice questions are taken from actual previous exams. On the day of the exam you'll see how closely this book follows the format of the real test.

This book will give you confidence *now*, while you are preparing for the test. It will build your self-confidence as you proceed and will prevent the kind of test anxiety that causes low test scores.

This book stresses the multiple-choice type of question because that's the kind you'll have on your test. You must not be satisfied with merely knowing the correct answer for each question. You must find out why the other choices are incorrect. This will help you remember a lot you thought you had forgotten.

After testing yourself, you may find that you are weak in a particular area. You should concentrate on improving your skills by using the specific practice sections in this book that apply to you.

THE KIND OF WORK YOU MAY BE DOING

This chapter provides essential information about the field in which you will be working. It gives you facts and figures concerning your chosen specialty and points up how desirable and interesting your job can be. When you know more about your job, you'll be more inclined to struggle and study for it.

POSTAL CLERKS

People are most familiar with the window clerk who sits behind the counter in post office lobbies selling stamps or accepting parcel post. However, the majority of postal clerks are distribution clerks who sort incoming and outgoing mail in workrooms. Only in a small post office does a clerk do both kinds of work.

When mail arrives at the post office it is dumped on long tables where distribution clerks and mail handlers separate it into groups of letters, parcel post, and magazines and newspapers. Clerks feed letters into stamp-canceling machines and cancel the rest by hand. The mail is then taken to other sections of the post office to be sorted by destination. Clerks first separate the mail into primary destination categories: mail for the local area, for each nearby State, for groups of distant States, and for some of the largest cities. This primary distribution is followed by one or more secondary distributions. For example, local mail is combined with mail coming in from other cities, and sorted according to street and number. In post offices with electronic mail-sorting machines, clerks simply push a but-

ton corresponding to the letter's destination, and the letter drops into the proper slot.

The clerks at post office windows provide a variety of services in addition to selling stamps and money orders. They weigh packages to determine postage and check to see if their size, shape, and condition are satisfactory for mailing. Clerks also register and insure mail and answer questions about postage rates, mailing restrictions, and other postal matters. Occasionally they may help a customer file a claim for a damaged package. In large post offices a window clerk may provide only one or two of these services and called a registry, stamp, or money order clerk.

Training and Advancement

Postal clerks must be at least 18 and pass a **two**-part written exmination. The first part tests reading accuracy by asking the applicant to compare pairs of addresses and indicate which are identical. The second part tests ability to **memorize mail distribution systems**.

Applicants who work with an electronic sorting machine must pass a special examination which includes a machine aptitude test. They must pass a physical examination and may be asked to show that they can lift and handle mail sacks weighing up to 70 pounds.

Applicants should apply at the post office where they wish to work because each post office keeps a separate list of those who have passed the examination. Applicants' names are listed in order of their scores. Five extra points are added to the score of an honorably discharged veteran, and 10 extra points to the score of a veteran wounded in combat or disabled. Disabled veterans who have a compensable, service—connected disability of 10 percent or more are placed at the top of the list. When a vacancy occurs, the appointing officer chooses one of the top three applicants; the rest of the names remain on the list for future appointments.

New clerks are trained on the job. Most clerks begin with simple tasks to learn regional groupings of States, cities, and ZIP codes. To help clerks learn these groups, many post offices offer classroom instruction.

A good memory, good coordination, and the ability to read rapidly and accurately are important.

Distribution clerks work closely with other clerks, frequently under the tension and strain of meeting mailing deadlines. Window clerks must be tactful when dealing with the public, especially when answering questions or receiving complaints.

Postal clerks are classified as casual, part-time flexible, part-time regular, or full-time. Casual workers are hired to help handle the large amounts of mail during the Christmas season. Part-time flexible employees do not have a regular work schedule, but replace absent workers or help with extra work loads as the need arises. Part-time regulars have a set work schedule—for example, 4 hours a day.

Most clerks begin as part-time flexible employees and become full-time workers as vacancies occur. As their seniority increases, they may bid for preferred assignments such as the day shift, a window job, or a higher level nonsupervisory position as stamp supply clerk or claims clerk. The supervisory examination may be taken after 4 to 5 years of service.

Employment Outlook

Employment of postal clerks —who numbered 286,000 in 1972— is expected to grow slowly through the mid-1980's. Most openings will result from the need to replace clerks who retire, die, or transfer to other occupations.

Although the amount of mail post offices handle is expected to grow as both population and the number of businesses grow, modernization of post offices and installation of new equipment will increase the amount of mail each clerk can handle. For example, machines which semiautomatically mark destination codes on envelopes are now being tested. These codes can be read by computer-controlled letter sorter machines which automatically drop each letter into the proper slot for its destination. With this system, clerks read addresses only once, at the time they are coded, instead of several times, as they now do. Eventually this equipment will be installed in all large post offices.

Earnings and Working Conditions

Earnings of postal clerks are related to the size of the post office where they work. Earnings are higher in larger post offices because clerks in these jobs process more regular mail, and more mail requiring special handling, than do clerks in smaller post offices.

Most clerks are at the grade 5 level. Clerks who worked in third- and fourth-class post offices were at the grade 3 level. All clerks who work night shifts receive 10 percent additional pay.

Working conditions of clerks differ according to the specific work assignments and the amount and kind of laborsaving machinery in the post office. In small post offices clerks must carry heavy mail sacks from one part of the building to another, and sort the mail by hand. In large post offices, chutes and conveyors move the mail and much of the sorting is done by machine. In either case, clerks are on their feet most of the time, reaching for sacks of mail, placing packages and bundles into sacks while sorting and walking around the workroom.

Distribution clerks may become bored with the routine of sorting mail unless they enjoy trying to improve their speed and accuracy. They also may have to work at night, because most large post offices process mail around the clock.

A window clerk, on the other hand, has a greater variety of duties, has frequent contact with the public, generally has a less strenuous job, and never has to work a night shift.

Sources of Additional Information

Local post offices and State employment service offices can supply details about entrance examinations and empoyment opportunities for postal clerks.

MAIL CARRIERS

Nature of the Work

Most mail carriers travel planned routes delivering and collecting mail. Carriers start work at the post office early in the morning, where they spend a few hours arranging their mail for delivery, readdressing letters to be forwarded, and taking care of other details.

A carrier typically covers the route on foot, toting a heavy load of mail in a satchel or pushing it in a cart. In outlying suburban areas where houses are far apart, a car or small truck is sometimes needed to deliver mail. Residential carriers cover their routes only once a day, but carriers assigned a business district may make two trips or more. Deliveries are made house-to-house except in large buildings, such as apartments, which have all the mailboxes on the first floor.

Besides making deliveries, carriers collect postage-due and c.o.d. fees and obtain signed receipts for registered and sometimes for insured mail. If a customer is not home the carrier leaves a notice that tells where special mail is being held. Carriers also pick up letters to be mailed.

After completing their routes, carriers return to the post office with mail gathered from street collection boxes and homes. They may separate letters and parcels so that stamps can be canceled easily, and they turn in the receipts and money collected during the day.

Many carriers have more specialized duties than those described above. Some deliver only parcel post. Others collect mail from street boxes and office mail chutes. Rural carriers provide a wide variety of postal services. In addition to delivering and picking up mail, they sell stamps and money orders and accept parcels and letters to be registered or insured.

All carriers answer customers' questions about postal regulations and service and provide change-of-address cards and other postal forms when requested.

Training, Other Qualifications, and Advancement

Mail carriers must be at least 18 and pass a two-part written examination. The first part tests clerical accuracy by asking the applicant to compare pairs of addresses and indicate which are identical. The second part tests ability to memorize mail distribution systems.

Applicants must have a driver's license and pass a road test if the job involves driving. They also must pass a physical examination and may be asked to show that they can lift and handle mail sacks weighing up to 70 pounds. Applicants who have had health conditions that might interfere with work must have a special review to determine their eligibility.

Applicants should apply at the post office where they wish to work because each post office keeps a separate list of those who have passed the examination. Applicants' names are listed in order of their scores. Five extra points are added to the score of an honorably discharged veteran, and 10 extra points to the score of a veteran wounded in combat or disabled. Disabled veterans who have a compensable, service-connected disability of 10 percent or more are placed at the top of the list. When a vacancy occurs, the appointing officer chooses one of the top three applicants; the rest of the names remain on the list to be considered for future openings.

Mail carriers are classified as casual, part-time flexible, part-time regular, or full time. Casual workers are hired to help handle the Christmas mail. Part-time flexible employees do not have a regular work schedule but replace absent workers and help with extra work as the need arises. Part-time regulars have a set work schedule—for example, 4 hours a day.

New carriers are trained on the job. They may begin as part-time flexible city carriers and become regular or full-time carriers in order of seniority as vacancies occur. Advancement possibilities are limited, but carriers can look forward to obtaining preferred routes as city carriers or to obtaining jobs as rural carriers or carrier technicians as their seniority increases. A relatively small number of carriers become supervisors.

Employment Outlook

Employment of mail carriers is expected to change very little through the mid-1980's. Although the amount of mail may increase along with growth in population and business activity, more efficient delivery of mail should limit the need for additional carriers. Most job openings will result from the need to replace experienced carriers who retire, die, or transfer to other occupations. Openings will be concentrated in metropolitan areas.

Working Conditions

A full-time city carrier works an 8-hour day 5 days a week. City carriers who work more than 8 hours a day or 40 hours a week are paid one and one-half times their regular rate of pay for the extra hours. City carriers who work either full or part time receive 10 percent additional pay for work between 6 p.m. and 6 a.m. Rural carriers work either a 5- or 6-day week.

Most carriers begin work early in the morning, in some cases as early as 6 a.m. if they have routes in the business district. Carriers spend most of their time outdoors in all kinds of weather, walking from house to house with their heavy mailbags. Even those who drive must walk when making deliveries, and must lift heavy sacks of parcel post when loading their vehicles.

The job, however, has its advantages. Carriers who begin work early in the morning are through by early afternoon. They are also free to work at their own pace as long as they cover their routes within a certain period of time. Moreover, full-time postal employees have more job security than workers in most other industries.

OCCUPATIONS IN THE POSTAL SERVICE

The U.S. Postal Service handles billions of pieces of mail a year, including letters, magazines, and parcels. Close to a million workers were required to process and deliver this mail. The vast majority of Postal Service jobs are open to workers with 4 years of high school or less. The work is steady. Some of the jobs, such as mail carrier, offer a good deal of personal freedom. Other jobs, however, are more closely supervised and more routine.

Nature and Location of the Industry

Most people are familiar with the duties of the mail carrier and the post office window clerk. Yet few are aware of the many different tasks required in processing mail and of the variety of occupations in the Postal Service.

At all hours of the day and night, a steady stream of letters, packages, magazines, and papers moves through the typical large post office. Mail carriers have collected some of this mail from neighborhood mailboxes; some has been trucked in from surrounding towns or from the airport. When a truck arrives at the post office, mail handlers unload the mail. Postal clerks then sort it according to destination. After being sorted, outgoing mail is loaded into trucks for delivery to the airport or nearby towns. Local mail is left for carriers to deliver the next morning.

To keep buildings and equipment clean and in good working order, the Postal Service employs a variety of service and maintenance workers. Included are janitors, laborers, truck mechanics, electricians, carpenters, and painters. Some workers specialize in repairing machines that process mail.

Postal inspectors audit post offices operations to see that they are run efficiently, that funds are spent properly, and that postal laws and regulations are observed. They also prevent and detect crimes such as theft, forgery, and fraud involving use of the mail.

Postmasters and supervisors are responsible for the day-to-day operation of the post office, for hiring and promoting employees, and for setting up work schedules.

The Postal Service also contracts with private businesses to transport mail. In 1974, there were about 12,500 of these "Star" route contracts. Most " Star" route carriers use trucks to haul mail, but in some remote areas horses or boats are used instead.

Almost 85 percent of all postal workers are in jobs directly related to processing and delivering mail. This group includes postal clerks, mail carriers, mail handlers, and truckdrivers. Postmasters and supervisors make up nearly 10 percent of total employment, and maintenance workers about 4 percent. The remainder includes such workers as postal inspectors, guards, personnel workers, and secretaries.

The Postal Service operates more than 41,000 installations. Most are post offices, but some serve special purposes, such as handling payroll records or supplying equipment.

Although every community receives mail service, employment is concentrated in large metropolitan areas. Post offices in cities such as New York, Chicago, and Los Angeles employ a great number of workers because they not only process huge amounts of mail for their own populations but also serve as mail processing points for the smaller communities that surround them.

Training, Other Qualifications, and Advancement

An applicant for a Postal Service job must pass an examination and meet minimum age requirements. Generally, the minimum age is 18, but a high school graduate may begin work at 16 if the job is not hazardous and does not require use of a motor vehicle. Many Postal Service jobs do not require formal education or special training. Applicants for these jobs are hired on the basis of their examination scores.

Applicants should apply at the post office where they wish to work and take the entrance examination for the job they want. Examinations for most jobs include a written test. A physical examination is required, as well. Applicants for jobs that require strength and stamina are sometimes given a special test. For example, mail handlers must be able to lift mail sacks weighing up to 70 pounds. The names of applicants who pass the examinations are placed on a list in the order of their scores. Separate eligibility lists are maintained for each post office. Five extra points are added to the score of an honorably discharged veteran, and 10 extra points to the score of a veteran wounded in combat or disabled. Disabled veterans who have a compensable, service-connected disability of 10 percent or more are placed at the top of the eligibility list. When a job opens, the appointing officer chooses one of the top three applicants. Others are left on the list so that they can be considered for future openings.

New employees are trained either on the job by supervisors and other experienced employees or in local training centers. Training ranges from a few days to several months, depending on the job. For example, mail handlers and mechanics' helpers can learn their jobs in a relatively short time. Postal inspectors, on the other hand, need months of training.

Postal workers are classified as casual, part-time flexible, part-time regular, or full-time. Casual workers are hired to help handle the large amounts of mail during the Christmas season and for other short-term assignments. Part-time flexible employees do not have a regular work schedule but replace absent workers or help with extra work loads as the need arises. Part-time regulars have a set work schedule—for example, 4 hours a day. Carriers, clerks, and mail handlers may start as part-time flexible workers and move into full-time jobs according to their seniority as vacancies occur.

Advancement opportunities are available for most postal workers because there is a management commitment to provide career development. Also, employees can get preferred assignments, such as the day shift or a more desirable delivery route, as their seniority increases. When an opening occurs, employees may submit written requests, called "bids," for assignment to the vacancy. The bidder who meets the qualifications and has the most seniority gets the job.

In addition, postal workers can advance to better paying positions by learning new skills. Training programs are available for low-skilled workers who wish to become technicians or mechanics.

Applicants for supervisory jobs must pass an examination. Additional requirements for promotion may include training or education, a satisfactory work record, and appropriate personal characteristics such as leadership ability. If the leading candidates are equally qualified, length of service also is considered.

Although opportunities for promotion to supervisory positions in smaller post offices are limited, workers may apply for vacancies in a larger post office and thus increase their chances.

Employment Outlook

Employment in the Postal Service is expected to grow more slowly than the average for all industries through the mid-1980's. Mechanization of mail processing and more efficient delivery should allow the Postal Service to handle increasing amounts of mail without corresponding increases in employment. Nevertheless, thousands of job openings will result as workers retire, die, or transfer to other fields.

Earnings and Working Conditions

Postal Service employees are paid under several separate pay schedules depending upon the duties of the job and the knowledge, experience, or skill required. For example, there are separate schedules for production workers, such as clerks and mail handlers; for rural carriers; for postal managers; and for postal executives. In all pay schedules, except that of executives, employees receive periodic "step" increases up to a specified maximum if their job performance is satisfactory. A distribution of employees in levels 1 through 8, with entrance and maximum salaries, is shown in table 1.

Most mail handlers are at level 4 and most postal clerks and mail carriers are at level 5.

Full-time employees work an 8-hour day 5 days a week. Both full-time and part-time employees who work more than 8 hours a day or 40 hours a week receive overtime pay of one and one-half times their hourly rates.

Postal employees earn 13 days of annual leave (vacation) during each of their first 3 years of service, including prior Federal civilian and military service; 20 days each year for 3 to 15 years of service; and 26 days after 15 years. In addition, they earn 13 days of paid sick leave a year regardless of length of service.

Other benefits include retirement and survivorship annuities, free group life insurance, and optional participation in health insurance programs supported in part by the Postal Service.

Most post office buildings are clean and well lighted, but some of the older ones are not. The Postal Service is in the process of replacing and remodeling its outmoded buildings, and conditions are expected to improve.

Most postal workers are members of unions and are covered by a national agreement between the Postal Service and the unions.

1

PART ONE

Applying and Studying For Your Exam

POST OFFICE CLERK-CARRIER

AN OFFICIAL ANNOUNCEMENT

THE OPPORTUNITY

Applications are now being accepted, and examinations will be given to establish a register of eligibles or to expand the current register of eligibles from which future clerk and carrier vacancies in this Post Office will be filled. All interested persons who meet the requirements described in this announcement are urged to apply.

QUALIFICATION REQUIREMENTS

No experience is required. All applicants will be required to take a written examination designed to test aptitude for learning and performing the duties of the position. The test will consist of 2 parts: (1) Address Checking, (2) Memory for Addresses. The test and completion of the forms will require approximately 1½ hours.

DUTIES

Clerks work indoors. Clerks have to handle sacks of mail weighing as much as 70 pounds. They sort mail and distribute it by using a complicated scheme which must be memorized. Some clerks work at a public counter or window doing such jobs as selling stamps and weighing parcels and are personally responsible for all money and stamps. A clerk may be on his feet all day. He also has to stretch, reach, and throw mail. Assignments to preferred positions, such as window clerks, typist and stenographic positions, etc., are filled by open bid and reassignment of the senior qualified clerk.

Carriers have to collect and deliver mail. Some carriers walk, other carriers drive. Carriers must be out in all kinds of weather. Almost all carriers have to carry mail bags on their shoulders; loads weigh as much as 35 pounds. Carriers sometimes have to load and unload sacks of mail weighing as much as 70 pounds.

The duties of newly appointed Clerks and Carriers are at times interchangeable. As representatives of the Postal Service, they must maintain pleasant and effective public relations with patrons and others, requiring a general familiarity with postal laws, regulations, and procedures commonly used.

Employees may be assigned to work in places exposed to public view. Their appearance influences the general public's confidence and attitude toward the entire Postal Service.

Employees appointed under this standard are therefore expected to maintain neat and proper personal attire and grooming appropriate to conducting public business, including the wearing of a uniform when required.

CARRIER POSITIONS REQUIRING DRIVING

Before eligibles may be appointed to carrier positions which require driving, they must demonstrate a Safe Driving record and must pass the Road Test to show they can safely drive a vehicle of the type used on the job.

Eligibles who fail to qualify in the Road Test will not be given the test again in the same group of hires. Those who fail the test a second time will not again be considered as a result of the same examination for appointment to a position that requires driving.

A valid driver's license from the state in which this post office is located must be presented at the time of appointment. Persons who do not have the license will not be appointed but their names will be restored to the register. They may not again be considered for carrier positions until they have obtained the required driver's license. After hire, individuals must also be able to obtain the required type of Government operator's permit.

PHYSICAL REQUIREMENTS

Applicants must be physically able to perform the duties described elsewhere in this announcement. Any physical condition which would cause the applicant to be a hazard to himself or to others will be disqualifying for appointment.

The distant vision for Clerk and Carrier positions not involving driving duties must test at least 20/30 (Snellen) in one eye, glasses permitted, and applicants generally must be able to hear ordinary conversation with or without a hearing aid, but some clerk positions may be filled by the deaf.

For Carrier positions which require driving, applicants must have at least 20/30 (Snellen) in one eye and 20/50 (Snellen) in the other with or without a corrective device, for unlimited operation of motor vehicles. Hearing must be at least 15/20 with or without a hearing aid.

A physical examination will be required before appointment.

AGE REQUIREMENT

The general age requirement is 18 years or 16 years for high school graduates, except for those for whom age limits are waived. For carrier positions which require driving, applicants must be 18 years of age or over. In general, there is no maximum age limit.

CITIZENSHIP

All applicants must be citizens of or owe allegiance to the United States of America or have been granted permanent resident alien status in the United States.

SALARY

Results from collective bargaining.

CONSIDERATION

Consideration to fill these positions will be made of the highest eligibles on the register who are available.

HOW TO APPLY

Submit application Form 2479-AB to the postmaster of this office or place designated by him.

Opening date for application _____
                                Month   Day   Year

CLOSING DATE FOR APPLICATION _____
                                Month   Day   Year

WRITTEN EXAMINATION

Applicants will be notified of date, time, and place of examination and will be sent sample questions.

POST OFFICE JOBS OFFER

JOB SECURITY	LIBERAL RETIREMENT	CASH FOR SUGGESTIONS
PAID VACATIONS	SICK LEAVE WITH PAY	PROMOTION OPPORTUNITIES
ON THE JOB TRAINING	LOW COST LIFE INSURANCE	PAID HOLIDAYS
	LOW COST HEALTH INSURANCE	

POST OFFICE CLERK-CARRIER

EXAMINATION FORECAST

If you want a preview of your exam, look these questions over carefully. We compiled them from official announcements and various other sources. Practice and study material in this book is geared closely to them. The time and effort you devote to the different parts of this book should be determined by the ease with which you answer the following questions.

Official Sample Questions That Forecast the Test

The test for Clerk-Carrier has two parts. They are:

Part A: Address Checking
> How quickly can you spot whether two addresses are alike or different?

Part B: Memory for Addresses
> How well can you memorize several groups of names and locations?

After you have passed this test, you will be placed on a list of eligibles on the basis of your score. If you are entitled to veterans' preference, you will be given the extra credit. (The higher your score the nearer the top of the list you will be.)

PRACTICE TESTS
How To Use These Practice Tests

On the following pages, you'll find questions just like the ones used in the Postal Service examinations for these jobs in the post office. Each type of question is explained separately. Study the samples and then do the practice tests.

Each practice test is timed.

When you have finished each practice test, go back and check your answers to find out what your score is. Then compare your score with the scale that goes with the test to determine how well you did. This will help you to find out where you need more practice.

Be sure to do the practice questions before you try the Clerk-Carrier examinations.

These tests are exactly like the ones you will have to take in the examinations. The time limit for each part and the types of questions in each part are exactly like they are in the Postal Service examinations.

TEST I. ADDRESS CHECKING

DESCRIPTION OF THE TEST AND SAMPLE QUESTIONS

Every member of the Postal work force is responsible for seeing that every letter reaches the right address. If one worker makes an error in reading an address, it can cause a serious delay in getting the letter to where it is supposed to go.

Can you spot whether or not two addresses are alike or different? It is as easy as that. But how fast can you do it accurately? Look at the sample questions below. Each question consists of a pair of addresses like this—

762 W 18th St   762 W 18th St

   Are they Alike or Different? They are exactly Alike.

9486 Hillsdale Rd   9489 Hillsdale Rd

   Alike or Different? They are Different. Do you see why?

1242 Regal St   1242 Regel St

   Alike or Different?

Remember that this test measures both speed and accuracy. So work as fast as you can without making any mistakes. Have a friend time you while you are working on the practice tests—you may find that you get faster as you become used to this type of question.

Hints for Answering Address-Checking Questions
- Do not spend too much time on any one question.
- The difference may not be noticeable at first, so be sure to check
  —all numbers (are they alike and in the same order or are they different)
  —abbreviations, such as St, Rd, NW, N Y (are they alike or are they different)
  —spellings of street, city, and state names
- Do not get nervous about the time limit. (In the official test no one is expected to do all the questions in the time allowed.)
- Make sure that you have marked the correct box for each question.

Address Checking—Sample Questions

Starting now, if the two addresses are ALIKE darken box A on the Sample Answer Sheet below. If the two addresses are DIFFERENT in any way darken box D. Answer every question.

1 ... 239 Windell Ave   239 Windell Ave
     Alike or Different? Alike. Mark space A for question 1.
2 ... 4667 Edgeworth Rd   4677 Edgeworth Rd
     Alike or Different? Different. Mark space D for question 2.
3 ... 2661 Kennel St SE   2661 Kennel St SW
4 ... 3709 Columbine St   3707 Columbine St
5 ... 969 W 14th St NW   969 W 14th St NW
6 ... 4439 Frederick Pkwy   4439 Frederick Pkwy
7 ... 77 Summers St   77 Summers St
8 ... 828 N Franklin Pl   828 S Franklin Pl

Check your answers with the correct answers. If you have any wrong answers, be sure you see why before you go on.

CONSOLIDATE YOUR KEY ANSWERS HERE

Practice using Answer Sheets. Make ONE mark for each answer. Additional and stray marks may be counted as mistakes. In making corrections erase errors COMPLETELY. Make glossy black marks. To arrive at an accurate estimate of your ability and progress cover the Correct Answers with a sheet of white paper while you are taking this test.

A B C D E	A B C D E	A B C D E	A B C D E	A B C D E	A B C D E	A B C D E	A B C D E
1 ⏐⏐⏐⏐⏐	2 ⏐⏐⏐⏐⏐	3 ⏐⏐⏐⏐⏐	4 ⏐⏐⏐⏐⏐	5 ⏐⏐⏐⏐⏐	6 ⏐⏐⏐⏐⏐	7 ⏐⏐⏐⏐⏐	8 ⏐⏐⏐⏐⏐

CORRECT KEY ANSWERS TO THE PRACTICE QUESTIONS

1.A   2.D   3.D   4.D   5.A   6.A   7.A   8.D

The addresses in the Practice Tests are like the ones you will have to check in the examinations. Work as fast as you can, but be careful because you will lose points for making mistakes. Be sure to take no more than the correct time for each test. Check your answers with the answers at the end of each test.

TEST II. MEMORY FOR ADDRESSES

DESCRIPTION OF THE TEST AND SAMPLE QUESTIONS

This test is part of the Clerk-Carrier examination.

All Clerks in the Post Office have to learn a scheme during their training period. The Clerk uses the scheme to sort the mail to where it is going. He must have a good memory in order to learn the scheme. Carriers also need good memories.

In this test you will be given 25 addresses to remember. The addresses are divided into five groups. Each group of five addresses is in a box such as those below. Each box has a letter—A, B, C, D, or E. You will have to learn which letter goes with each address. You will be given time to study in the examination room. In order to practice for this test, you need to be timed.

While you are doing the practice test, find out what is the best way for you to memorize which letter goes with each address. Some people learn best by studying the addresses in one box; then covering it and seeing whether they can say the addresses to themselves. If they can say them, they then try to learn the next box. If they cannot, they study the names in the first box again; and then try to say the names with the box covered. They do this for all the boxes. Other people learn best by studying across the page. Still others do best by memorizing everything at once. If you do not know your best way, try different ways and see which one is best for you. Do not try to memorize the names by writing them down because you won't be allowed to write them in the official examination.

Hints for Memory for Addresses Test

- Be sure to spend the study period studying.
- Be sure to try to learn which letter goes with each address. It is to your advantage to learn as many as you can.
- Do not spend too much time on any one question.
- Do not get nervous about the time limit. (In the official test no one is expected to do all the questions in the time allowed.)
- If you are not sure of an answer, guess.

NOTE: Be sure to memorize the addresses for the Practice Test, as instructed. In the past, the addresses learned for the Practice Test have been the same addresses used for the actual test.

Sample Questions for Memory for Addresses

In this test you will have five boxes labeled A, B, C, D, and E. Each box contains five addresses. Three of the five are groups of street addresses like 1700–2599 Wood, 8500–8699 Lang, and 6200–6399 James, and two are names of places. They are different in each box.

You will also be given two lists of names. You will have to decide which box each name belongs in. When you are working on the first list, you will have the boxes with the names in front of you. When you are working on the second list, you will not be able to look at the boxes.

The addresses you will use for the Practice Test are given in the boxes below.

A	B	C	D	E
1700–2599 Wood Dushore 8500–8699 Lang Lott 6200–6399 James	2700–3299 Wood Jeriel 8700–9399 Lang Vanna 5700–6199 James	1300–1699 Wood Levering 9400–9499 Lang Ekron 6400–6499 James	3300–3599 Wood Bair 8000–8499 Lang Viborg 5000–5699 James	2600–2699 Wood Danby 9500–9999 Lang Lycan 4700–4999 James

Questions 1 through 5 show the way the questions look. You have to decide in which lettered box (A, B, C, D, or E) the address belongs and then mark that answer on the Sample Answer Sheet on this page.

1. Levering

   This address is in box C. So darken box C on the Sample Answer Sheet.

2. 2700–3299 Wood

   This address is in box B. So darken box B on the Sample Answer Sheet.

3. Vanna

   This address is in box B. So darken box B on the Sample Answer Sheet.
Now, you do questions 4 and 5.

4. 6200–6399 James

5. Bair

CONSOLIDATE YOUR KEY ANSWERS HERE

Practice using Answer Sheets. Make ONE mark for each answer. Additional and stray marks may be counted as mistakes. In making corrections erase errors COMPLETELY. Make glossy black marks. To arrive at an accurate estimate of your ability and progress cover the Correct Answers with a sheet of white paper while you are taking this test.

```
   A B C D E      A B C D E      A B C D E      A B C D E      A B C D E
1 [] [] [] [] []  2 [] [] [] [] []  3 [] [] [] [] []  4 [] [] [] [] []  5 [] [] [] [] []
```

CORRECT ANSWERS TO THE FOREGOING PRACTICE QUESTIONS

Now compare your answers with these Correct Answers to the Practice Questions. If your answers differ from these, go back and study those questions to see where and how you made your mistakes.

1. C   2. B   3. B   4. A   5. D

TECHNIQUES OF
STUDY AND TEST-TAKING

Although a thorough knowledge of the subject matter is the most important factor in succeeding on your exam, the following suggestions could raise your score substantially. These few pointers will give you the strategy employed on tests by those who are most successful in this not-so-mysterious art. It's really quite simple. Do things right . . . right from the beginning. Make these successful methods a habit. Then you'll get the greatest dividends from the time you invest in this book.

PREPARING FOR THE EXAM

1. *Budget your time.* Set aside definite hours each day for concentrated study. Keep to your schedule.

2. *Study alone.* You will concentrate better when you work by yourself. Keep a list of questions you cannot answer and points you are unsure of to talk over with a friend who is preparing for the same exam. Plan to exchange ideas at a joint review session just before the test.

3. *Eliminate distractions.* Disturbances caused by family and neighbor activities (telephone calls, chit-chat, TV programs, etc.) work to your disadvantage. Study in a quiet, private room.

4. *Use the library.* Most colleges and universities have excellent library facilities. Some institutions have special libraries for the various subject areas: physics library, education library, psychology library, etc. Take full advantage of such valuable facilities. The library is free from those distractions that may inhibit your home study. Moreover, research in your subject area is more convenient in a library since it can provide more study material than you have at home.

5. *Answer all the questions in this book.* Don't be satisfied merely with the correct answer to each question. Do additional research on the other choices which are given. You will broaden your background and be more adequately prepared for the "real" exam. It's quite possible that a question on the exam which you are going to take may require you to be familiar with the other choices.

6. *Get the "feel" of the exam.* The sample questions which this book contains will give you that "feel" since they are virtually the same as those you will find on the test.

7. *Take the Sample Tests as "real" tests.* With this attitude, you will derive greater benefit. Put yourself under strict examination conditions. Tolerate no interruptions while you are taking the sample tests. Work steadily. Do not spend too much time on any one question. If a question seems too difficult go to the next one. If time permits, go back to the omitted question.

8. *Tailor your study to the subject matter. Skim or scan.* Don't study everything in the same manner. Obviously, certain areas are more important than others.

9. *Organize yourself.* Make sure that your notes are in good order—valuable time is unnecessarily consumed when you can't find quickly what you are looking for.

10. *Keep physically fit.* You cannot retain information well when you are uncomfortable, headachy, or tense. Physical health promotes mental efficiency.

HOW TO TAKE AN EXAM

1. *Get to the Examination Room about Ten Minutes Ahead of Time.* You'll get a better start when you are accustomed to the room. If the room is too cold, or too warm, or not well ventilated, call these conditions to the attention of the person in charge.

2. *Make Sure that You Read the Instructions Carefully.* In many cases, test-takers lose credits because they misread some important point in the given directions—example: the *incorrect* choice instead of the *correct* choice.

3. *Be Confident.* Statistics conclusively show that high scores are more likely when you are prepared. It is important to know that you are not expected to answer every question correctly. The questions usually have a range of difficulty and differentiate between several levels of skill.

4. *Skip Hard Questions and Go Back Later.* It is a good idea to make a mark on the question sheet next to all questions you cannot answer easily, and to go back to those questions later. First answer the questions you are sure about. Do not

panic if you cannot answer a question. Go on and answer the questions you know. Usually the easier questions are presented at the beginning of the exam and the questions become gradually more difficult.

If you do skip ahead on the exam, be sure to skip ahead also on your answer sheet. A good technique is periodically to check the number of the question on the answer sheet with the number of the question on the test. You should do this every time you decide to skip a question. If you fail to skip the corresponding answer blank for that question, all of your following answers will be wrong.

Each student is stronger in some areas than in others. No one is expected to know all the answers. Do not waste time agonizing over a difficult question because it may keep you from getting to other questions that you can answer correctly.

5. *Guess If You Are Not Sure.* No penalty is given for guessing when these exams are scored. Therefore, it is better to guess than to omit an answer.

6. *Mark the Answer Sheet Clearly.* When you take the examination, you will mark your answers to the multiple-choice questions on a separate answer sheet that will be given to you at the test center. If you have not worked with an answer sheet before, it is in your best interest to become familiar with the procedures involved. Remember, knowing the correct answer is not enough! If you do not mark the sheet correctly, so that it can be machine-scored, you will not get credit for your answers!

In addition to marking answers on the separate answer sheet, you will be asked to give your name and other information, including your social security number. As a precaution bring along your social security number for identification purposes.

Read the directions carefully and follow them exactly. If they ask you to print your name in the boxes provided, write only one letter in each box. If your name is longer than the number of boxes provided, omit the letters that do not fit. Remember, you are writing for a machine; it does not have judgment. It can only record the pencil marks you make on the answer sheet.

Use the answer sheet to record all your answers to questions. Each question, or item, has four or five answer choices labeled (A), (B), (C), (D), (E). You will be asked to choose the letter that stands for the best answer. Then you will be asked to mark your answer by blackening the appropriate space on your answer sheet. Be sure that each space you choose and blacken with your pencil is *completely* blackened. The machine will "read" your answers in terms of spaces blackened. Make sure that only one answer is clearly blackened. If you erase an answer, erase it completely and mark your new answer clearly. The machine will give credit only for clearly marked answers. It does not pause to decide whether you really meant (B) or (C).

Make sure that the number of the question you are being asked on the question sheet corresponds to the number of the question you are answering on the answer sheet. It is a good idea to check the numbers of questions and answers frequently. If you decide to skip a question, but fail to skip the corresponding answer blank for that question, all your answers after that will be wrong.

7. *Read Each Question Carefully.* The exam questions are not designed to trick you through misleading or ambiguous alternative choices. On the other hand, they are not all direct questions of factual information. Some are designed to elicit responses that reveal your ability to reason, or to interpret a fact or idea. It's up to you to read each question carefully, so you know what is being asked. The exam authors have tried to make the questions clear. Do not go astray looking for hidden meanings.

8. *Don't Answer Too Fast.* The multiple-choice questions which you will meet are not superficial exercises. They are designed to test not only your memory but also your understanding and insight. Do not place too much emphasis on speed. The time element is a factor, but it is not all-important. Accuracy should not be sacrificed for speed.

9. *Materials and Conduct at the Test Center.* You need to bring with you to the test center your Admission Form, your social security number, and several No. 2 pencils. Arrive on time as you may not be admitted after testing has begun. Instructions for taking the tests will be read to you by the test supervisor and time will be called when the test is over. If you have questions, you may ask them of the supervisor. Do not give or receive assistance while taking the exams. If you do, you will be asked to turn in all test materials and told to leave the room. You will not be permitted to return and your tests will not be scored.

THE GIST OF TEST STRATEGY

HOW TO BE A MASTER TEST TAKER

- APPROACH THE TEST CONFIDENTLY. TAKE IT CALMLY.

- REMEMBER TO REVIEW, THE WEEK BEFORE THE TEST.

- DON'T "CRAM." BE CAREFUL OF YOUR DIET AND SLEEP. . . . ESPECIALLY AS THE TEST DRAWS NIGH.

- ARRIVE ON TIME . . . AND READY.

- CHOOSE A GOOD SEAT. GET COMFORTABLE AND RELAX.

- BRING THE COMPLETE KIT OF "TOOLS" YOU'LL NEED.

- LISTEN CAREFULLY TO ALL DIRECTIONS.

- APPORTION YOUR TIME INTELLIGENTLY WITH AN "EXAM BUDGET."

- READ ALL DIRECTIONS CAREFULLY. TWICE IF NECESSARY. PAY PARTICULAR ATTENTION TO THE SCORING PLAN.

- LOOK OVER THE WHOLE TEST BEFORE ANSWERING ANY QUESTIONS.

- START RIGHT IN, IF POSSIBLE. STAY WITH IT. USE EVERY SECOND EFFECTIVELY.

- DO THE EASY QUESTIONS FIRST; POSTPONE HARDER QUESTIONS UNTIL LATER.

- DETERMINE THE PATTERN OF THE TEST QUESTIONS. IF IT'S HARD-EASY ETC., ANSWER ACCORDINGLY.

- READ EACH QUESTION CAREFULLY. MAKE SURE YOU UNDERSTAND EACH ONE BEFORE YOU ANSWER. RE-READ, IF NECESSARY.

- THINK! AVOID HURRIED ANSWERS. GUESS INTELLIGENTLY.

- WATCH YOUR WATCH AND "EXAM BUDGET," BUT DO A LITTLE BALANCING OF THE TIME YOU DEVOTE TO EACH QUESTION.

- GET ALL THE HELP YOU CAN FROM "CUE" WORDS.

- REPHRASE DIFFICULT QUESTIONS FOR YOURSELF. WATCH OUT FOR "SPOILERS."

- REFRESH YOURSELF WITH A FEW, WELL-CHOSEN REST PAUSES DURING THE TEST.

- USE CONTROLLED ASSOCIATION TO SEE THE RELATION OF ONE QUESTION TO ANOTHER AND WITH AS MANY IMPORTANT IDEAS AS YOU CAN DEVELOP.

- NOW THAT YOU'RE A "COOL" TEST-TAKER, STAY CALM AND CONFIDENT THROUGHOUT THE TEST. DON'T LET ANYTHING THROW YOU.

- EDIT, CHECK, PROOFREAD YOUR ANSWERS. BE A "BITTER ENDER." STAY WORKING UNTIL THEY MAKE YOU GO.

2

PART TWO

Three Model Exams to Direct Your Study

ANSWER SHEET FOR VERISIMILAR EXAMINATION I.

TEST I. ADDRESS CHECKING

TEST II. MEMORY FOR ADDRESSES

TEAR OUT ALONG THIS LINE AND MARK YOUR ANSWERS AS INSTRUCTED IN THE TEXT

POST OFFICE CLERK-CARRIER

SAMPLE EXAM I

To begin your studies, test yourself now to see how you measure up. This examination is similar to the one you'll get, and is therefore a practical yardstick for charting your progress and planning your course. Adhere strictly to all test instructions. Mark yourself honestly and you'll find where your weaknesses are and where to concentrate your study.

Time allowed for the entire Examination: 1½ Hours

This includes the time for filling out forms as well as for reviewing instructions and trying out practice questions. The actual test time is 11 minutes.

In constructing this Examination we tried to visualize the questions you are *likely* to face on your actual exam. We included those subjects on which they are *probably* going to test you.

Although copies of past exams are not released, we were able to piece together a fairly complete picture of the forthcoming exam.

A principal source of information was our analysis of official announcements going back several years.

Critical comparison of these announcements, particularly the sample questions, revealed the testing trend; foretold the important subjects, and those that are likely to recur.

In making up the Tests we predict for your exam, great care was exercised to prepare questions having just the difficulty level you'll encounter on your exam. Not easier; not harder, but just what you may expect.

The various subjects expected on your exam are represented by separate Tests. Each Test has just about the number of questions you may find on the actual exam. And each Test is timed accordingly.

The questions on each Test are represented exactly on the special Answer Sheet provided. Mark your answers on this sheet. It's just about the way you'll have to do it on the real exam.

Correct answers for all the questions in all the Tests of this Exam appear at the end of the Exam.

Don't cheat yourself by looking at these answers while taking the Exam. They are to be compared with your own answers *after* the time limit is up.

TEST-TAKING TECHNIQUES

The examination sections titled "Address Checking" and "Memory for Addresses" are both timed. Your success in these two parts of the examination will be governed strictly by your use of proper test techniques.

In the section on address checking you will be required to compare two columns of addresses to see if they are exactly alike or different in any way. Even the slightest difference should be noted and appropriately recorded on your answer sheet. A reversal of numbers, a slight change in spelling, an abbreviation in one and not in the other, makes them different. Only if they are exactly alike in all respects are they to be considered alike.

The most effective way of coping with this part of the examination is through the use of your index fingers. Use your left index finger on the left column and use your right index finger on the column on the right hand side of the page. Follow your two index fingers across both addresses to the point of difference, then record your answer promptly. If you find no difference, record your answer appropriately. Do not linger over any one set of answers. Time is important. Checking with your fingers should make it possible for you to detect a difference between two addresses quickly, *if there is one,* otherwise record your answer as "alike" and go on to the next set.

You can assure yourself of a better score on the examination called "Memory for Addresses" by the use of little "tricks" which can vary with each candidate. This section of the examination is truly an evaluation of your ability to memorize addresses. Your skill in this area will be put to work after you're appointed and assigned the duty of sorting mail.

Most people use a variety of techniques to jog their memories in day to day activities. Most of these techniques are implemented through the use of associations. For instance, passing a fruit store may remind you that you need apples. Somebody's mention of a birthday party can send you running to the store for a card for your cousin. The use of associations or "key words" which you must form in your own mind during the period you are given to study the test addresses should form the basis for success on your examination.

However, you should go beyond the technique of association. Your approach should be entirely practical and you should limit your memorization to the absolute minimum.

Turn to page 25, the sample questions for "Memory of Addresses." There are three addresses in each box preceded by a number. Even though each number consists of four digits there is no need to memorize all twenty four digits in each box. You can do the job by memorizing the first two digits in each of the numbers. Therefore for box A you should memorize 17-25, 85-86, 62-63. You need not even memorize the names of the street. You can correctly identify any address on the examination by referring to the numbers. Additionally, there are two streets in each box without numbers. Here is where the association technique comes into operation. Use your own key word, something which will stay with you. For instance in Box A you have Dushore and Lott. Form your own key word, Dulo. Box B, Jeriel and Vanna, your key work is Jeva; Box C, Levering and Ekron, key work, Leek; Box D, Bair and Viborg, key work Bavi; Box E, Danby and Lycan, key word Daly.

Therefore at the termination of your memorization period you should remember the following, Box A, 17-25, 85-86, 62-63 Dulo; Box B, 27-32, 87-93, 57-61 Jeva; Box C, 13-16, 94, 64, Leek; Box D, 33-35, 80-84, 50, 56 Bavi; Box E, 26, 95-99, 47, 49 Daly. With this limited amount of memorization you cannot help but get 100% on this part of the examination, if you move along with a reasonable amount of speed.

The technique we have put to work here is limiting your need to memorize to the absolute minimum amount which will enable you to successfully cope with this part of the examination.

TEST I. ADDRESS CHECKING

TIME: 6 Minutes. 95 Questions.

DIRECTIONS: This is a test of your speed and accuracy in comparing addresses. Blacken the proper space under A in the Answer Sheet if the two addresses are exactly alike in every way. Blacken D if they are not alike in every way.

1 ...	Las Vegas Nev	Las Vegas N Mex
2 ...	New Sarpy La	New Sarpy La
3 ...	Loma Mont	Loma Mont
4 ...	Pitsburg Ohio	Pitsburg Ohio
5 ...	Bloomington Ind	Bloomingdale Ind
6 ...	Eastabuchie Miss	Eastabuchie Minn
7 ...	Newberg Oreg	Newberg Oreg
8 ...	Arco Ga	Atco Ga
9 ...	Orocovis P R	Orocovis P R
10 ...	Bloomingburg Ohio	Bloomingdale Ohio
11 ...	Crumpton Md	Crampton Md
12 ...	Nashville Tenn 37214	Nashville Tenn 37214
13 ...	Charlson N Dak	Charlson N Dak
14 ...	Florence S C	Florence S Dak
15 ...	Burnett Minn	Barnett Minn
16 ...	Lakewood Wash	Lakewood Wash
17 ...	Moodus Conn	Moosup Conn
18 ...	Brighton N Y 11200	Brighton N Y 14600
19 ...	Akiak Alaska	Aniak Alaska
20 ...	Maskell Nebr	Maskell Nebr
21 ...	Gaston S C	Gasden S C
22 ...	Sonora Calif 95370	Sonora Calif 95310
23 ...	Glovergap W Va	Clovergap W Va
24 ...	Fairfax Ala	Fairfield Ala
25 ...	Cubero N Mex	Cubero N Mex
26 ...	Reedsville Wis	Reeseville Wis
27 ...	Ada Ohio	Ava Ohio
28 ...	Cheektowaga N Y 14278	Cheektowaga N Y 14278
29 ...	Cayuga N Y	Cayuta N Y
30 ...	Fruitland Idaho	Fruitland Idaho
31 ...	Cora W Va	Cord W Va
32 ...	Afton Tex	Anton Tex
33 ...	Hamptonville N C	Hamptonville N C
34 ...	Portola Calif 96100	Portola Calif 96100
35 ...	Sonoita Ariz	Sonoita Ariz
36 ...	Dunbarton N H 03300	Dunbarton N H 03300
37 ...	Benson Ill	Benton Ill
38 ...	Portland Oreg 97206	Portland Oreg 97206
39 ...	Flayton N Dak	Flaston N Dak
40 ...	Barnsdall Okla	Barnsdall Okla
41 ...	Irmo S C	Irmo S C
42 ...	East Barnet Vt	East Barnet Vt
43 ...	Ellenburg Center N Y 12900	Ellenburg Depot N Y 12900
44 ...	Helena Mo	Helena Mo
45 ...	Grafton Wis	Granton Wis
46 ...	Columbia N C	Columbus N C
47 ...	Dumont Colo	Dupont Colo

48	McClusky N Dak	McClosky N Dak
49	Sheldon S C	Shelton S C
50	Fredericksburg Iowa	Fredericksburg Iowa
51	Holden Vt	Holton Vt
52	Karlsruhe N Dak	Karlsruhe N Dak
53	East Springfield Pa	West Springfield Pa
54	Villa Prades P R	Villa Prades P R
55	Cadmus Mich	Cadmus Mich
56	New London N H 03200	New London N H 03200
57	Anchorage Alaska 95501	Anchorage Alaska 99501
58	Garciasville Tex 78547	Garciasville Tex 78547
59	Edenton Ohio	Edenton Ohio
60	Vernal Utah	Vernon Utah
61	Tullahassee Okla	Tallahassee Okla
62	Carlton Wash	Carson Wash
63	Tucson Ariz 85721	Tucson Ariz 85751
64	Vermillion S Dak 57069	Vermillion S Dak 57069
65	Oxford N H	Orford N H
66	Evanston Wyo	Evanston Wyo
67	Gonzalez Fla 32560	Gonzalez Fla 32560
68	Clifton Tenn	Clinton Tenn
69	Lindsborg Kans	Lindsborg Kans
70	Greenbush Va	Greenbush Va
71	Paterson N J 07400	Paterson N J 07500
72	Monticello Minn	Monticello Minn
73	Haina Hawaii	Hana Hawaii
74	Barre Mass	Barre Mass
75	Beech Creek Ky 42300	Beech Grove Ky 42300
76	Biddeford Maine 04005	Biddeford Maine 04006
77	Richford N Y	Richland N Y
78	Shamko Oreg 97057	Shaneko Oreg 97057
79	Farmington N Mex	Framington N Mex
80	Goodwell Okla	Goodwell Okla
81	Saginaw Tex	Saginaw Tex
82	Jersey City N J 07323	Jersey City N J 07328
83	Fremont N C	Fremont N C
84	Ottumwa S Dak	Ottumwa S Dak
85	Alasha S Dak	Alaska S Dak
86	Oklahoma City Okla 73106	Oklahoma City Okla 73106
87	Slocum R I	Slocam R I
88	Leesburg Va	Leesburg Va
89	Wilmot Ark	Wilmor Ark
90	Seaford Del 19973	Seaford Del 19973
91	Aldan Pa	Alden Pa
92	Washington D C 20008	Washington D C 20018
93	Wilson Ark	Wilton Ark
94	Fresno Calif 93705	Fresno Calif 93705
95	Clearmont Wyo	Clearmont Wyo

END OF PART

If you finish before the allotted time is up, work on this part only.
When time is up, proceed directly to the next part and do not
return to this part.

PRACTICE FOR MEMORIZING ADDRESSES

MEMORIZING TIME: 5 Minutes

DIRECTIONS: This is a test of memory, speed, and accuracy in which you will be given names, numbers, and addresses to remember. They are divided into five groups, boxed and lettered A, B, C, D, E. For each question, mark the Answer Sheet to show the letter of the box in which the item belongs. If you are not sure of an answer you should guess. Try to remember the box-location of as many items as you can.

A	B	C	D	E
2100–2799 Mall	3900–4399 Mall	4400–4599 Mall	3400–3899 Mall	2800–3399 Mall
Ceres	Cedar	Niles	Cicero	Delhi
4800–4999 Cliff	4000–4299 Cliff	3300–3999 Cliff	4500–4799 Cliff	4300–4499 Cliff
Natoma	Foster	Dexter	Pearl	Magnet
1900–2299 Laurel	2300–2999 Laurel	3200–3799 Laurel	3000–3199 Laurel	1500–1899 Laurel

1. Magnet
2. Niles
3. 1500–1899 Laurel
4. 4000–4299 Cliff
5. 3300–3999 Cliff
6. Cicero
7. Cicero
8. Cedar

SAMPLE ANSWER SHEET

ADDITIONAL MEMORIZING TIME: 3 Minutes

DIRECTIONS: Cover the lettered boxes. Answer as best you can from memory.

9. 3200–3799 Laurel
10. 2100–2799 Mall
11. 1900–2299 Laurel
12. Cedar
13. 4500–4799 Cliff
14. 2100–2799 Mall
15. Foster
16. 4800–4999 Cliff

CORRECT KEY ANSWERS TO THE PRACTICE QUESTIONS

1.E	3.E	5.C	7.D	9.C	11.A	13.D	15.B
2.C	4.B	6.D	8.B	10.A	12.B	14.A	16.A

NOTE: Be sure to memorize the addresses for the Practice Test, as instructed. In the past, the addresses learned for the Practice Test have been the same addresses used for the actual test.

TEST II. MEMORY FOR ADDRESSES

TIME: 5 Minutes. 88 Questions.

DIRECTIONS: Having committed to memory the box-locations in the previous Memorizing test, you must now mark your Answer Sheet for each question to show the letter of the box in which the item belongs. Do not turn back to the lettered boxes in the previous Memorizing test. Answer as best you can from memory.

1. Magnet
2. Niles
3. 3400–3899 Mall
4. 1900–2299 Laurel
5. Cicero
6. Dexter
7. 2300–2999 Laurel
8. 3300–3999 Cliff

9. 3200–3799 Laurel
10. 2100–2799 Mall
11. Pearl
12. 3200–3799 Laurel
13. Ceres
14. 4500–4799 Cliff
15. 3900–4399 Mall
16. Delhi

17. 4300–4499 Cliff
18. 3000–3199 Laurel
19. Ceres
20. Foster
21. Natoma
22. 4400–4599 Mall
23. Cedar
24. 2300–2999 Laurel

25. 1500–1899 Laurel
26. 4000–4299 Cliff
27. Dexter
28. Magnet
29. 3300–3999 Cliff
30. 3400–3899 Mall
31. Niles
32. 2100–2799 Mall

33. 1900–2299 Laurel
34. Cedar
35. Pearl
36. 2800–3399 Mall
37. 4800–4999 Cliff
38. 3900–4399 Mall
39. Foster
40. 3000–3199 Laurel

41. Ceres
42. Niles
43. 3400–3899 Mall
44. Delhi
45. 2300–2999 Laurel
46. 4500–4799 Cliff
47. Dexter
48. Magnet

49. 3300–3999 Cliff
50. Cicero
51. 4300–4499 Cliff
52. 3900–4399 Mall
53. Natoma
54. 3200–3799 Laurel
55. Pearl
56. 4000–4299 Cliff

57. 4500–4799 Cliff
58. 2100–2799 Mall
59. Foster
60. 4400–4599 Mall
61. 4800–4999 Cliff
62. Ceres
63. 2800–3399 Mall
64. 1500–1899 Laurel

65. Natoma
66. 3000–3199 Laurel
67. 4000–4299 Cliff
68. Niles
69. 2300–2999 Laurel
70. Magnet
71. Delhi
72. 4400–4599 Mall

73. Cicero
74. Cedar
75. 2800–3399 Mall
76. 1900–2299 Laurel
77. Dexter
78. Pearl
79. 4300–4499 Cliff
80. 3900–4399 Mall

81. Foster
82. 4800–4999 Cliff
83. Delhi
84. Ceres
85. 1500–1899 Laurel
86. Natoma
87. 2800–3399 Mall
88. Niles

STOP.

If you finish before the time is up, go back and check your answers for the questions on this page. Do not go to any other page until the time is up.

END OF EXAMINATION

CORRECT ANSWERS FOR SAMPLE EXAMINATION I

(Please try to answer the questions on your own before looking at our answers. You'll do much better on your test if you follow this rule.)

TEST I. ADDRESS CHECKING

1.D	13.A	25.A	37.D	49.D	61.D	73.D	85.D
2.A	14.D	26.D	38.A	50.A	62.D	74.A	86.A
3.A	15.D	27.D	39.D	51.D	63.D	75.D	87.D
4.A	16.A	28.A	40.A	52.A	64.A	76.D	88.A
5.D	17.D	29.D	41.A	53.D	65.D	77.D	89.D
6.D	18.D	30.A	42.A	54.A	66.A	78.D	90.A
7.A	19.D	31.D	43.D	55.A	67.A	79.D	91.D
8.D	20.A	32.D	44.A	56.A	68.D	80.A	92.D
9.A	21.D	33.A	45.D	57.D	69.A	81.A	93.D
10.D	22.D	34.A	46.D	58.A	70.A	82.D	94.A
11.D	23.D	35.A	47.D	59.A	71.D	83.A	95.A
12.A	24.D	36.A	48.D	60.D	72.A	84.A	

TEST II. MEMORY FOR ADDRESSES

1.E	12.C	23.B	34.B	45.B	56.B	67.B	78.D
2.C	13.A	24.B	35.D	46.D	57.D	68.C	79.E
3.D	14.D	25.E	36.E	47.C	58.A	69.B	80.B
4.A	15.B	26.B	37.A	48.E	59.B	70.E	81.B
5.D	16.E	27.C	38.B	49.C	60.C	71.E	82.A
6.C	17.E	28.E	39.B	50.D	61.A	72.C	83.E
7.B	18.D	29.C	40.D	51.E	62.A	73.D	84.A
8.C	19.A	30.D	41.A	52.B	63.E	74.B	85.E
9.C	20.B	31.C	42.C	53.A	64.E	75.E	86.A
10.A	21.A	32.A	43.D	54.C	65.A	76.A	87.E
11.D	22.C	33.A	44.E	55.D	66.D	77.C	88.C

HOW TO SCORE THE SAMPLE EXAMINATION

For the Address Checking, count the number that you got right and the number that you got wrong. (If you didn't mark anything for a question, it doesn't get counted.)

From the number right   _____

Subtract the number wrong   ==========

This number (the difference) is your score————————————→ _____

Go back and see where you made your mistakes. Were you careless? Did you work too slowly? In the Memory for Addresses, count the number that you got right and the number that you got wrong. (If you didn't mark anything for a question, it doesn't get counted.)

Divide the number wrong by 4. _____

From the number right   _____

Subtract ¼ the number wrong   ==========

This number (the difference) is your score————————————→ _____

Go back and see where you made your mistakes. Were you careless? Did you work too slowly? Try to find out what is the best way for you to memorize.

POST OFFICE CLERK-CARRIER

SAMPLE EXAM II

This Examination is very much like the one you'll take. It was constructed by professionals who utilized all the latest information available. They derived a series of Tests which neatly cover all the subjects you are likely to encounter on the actual examination. Stick to business; follow all instructions closely; and score yourself objectively. If you do poorly . . . review. If necessary, take this Examination again for comparison.

Time allowed for the entire Examination: 1½ Hours

This includes the time for filling out forms as well as for reviewing instructions and trying out practice questions. The actual test time is 11 minutes.

In order to create the climate of the actual exam, that's exactly what you should allow yourself . . . no more, no less. Use a watch to keep a record of your time, since it might suit your convenience to try this practice exam in several short takes.

ANALYSIS AND TIMETABLE: SAMPLE EXAMINATION II.

This table is both an analysis of the exam that follows and a priceless preview of the actual test. Look it over carefully and use it well. Since it lists both subjects and times, it points up not only what to study, but also how much time to spend on each topic. Making the most of your study time adds valuable points to your examination score.

SUBJECT TESTED	Time Allowed	SUBJECT TESTED	Time Allowed
ADDRESS CHECKING	6 Minutes	MEMORY FOR ADDRESSES	5 Minutes

B3716

ANSWER SHEET FOR VERISIMILAR EXAMINATION II.

Consolidate your key answers here just as you would do on the actual exam. Using this type of Answer Sheet will provide valuable practice. Tear it out along the indicated lines and mark it up correctly. Use a No. 2 (medium) pencil. Make only ONE mark for each answer. Additional and stray marks may be counted as mistakes. In making corrections erase errors COMPLETELY. Make glossy black marks.

TEST I. ADDRESS CHECKING

TEST II. ADDRESS CHECKING

TEST III. MEMORY FOR ADDRESSES

TEST I. ADDRESS CHECKING

TIME: 3 Minutes. 40 Questions.

DIRECTIONS: This is a test of your speed and accuracy in comparing addresses. Blacken the proper space under A in the Answer Sheet if the two addresses are exactly alike in every way. Blacken D if they are not alike in every way.

1	7961 Eastern Ave SE	7961 Eastern Ave SE
2	3809 20th Rd N	3309 20th Rd N
3	Smicksburg Pa	Smithsburg Pa
4	Sherman Conn	Sherman Conn
5	Richland Ga	Richland La
6	8520 Leesburg Pike SE	8520 Leesburg Pike SE
7	Genevia Ark	Geneva Ark
8	104 W Jefferson St	104 W Jefferson St
9	Meandor W Va	Meander W Va
10	6327 W Mari Ct	6327 W Mari Ct
11	3191 Draper Dr SE	3191 Draper Dr SW
12	1415 W Green Spring Rd	1415 W Green Spring Rd
13	Parr Ind	Parr Ind
14	East Falmouth Mass 02536	East Falmouth Miss 02536
15	3016 N St NW	3016 M St NW
16	Yukon Mo	Yukon Mo
17	7057 Brookfield Plaza	7057 Brookfield Plaza
18	Bethel Ohio 45106	Bethel Ohio 45106
19	Littleton N H	Littleton N C
20	8909 Bowie Dr	8909 Bowie Dr
21	Colmar Ill	Colmar Ill
22	784 Matthews Dr NE	784 Matthews Dr NE
23	2923 John Marshall Dr	2932 John Marshall Dr
24	6023 Woodmont Rd	6023 Woodmount Rd
25	Nolan Tex	Noland Tex
26	342 E Lincolnia Rd	342 E Lincolnia Dr
27	Jane Calif	Jane Calif
28	4921 Seminary Rd	4912 Seminary Rd
29	Ulmers S C	Ullmers S C
30	4804 Montgomery Lane SW	4804 Montgomery Lane SW
31	210 E Fairfax Dr	210 W Fairfax Dr
32	Hanapepe Hawaii	Hanapepe Hawaii
33	450 La Calle del Punto	450 La Calle del Punto
34	Walland Tenn 37886	Walland Tenn 37836
35	Villamont Va	Villamont Va
36	4102 Georgia Ave NW	4102 Georgia Rd NW
37	Aroch Oreg	Aroch Oreg
38	6531 N Walton Ave	6531 N Waldon Ave
39	Jeff Ky	Jeff Ky
40	Delphos Iowa	Delphis Iowa

TEST II. ADDRESS CHECKING

TIME: 3 Minutes. 40 Questions.

DIRECTIONS: This is a test of your speed and accuracy in comparing addresses. Blacken the proper space under A in the Answer Sheet if the two addresses are exactly alike in every way. Blacken D if they are not alike in every way.

1	2134 S 20th St	2134 S 20th St
2	4608 N Warnock St	4806 N Warnock St
3	1202 W Girard Dr	1202 W Girard Rd
4	3120 S Harcourt St	3120 S Harcourt St
5	4618 W Addison St	4618 E Addison St
6	Sessums Miss	Sessoms Miss
7	6425 N Delancey	6425 N Delancey
8	5407 Columbia Rd	5407 Columbia Rd
9	2106 Southern Ave	2106 Southern Ave
10	Highfalls N C 27259	Highlands NC 27259
11	2873 Pershing Dr	2873 Pershing Dr
12	1329 N H Ave NW	1329 N J Ave NW
13	1316 N Quinn St	1316 N Quinn St
14	7507 Wyngate Dr	7505 Wyngate Dr
15	2918 Colesville Rd	2918 Colesvale Rd
16	2071 E Belvedere Dr	2071 E Belvedere Dr
17	Palmer Wash	Palmer Mich
18	2106 16th St SW	2106 16th St SW
19	2207 Markland Ave	2207 Markham Ave
20	5345 16th St SW	5345 16th St SE
21	239 Summit Pl NE	239 Summit Pl NE
22	152 Continental Pkwy	152 Continental Blvd
23	8092 13th Rd S	8029 13th Rd S
24	3906 Queensbury Rd	3906 Queensbury Rd
25	4719 Linnean Ave NW	4719 Linnean Ave NE
26	Bradford Me	Bradley Me
27	Parrott Ga 31777	Parrott Ga 31177
28	4312 Lowell Lane	4312 Lowell Lane
29	6929 W 135th Place	6929 W 135th Plaza
30	5143 Somerset Cir	5143 Somerset Cir
31	8501 Kennedy St	8501 Kennedy St
32	2164 E McLean Ave	2164 E McLean Ave
33	7186 E St NW	7186 F St NW
34	2121 Beechcrest Rd	2121 Beechcroft Rd
35	3609 E Montrose St	3609 E Montrose St
36	324 S Alvadero St	324 S Alverado St
37	2908 Plaza de las Estrellas	2908 Plaza de las Estrellas
38	223 Great Falls Rd SE	223 Great Falls Dr SE
39	Kelton S C 29354	Kelton S C 29354
40	3201 Landover Rd	3201 Landover Rd

PRACTICE FOR MEMORIZING ADDRESSES

MEMORIZING TIME: 5 Minutes

DIRECTIONS: This is a test of memory, speed, and accuracy in which you will be given names, numbers, and addresses to remember. They are divided into five groups, boxed and lettered A, B, C, D, E. For each question, mark the Answer Sheet to show the letter of the box in which the item belongs. If you are not sure of an answer you should guess. Try to remember the box-location of as many items as you can.

A	B	C	D	E
1700–2599 Wood Dushore 8500–8699 Lang Lott 6200–6399 James	2700–3299 Wood Jeriel 8700–9399 Lang Vanna 5700–6199 James	1300–1699 Wood Levering 9400–9499 Lang Ekron 6400–6499 James	3300–3599 Wood Bair 8000–8499 Lang Viborg 5000–5699 James	2600–2699 Wood Danby 9500–9999 Lang Lycan 4700–4999 James

1. 6200–6399 James
2. 1700–2599 Wood
3. Lott
4. Viborg
5. 1700–2599 Wood
6. 6200–6399 James
7. 6200–6399 James
8. 2600–2699 Wood

ADDITIONAL MEMORIZING TIME: 3 Minutes

DIRECTIONS: Cover the lettered boxes. Answer as best you can from memory.

9. Lycan
10. 8000–8499 Lang
11. Ekron
12. 3300–3599 Wood
13. 5700–6199 James
14. 1300–1699 Wood
15. Levering
16. 8700–9399 Lang

CORRECT ANSWERS FOR THE FOREGOING QUESTIONS.

1.A 3.A 5.A 7.A 9.E 11.C 13.B 15.C
2.A 4.D 6.A 8.E 10.D 12.D 14.C 16.B

NOTE: Be sure to memorize the addresses for the Practice Test, as instructed. In the past, the addresses learned for the Practice Test have been the same addresses used for the actual test.

TEST III. MEMORY FOR ADDRESSES

TIME: 5 Minutes. 88 Questions.

DIRECTIONS: Having committed to memory the box-locations in the previous Memorizing test, you must now mark your Answer Sheet for each question to show the letter of the box in which the item belongs. Do not turn back to the lettered boxes in the previous Memorizing test. Answer as best you can from memory.

1. 6200–6399 James
2. 1700–2599 Wood
3. Bair
4. 1700–2599 Wood
5. Ekron
6. Viborg
7. Danby
8. 8500–8699 Lang

9. Lycan
10. 8000–8499 Lang
11. 4700–4999 James
12. 9400–9499 Lang
13. 2700–3299 Wood
14. Jeriel
15. 9500–9999 Lang
16. 1300–1699 Wood

17. 8700–9399 Lang
18. Levering
19. Vanna
20. 6400–6499 James
21. 3300–3599 Wood
22. Dushore
23. Lycan
24. 5700–6199 James

25. Lott
26. Viborg
27. Jeriel
28. 5000–5699 James
29. 2600–2699 Wood
30. 4700–4999 James
31. 2700–3299 Wood
32. 8000–8499 Lang

33. Ekron
34. 3300–3599 Wood
35. 9400–9499 Lang
36. 6200–6399 James
37. 2600–2699 Wood
38. 8500–8699 Lang
39. Levering
40. Lott

41. Bair
42. 1700–2599 Wood
43. 6400–6499 James
44. 9500–9999 Lang
45. Jeriel
46. 4700–4999 James
47. Dushore
48. Lycan

49. 1700–2599 Wood
50. 6200–6399 James
51. Vanna
52. Ekron
53. 8700–9399 Lang
54. Bair
55. 2600–2699 Wood
56. Dushore

57. 5700–6199 James
58. 1300–1699 Wood
59. Levering
60. Lott
61. Jeriel
62. 2600–2699 Wood
63. Lott
64. 4700–4999 James

65. Dushore
66. Danby
67. 8500–8699 Lang
68. Vanna
69. 2700–3299 Wood
70. 9500–9999 Lang
71. Viborg
72. Ekron

73. 6200–6399 James
74. 2600–2699 Wood
75. Levering
76. Lott
77. 1300–1699 Wood
78. Bair
79. Lycan
80. 5700–6199 James

81. Levering
82. 8700–9399 Lang
83. 5000–5699 James
84. 1700–2599 Wood
85. Jeriel
86. 6200–6399 James
87. Ekron
88. 2700–3299 Wood

STOP.

If you finish before the 5 minutes are up, go back and check your answers for the questions on this page.

END OF EXAMINATION

CORRECT ANSWERS FOR SAMPLE EXAMINATION II

(Please try to answer the questions on your own before looking at our answers. You'll do much better on your test if you follow this rule.)

TEST I. ADDRESS CHECKING

1.A	6.A	11.D	16.A	21.A	26.D	31.D	36.D
2.D	7.D	12.A	17.A	22.A	27.A	32.A	37.A
3.D	8.A	13.A	18.A	23.D	28.D	33.A	38.D
4.A	9.D	14.D	19.D	24.D	29.D	34.D	39.A
5.D	10.A	15.D	20.A	25.D	30.A	35.A	40.D

TEST II. ADDRESS CHECKING

1.A	6.D	11.A	16.A	21.A	26.D	31.A	36.D
2.D	7.A	12.D	17.D	22.D	27.D	32.A	37.A
3.D	8.A	13.A	18.A	23.D	28.A	33.D	38.D
4.A	9.A	14.D	19.D	24.A	29.D	34.D	39.A
5.D	10.D	15.D	20.D	25.D	30.A	35.A	40.A

TEST III. MEMORY FOR ADDRESSES

1.A	12.C	23.E	34.D	45.B	56.A	67.A	78.D
2.A	13.B	24.B	35.C	46.E	57.B	68.B	79.E
3.D	14.B	25.A	36.A	47.A	58.C	69.B	80.B
4.A	15.E	26.D	37.E	48.E	59.C	70.E	81.C
5.C	16.C	27.B	38.A	49.A	60.A	71.D	82.B
6.D	17.B	28.D	39.C	50.A	61.B	72.C	83.D
7.E	18.C	29.E	40.A	51.B	62.E	73.A	84.A
8.A	19.B	30.E	41.D	52.C	63.A	74.E	85.B
9.E	20.C	31.B	42.A	53.B	64.E	75.C	86.A
10.D	21.D	32.D	43.C	54.D	65.A	76.A	87.C
11.E	22.A	33.C	44.E	55.E	66.E	77.C	88.B

AFTER TAKING THE VERISIMILAR EXAMINATION

STEP ONE — Check all your answers with the Correct Answers

STEP TWO — Use the results of the Examination you have just taken to diagnose yourself. Pinpoint the areas in which you show the greatest weakness. Fill in the Diagnostic Table to spotlight the subjects in which you need the most practice.

SUBJECT TESTED	SCORE ON EXAM		
	Strong	Average	Weak
ADDRESS CHECKING	55-80	36-54	0-35
MEMORY FOR ADDRESSES	66-88	41-65	0-40

DIAGNOSTIC TABLE FOR EXAMINATION II.

STEP THREE—Use the following Check List to establish areas that require the greatest application on your part. One check (√) after the item means moderately weak; two checks (√ √) means seriously weak.

AREA OF WEAKNESS	CHECK BELOW	AREA OF WEAKNESS	CHECK BELOW
ADDRESS CHECKING		MEMORY FOR ADDRESSES	

POST OFFICE CLERK-CARRIER

SAMPLE EXAM III

In this comprehensive examination we have sought to predict the content of your test, and to provide you with the kind of practice you really require. It has approximately the same number of questions as the official test. The topics tested, the form of the questions, the level of difficulty, and the number of questions for each topic . . . all are quite similar to the official test. In every respect it simulates the actual conditions you will encounter. Test yourself to get an overview, to review your strengths and weaknesses, and to put yourself in the right frame of mind for scoring high.

Time allowed for the entire Examination: 1½ Hours

This includes the time for filling out forms as well as for reviewing instructions and trying out practice questions. The actual test time is 11 minutes.

In order to create the climate of the actual exam, that's exactly what you should allow yourself . . . no more, no less. Use a watch to keep a record of your time, since it might suit your convenience to try this practice exam in several short takes.

ANALYSIS AND TIMETABLE: SAMPLE EXAMINATION III.			
The timetable below is both an index to your practice test and a preview of the actual exam. In constructing this examination, we have analyzed every available announcement and official statement about the exam and thus predict that this is what you may face. *It is well known that examiners like to experiment with various types of questions, so the test you take may be slightly different in form or content. However, we feel certain that if you have mastered each subject covered here, you will be well on your way to scoring high.*			
SUBJECT TESTED	*Time Allowed*	*SUBJECT TESTED*	*Time Allowed*
ADDRESS CHECKING	6 min.	MEMORY FOR ADDRESSES	5 min.

ANSWER SHEET FOR VERISIMILAR EXAMINATION III.

Consolidate your key answers here just as you would do on the actual exam. Using this type of Answer Sheet will provide valuable practice. Tear it out along the indicated lines and mark it up correctly. Use a No. 2 (medium) pencil. Make only ONE mark for each answer. Additional and stray marks may be counted as mistakes. In making corrections erase errors COMPLETELY. Make glossy black marks.

TEST I. ADDRESS CHECKING

TEST II. ADDRESS CHECKING

TEST III. MEMORY FOR ADDRESSES

TEST I. ADDRESS CHECKING

TIME: 3 Minutes. 40 Questions.

DIRECTIONS: This is a test of your speed and accuracy in comparing addresses. Blacken the proper space under A in the Answer Sheet if the two addresses are exactly alike in every way. Blacken D if they are not alike in every way.

1	Purdin Mo	Purdon Mo
2	Hobart Ind 46342	Hobart Ind 46342
3	Kuna Idaho	Kuna Idaho
4	Janesville Calif 96114	Janesville Calif 96119
5	Sioux Falls S Dak	Sioux Falls S Dak
6	Homewood Miss	Homewood Miss
7	Kaweah Calif	Kawaeh Calif
8	Unionport Ohio	Unionport Ohio
9	Meyersdale Pa	Meyersdale Va
10	Coquille Oreg 97423	Coqville Oreg 97423
11	Milan Wis	Milam Wis
12	Prospect Ky	Prospect Ky
13	Cloversville N Y	Cloverville N Y
14	Locate Mont 59340	Locate Mont 59340
15	Bozman Md	Bozeman Md
16	Orient Ill	Orient Ill
17	Yosemite Ky 42566	Yosemite Ky 42566
18	Camden Miss 39045	Camden Miss 39054
19	Bennington Vt	Bennington Vt
20	La Farge Wis	La Farge Wis
21	Fairfield N Y	Fairfield N C
22	Wynot Nebr	Wynot Nebr
23	Arona Pa	Aroda Pa
24	Thurman N C 28683	Thurmond N C 28683
25	Zenda Kans	Zenba Kans
26	Pike N H	Pike N H
27	Gorst Wash 98337	Gorst Wash 98837
28	Joiner Ark	Joiner Ark
29	Normangee Tex	Normangee Tex
30	Toccoa Ga	Tococa Ga
31	Small Point Maine 04567	Small Point Maine 04567
32	Eagan Tenn	Eagar Tenn
33	Belfield N Dak	Belford N Dak
34	De Ridder La 70634	De Ridder La 70634
35	Van Meter Iowa	Van Meter Iowa
36	Valparaiso Fla	Valparaiso Ind
37	Souris N Dak	Souris N Dak
38	Robbinston Maine	Robbinstown Maine
39	Dawes W Va 25054	Dawes W Va 25054
40	Goltry Okla	Goltrey Okla

TEST II. ADDRESS CHECKING

TIME: 3 Minutes. 36 Questions.

DIRECTIONS: This is a test of your speed and accuracy in comparing addresses. For each question in the test blacken the correspondingly-numbered answer space as follows.

Blacken ''A'' if the two addresses are exactly ALIKE in every way.

Blacken ''D'' if the two addresses are DIFFERENT in any way.

Work as fast as you can without making mistakes. Do as many questions as you can in the time allowed.

1.	Hornell, N.Y.	Hornell, N.Y.
2.	Camden, N.J.	Camden, Me.
3.	523 Greenwich Rd.	532 Greenwich Rd.
4.	Salina, Kansas	Salina, Kansas
5.	8203 Sandhurst	8203 Sandhurst
6.	Garfield, N.J.	Garfield, N.J.
7.	428 Mulberry Lane	428 Mulburry Lane
8.	Durham, N.C.	Durham, N.C.
9.	Chelsea, Mass.	Chelsey, Mass.
10.	Abilene, Kansas	Abilene, Kansas
11.	3893 Asher Rd.	3839 Asher Rd.
12.	Madison, Wisc.	Madison, Wisconsin
13.	Miami, Florida	Miami Beach
14.	7009 Terry Drive	7900 Terry Drive
15.	3425 Crown Ave.	3245 Crown Ave.
16.	Sioux City, Iowa	Sioux City, Iowa
17.	Houston, Texas	Huston, Texas
18.	5850 Green Street	5850 Green Street
19.	Woodbridge, Conn.	Woodbridge, N.J.
20.	867 Abington Ave.	867 Abington Ave.
21.	2857 Baxter Blvd.	2857 Baxter Blvd.
22.	London Terrace	London Terraces
23.	9089 Bay View Drive	9809 Bay View Drive
24.	489 St. Kevin	489 St. Kevin
25.	5005 Decelles	5050 Decelles
26.	Banger, Maine	Bangor, Maine
27.	119 Washburn Ave.	119 Washburn Ave.
28.	80 Chenery Street	80 Chenery St.
29.	480 Lexington Avenue	480 Lexington Avenue
30.	Greenbrier, Vt.	Greenbrier, Va.
31.	Rangley Lakes	Rangely Lake
32.	9669 Hope Ave.	9669 Hope Ave.
33.	3532 Ruse Road	3532 Ruse Road
34.	Forest Hills, N.Y.	Forest Hill, N.Y.
35.	4050 Laurel Lane	4005 Laurel Lane
36.	Greenwhich, Conn.	Greenwich, Conn.

END OF TEST

PRACTICE FOR MEMORIZING ADDRESSES

MEMORIZING TIME: 5 Minutes

DIRECTIONS: This is a test of memory, speed, and accuracy in which you will be given names, numbers, and addresses to remember. They are divided into five groups, boxed and lettered A, B, C, D, E. For each question, mark the Answer Sheet to show the letter of the box in which the item belongs. If you are not sure of an answer you should guess. Try to remember the box-location of as many items as you can.

A	B	C	D	E
2100–2799 Mall	3900–4399 Mall	4400–4599 Mall	3400–3899 Mall	2800–3399 Mall
Ceres	Cedar	Niles	Cicero	Delhi
4800–4999 Cliff	4000–4299 Cliff	3300–3999 Cliff	4500–4799 Cliff	4300–4499 Cliff
Natoma	Foster	Dexter	Pearl	Magnet
1900–2299 Laurel	2300–2999 Laurel	3200–3799 Laurel	3000–3199 Laurel	1500–1899 Laurel

1. Cedar
2. 4300–4999 Cliff
3. 4800–4999 Cliff
4. 1500–1899 Laurel
5. 4500–4799 Cliff
6. 1900–2299 Laurel
7. 4000–4299 Cliff
8. 3400–3899 Mall

ADDITIONAL MEMORIZING TIME: 3 Minutes

DIRECTIONS: Cover the lettered boxes. Answer as best you can from memory.

9. Delhi
10. Dexter
11. Delhi
12. 3900–4399 Mall
13. Dexter
14. Magnet
15. 3000–3199 Laurel
16. 3900–4399 Mall

CORRECT ANSWERS FOR THE FOREGOING QUESTIONS.

1.B	3.A	5.D	7.B	9.E	11.E	13.C	15.D
2.E	4.E	6.A	8.D	10.C	12.B	14.E	16.B

NOTE: Be sure to memorize the addresses for the Practice Test, as instructed. In the past, the addresses learned for the Practice Test have been the same addresses used for the actual test.

TEST III. MEMORY FOR ADDRESSES

TIME: 5 Minutes. 88 Questions.

DIRECTIONS: Having committed to memory the box-locations in the previous Memorizing test, you must now mark your Answer Sheet for each question to show the letter of the box in which the item belongs. Do not turn back to the lettered boxes in the previous Memorizing test. Answer as best you can from memory.

1. Cedar
2. 4300–4499 Cliff
3. 4400–4599 Mall
4. Natoma
5. 2300–2999 Laurel
6. 4500–4799 Cliff
7. Ceres
8. 3400–3899 Mall

25. 4800–4999 Cliff
26. 1500–1899 Laurel
27. Cedar
28. 4400–4599 Mall
29. 4500–4799 Cliff
30. Dexter
31. 3000–3199 Laurel
32. Niles

49. 4500–4799 Cliff
50. 1900–2299 Laurel
51. Niles
52. 3300–3999 Cliff
53. 2800–3399 Mall
54. Cicero
55. Delhi
56. 4000–4299 Cliff

73. 4000–4299 Cliff
74. 3400–3899 Mall
75. 1900–2299 Laurel
76. 2800–3399 Mall
77. Ceres
78. Magnet
79. Cicero
80. 3200–3799 Laurel

9. Delhi
10. Dexter
11. 1900–2299 Laurel
12. 3300–3999 Cliff
13. Cicero
14. 4000–4299 Cliff
15. 2100–2799 Mall
16. Foster

33. Delhi
34. 3900–4399 Mall
35. Cicero
36. Dexter
37. 4800–4999 Cliff
38. 2300–2999 Laurel
39. 2100–2799 Mall
40. 3300–3999 Cliff

57. Dexter
58. Magnet
59. 3000–3199 Laurel
60. 3900–4399 Mall
61. Natoma
62. 3000–3199 Laurel
63. 4300–4499 Cliff
64. Cedar

81. 3000–3199 Laurel
82. 3900–4399 Mall
83. Natoma
84. 3300–3999 Cliff
85. 3400–3899 Mall
86. Foster
87. 2100–2799 Mall
88. 4300–4499 Cliff

17. Magnet
18. Ceres
19. 2800–3399 Mall
20. 3200–3799 Laurel
21. 4300–4499 Cliff
22. Pearl
23. 3900–4399 Mall
24. Natoma

41. 3400–3899 Mall
42. 4300–4499 Cliff
43. Ceres
44. Foster
45. Magnet
46. 3200–3799 Laurel
47. Pearl
48. 1500–1899 Laurel

65. 4400–4599 Mall
66. 1500–1899 Laurel
67. 4800–4999 Cliff
68. Delhi
69. Pearl
70. 2300–2999 Laurel
71. 4500–4799 Cliff
72. Niles

STOP.

If you finish before the time is up, go back and rework the questions on this page only.

END OF EXAMINATION

CORRECT ANSWERS FOR SAMPLE EXAMINATION III

(Please make every effort to answer the questions on your own before looking at these answers. You'll make faster progress by following this rule.)

TEST I. ADDRESS CHECKING

1.D	6.A	11.D	16.A	21.D	26.A	31.A	36.D
2.A	7.D	12.A	17.A	22.A	27.D	32.D	37.A
3.A	8.A	13.D	18.D	23.D	28.A	33.D	38.D
4.D	9.D	14.A	19.A	24.D	29.A	34.A	39.A
5.A	10.D	15.D	20.A	25.D	30.D	35.A	40.D

TEST II. ADDRESS CHECKING

1.A	7.D	13.D	19.D	25.D	31.D
2.D	8.A	14.D	20.A	26.D	32.A
3.D	9.D	15.D	21.A	27.A	33.A
4.A	10.A	16.A	22.D	28.D	34.D
5.A	11.D	17.D	23.D	29.A	35.D
6.A	12.D	18.A	24.A	30.D	36.D

TEST III. MEMORY FOR ADDRESSES

1.B	12.C	23.B	34.B	45.E	56.B	67.A	78.E
2.E	13.D	24.A	35.D	46.C	57.C	68.E	79.D
3.C	14.B	25.A	36.C	47.D	58.E	69.D	80.C
4.A	15.A	26.E	37.A	48.E	59.D	70.B	81.D
5.B	16.B	27.B	38.B	49.D	60.B	71.D	82.B
6.D	17.E	28.C	39.A	50.A	61.A	72.C	83.A
7.A	18.A	29.D	40.C	51.C	62.D	73.B	84.C
8.D	19.E	30.C	41.D	52.C	63.E	74.D	85.D
9.E	20.C	31.D	42.E	53.E	64.B	75.A	86.B
10.C	21.E	32.C	43.A	54.D	65.C	76.E	87.A
11.A	22.D	33.E	44.B	55.E	66.E	77.A	88.E

PART THREE

Practice With Exam Subjects

3

U.S. MAIL

U.S. MAIL

POST OFFICE CLERK-CARRIER

ADDRESS CHECKING

HOW TO PROFIT FROM THE PRACTICE TESTS

On the following pages you are furnished practice tests consisting of questions like those on the actual exam. The time limit here is just about what you may expect. Take these tests as a series of dress rehearsals strengthening your ability to score high on this type of question. For each test use the Answer Sheet provided to mark down your answers. If the Answer Sheet is separated from the questions, tear it out so you can mark it more easily. As you finish each test, go back and check your answers to find your score, and to determine how well you did. This will help you discover where you need more practice.

DESCRIPTION OF THE TEST AND SAMPLE QUESTIONS

Here are some sample questions for you to do. Mark your answers on the Sample Answer Sheet, making sure to keep your mark inside the correct box. If you want to change an answer, erase the mark you don't want to count. Then mark your new answer. Use a No. 2 (medium) pencil.

Can you spot whether or not two addresses are alike or different? It is as easy as that. But how fast can you do it accurately? Look at the sample questions below. Each question consists of a pair of addresses like this—

762 W 18th St	762 W 18th St

Are they Alike or Different? They are exactly Alike.

9486 Hillsdale Rd	9489 Hillsdale Rd

Alike or Different? They are Different. Do you see why?

1242 Regal St	1242 Regel St

Alike or Different?

Remember that this test measures both speed and accuracy. So work as fast as you can without making any mistakes. Have a friend time you while you are working on the practice tests—you may find that you get faster as you become used to this type of question.

Address Checking—Sample Questions

ADDRESS CHECKING

DIRECTIONS: This is a test of your speed and accuracy in comparing addresses. For each question in the test blacken the correspondingly-numbered answer space as follows.

Blacken "A" if the two addresses are exactly ALIKE in every way.

Blacken "D" if the two addresses are DIFFERENT in any way.

Work as fast as you can without making mistakes. Do as many questions as you can in the time allowed.

It will be to your advantage to work as quickly and accurately as possible since your score on this part of the test will be based on the number of wrong answers as well as the number of right answers. It is not expected that you will be able to finish all the questions in the time allowed.

Be sure to use a pencil so that you can make erasures.

When you begin the test, work as fast as you can without making mistakes. Do as many questions as you can in the time allowed.

You will have *6 minutes* to answer as many of the questions as you can.

Starting now, if the two addresses are ALIKE darken box A on the Sample Answer Sheet below. If the two addresses are DIFFERENT in any way darken box D. Answer every question.

1. ... 239 Windell Ave   239 Windell Ave
Alike or Different? Alike. Mark space A for question 1.

2. ... 4667 Edgeworth Rd   4677 Edgeworth Rd
Alike or Different? Different. Mark space D for question 2.

3. ... 2661 Kennel St SE   2661 Kennel St SW

4. ... 3709 Columbine St   3707 Columbine St

5. ... 969 W 14th St NW   969 W 14th St NW

6. ... 4439 Frederick Pkwy   4439 Frederick Pkwy

7. ... 77 Summers St   77 Summers St

8. ... 828 N Franklin Pl   828 S Franklin Pl

9. ... Acme La   Acme La
Since the two addresses are exactly alike, you should have darkened box A for question 9 on the Sample Answer Sheet. Now do the other sample questions.

10. ... Orleans Mass   Orleans Mich

11. ... Saxe Va   Saxis Va

12. ... Chappaqua N Y 10514   Chappaqua N Y 10514

13. ... Los Angeles Calif 90013   Los Angeles Calif 90018

14. ... 2134 S 20th St   2134 S 20th St
Since the two addresses are exactly alike, mark A for question 14 on the Sample Answer Sheet.

15. ... 4608 N Warnock St   4806 N Warnock St

16. ... 1202 W Girard Dr   1202 W Girard Rd

17. ... Chappaqua N Y 10514   Chappaqua N Y 10514

18. ... 2207 Markland Ave   2207 Markham Ave

END OF TEST

CONSOLIDATE YOUR KEY ANSWERS HERE

Practice using Answer Sheets. Make ONE mark for each answer. Additional and stray marks may be counted as mistakes. In making corrections erase errors COMPLETELY. Make glossy black marks. To arrive at an accurate estimate of your ability and progress, cover the Correct Answers with a sheet of white paper while you are taking this test.

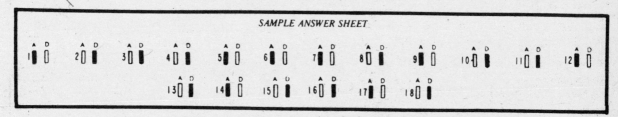

SAMPLE ANSWER SHEET

CORRECT ANSWERS TO SAMPLE QUESTIONS

Now compare your answers with the Correct Answers to Sample Questions. If your answers are not the same as the correct answers shown, go back and study the samples to see where you made a mistake.

INTERPRETATION OF TEST SCORES

After you have finished the Address Checking test, having taken all the time you are allowed, compare your answers with those given in the Correct Answers. Count the number that you got right and the number that you got wrong. If you didn't mark anything for a question, it doesn't get counted.

> *From the number right*
> *Subtract the number wrong*
> *This number (the difference) is your score*

The meaning of the score is as follows:

> *10 or higher* ....*Good.*
> *Between 6 and 9* ....*Fair.*
> *Below 6* ....*You need more practice.*

Hints for Answering Address-Checking Questions

- Do not spend too much time on any one question.
- The difference may not be noticeable at first, so be sure to check
  —all numbers (are they alike and in the same order or are they different)
  —abbreviations, such as St, Rd, NW, N Y (are they alike or are they different)
  —spellings of street, city, and state names
- Do not get nervous about the time limit. (In the official test no one is expected to do all the questions in the time allowed.)
- Make sure that you have marked the correct box for each question.

DO NOT TURN THIS PAGE UNTIL YOU ARE READY TO BEGIN THE TEST.

ADDRESS CHECKING TEST ONE

DIRECTIONS: This is a test of your speed and accuracy in comparing addresses. For Part I of the test, blacken the proper space under A in the Answer Sheet if the two addresses are exactly alike in every way. Blacken B if they are not alike in every way. For Part II of the test, go back to number 1 on the Answer Sheet. But this time blacken the space under D if the two addresses are exactly alike in every way. Blacken the space under E if they are not exactly alike in every way. Allow exactly five minutes.

PART I

1.	2121 South Drive	2121 South Drive
2.	6354 Forest Ave.	6543 Forest Ave.
3.	Tuckahoe, N.Y.	Tuckahoe, New York
4.	140 Bay State Road	140 Bay State Road
5.	5689 Park Place	5689 Park Place
6.	6709 Dewey Ave.	6709 Dewey Ave.
7.	Eastern Parkway	Easten Parkway
8.	6790 Beekman	6709 Beekman
9.	4786 Catalana Dr.	4786 Catalina Dr.
10.	Stuyvesant Town	Stuyvesant Town
11.	Newport, Va.	Newport, R.I.
12.	Woodmere, L.I.	Woodmere, L.I.
13.	7809 Greer Garden	7890 Greer Garden
14.	334 N.W. Lane	334 N.W. Lake
15.	195 Craig St.	195 Craigie St.
16.	Brunswick, Maine	Brunswick, Maine
17.	7543 Stevens Ave.	7435 Stevens Avenue

PART II

1.	248 Love Lane	248 Love Lane
2.	Niagra Falls	Niagra Falls
3.	5329 Jefferson Ave.	5392 Jefferson Ave.
4.	7809 Windy Way	7809 Windy Way
5.	8218 Bedel St.	8218 Bedel St.
6.	3090 Catherine Road	3090 Catherine Road
7.	Cape Porpoise	Cape Porpose
8.	9669 Wrange Rd.	9669 Wrange Rd.
9.	418 N. Wallace St.	418 N. Wallace St.
10.	2144 W. Tenth Ave.	2144 W. Tenth Ave.
11.	1618 N. Tecumseh	1618 N. Tecumseh
12.	5856 S. Pershing Rd.	5866 S. Pershing Rd.
13.	4231 Kealing Ave. N.	4231 Kelling Ave. N.
14.	6349 Ewing Ave.	349 Ewing Ave.
15.	1322 E. Hampton Dr.	1322 E. Hampton St.
16.	3343 London Rd. N.E.	3343 London Pl. N.E.
17.	Paoli, Ill.	Paoli, Ind.

Correct Answers

	A	B	C	D	E
1	■			■	
2		■		■	
3	■			■	
4	■			■	
5	■			■	
6	■				■
7		■			■
8		■			■
9		■		■	
10	■			■	
11		■		■	
12	■				■
13		■			■
14		■			■
15		■			■
16	■				■
17		■			■

Answer Sheet

	A	B	C	D	E
1					
2					
3					
4					
5					
6					
7					
8					
9					
10					
11					
12					
13					
14					
15					
16					
17					

ADDRESS CHECKING TEST TWO

DIRECTIONS: This is a test of your speed and accuracy in comparing addresses. For Part I of the test, blacken the proper space under A in the Answer Sheet if the two addresses are exactly alike in every way. Blacken B if they are not alike in every way. For Part II of the test, go back to number 1 on the Answer Sheet. But this time blacken the space under D if the two addresses are exactly alike in every way. Blacken the space under E if they are not exactly alike in every way. Allow exactly five minutes.

PART I

1.	418 N. Wallac St.	418 N. Wallace St.
2.	2144 W. Tenth Ave.	144 W. Tenth Ave.
3.	1618 N. Tecumseh	1618 N. Tecumse
4.	5856 S. Pershing Rd.	5866 S. Pershing
5.	4231 Kealing Ave. N.	4231 Keeling Ave. N.
6.	6349 Ewing Ave.	6349 Ewing Ave.
7.	132 E. Hampton Dr.	1322 E. Hampton St.
8.	3343 London Rd. N.E.	334 London Pl. N.E.
9.	Paoli, Ill.	Poli, Ind.
10.	6892 Beech Grove Ave.	6892 Beech Grove Ave.
11.	2939 E. Division	2939 E. Diversey
12.	1066 Goethe Sq. S.	1096 Goethe Sq. S.
13.	1108 Lyndhurst Dr.	1108 Lyndhurst Dr.
14.	Berne, Wyo.	Berne, Wis.
15.	1468 Woodruff Pl.	1468 Woodruff Pl.
16.	992 S. Highland Ave.	992 S. Highland Ave.
17.	2478 Berkeley Rd.	2478 Barclay Rd.

PART II

1.	4718 N. Central St.	4718 S. Central St.
2.	1118 W. Jerriman	1218 W. Jerriman
3.	2541 Appleton St.	2541 Appleton St.
4.	6439 Kessler Blvd. S.	6439 Kessler Blvd. S.
5.	928 Miramar Rd.	928 Miramar Bldg.
6.	1929 Connecticut Ave. N.E.	1929 Connecticut Ave. N.E.
7.	9452 N. Gale St.	9452 N. Gale St.
8.	1815 Ridgewood Dr.	1815 Ridgewood Dr.
9.	25 92nd Elm	25 97th Elm
10.	389 Woodward Hts.	389 Woodward Ave.
11.	7718 Lincoln Pkwy.	7718 Lincoln Blvd.
12.	5798 Gd. Central Dr.	5798 Gd. Central Dr.
13.	108-46 159 Ave.	108-36 159 Ave.
14.	5 Willow Rd.	5 Willow Rd.
15.	3213 Brookhaven	3213 Brookhale
16.	186 Fr. Meadows	186 Fr. Meadows
17.	1109 Liberty Ave.	1109 Liberty St.

Correct Answers and **Answer Sheet** grids (columns A B C D E, rows 1–17).

ADDRESS CHECKING TEST THREE

DIRECTIONS: This is a test of your speed and accuracy in comparing addresses. For Part I of the test, blacken the proper space under A in the Answer Sheet if the two addresses are exactly alike in every way. Blacken B if they are not alike in every way. For Part II of the test, go back to number 1 on the Answer Sheet. But this time blacken the space under D if the two addresses are exactly alike in every way. Blacken the space under E if they are not exactly alike in every way. Allow exactly five minutes.

PART I

1.	2439 Langston Ave.	2449 Langston Ave.
2.	408 W. Hamilton Dr.	408 E. Hamilton Dr.
3.	20 Hammerly Sq.	20 Hammerly Sq.
4.	193-08 50th Ave.	193-05 50th Ave.
5.	8949 Astoria Blvd.	8949 Astoria Pl.
6.	155 S.W. Flushing	155 S.W. Flusher
7.	4319 S. Elmont Rd.	4319 S. Elmont Rd.
8.	64 Woodbourne Ave.	64 Woodburn Ave.
9.	1421 N. 38th Ave.	1421 N. 38th Ave.
10.	289 Continental Pl.	289 Continental Pl.
11.	1654 Putnam St.	1644 Putnam St.
12.	1610 Mott Haven	1610 Mott Ave.
13.	4335 W. 167 Ave.	4335 W. 267 Ave.
14.	4192 N.W. Illinois	4192 N.W. Illinois
15.	3374 Ashburne House	3374 Adbourne House
16.	1719 Pleasant Run Blvd.	1719 Pleasant Run Blvd.
17.	3857 S. Morris St.	3857 S. Morris St.

PART II

1.	Bradford, O.	Bradford, O.
2.	2131 W. 18th Dr.	2131 W. 18th Dr.
3.	Townley, Texas	Townley, Tenn.
4.	2525 Wavecrest Ave.	2825 Wavecrest Dr.
5.	123 Linden Pl.	123 Linton Pl.
6.	5929 Washington Blvd.	5929 Washington Blvd.
7.	4628 Park Ave. N.	4628 Park Ave. E.
8.	1235 Meridian St.	1235 Meridian St.
9.	7832 Ruckle Pl. S.W.	7832 Ruckle Pl. S.W.
10.	3422 E. Tenth St.	3422 E. Tenth St.
11.	629 Beveridge Cir.	621 Beveridge Cir.
12.	6888 Forster Ave. W.	6888 Forester Ave. W.
13.	4531 E. 59th St.	4531 E. 59th St.
14.	Melrose Park Mich.	Melray Park Mich.
15.	1871 De Quincey Blvd.	1871 DeQuincy Blvd.
16.	2436 Massachusetts Ave.	2436 Massachusetts Ave.
17.	3951-D 29th St. E.	3951-D 29th St. E.

Correct Answers

Answer Sheet

ADDRESS CHECKING TEST FOUR

DIRECTIONS: This is a test of your speed and accuracy in comparing addresses. For Part I of the test, blacken the proper space under A in the Answer Sheet if the two addresses are exactly alike in every way. Blacken B if they are not alike in every way. For Part II of the test, go back to number 1 on the Answer Sheet. But this time blacken the space under D if the two addresses are exactly alike in every way. Blacken the space under E if they are not exactly alike in every way. Allow exactly five minutes.

PART I

1. 4389 N. De Kalb St.   4389 N. De Kalb St.
2. 1982 Grosvenor St.   1982 Governor St.
3. 3923 Kansas St.   3923 Kansan St.
4. 1408 E. Jefferson Ave.   1408 E. Jerrison Ave.
5. 838 S. Harrison St.   838 S. Harrison St.
6. 1629 N.W. Pike Dr.   1629 N.W. Pike Dr.
7. 9800 S. Rural St.   8900 S. Rural St.
8. Weston, N.Y.   Weston, N. J.
9. 2318 F St. N.W.   2318 F St. N.W.
10. 4121 S. Eastern Ave.   4121 S. Eastern Ave.
11. 1517 La Salle Ave.   1517 La Salle Ave.
12. Elmhurst, L.I.   Elmhurst, Ill.
13. 6807 Forest Ave.   6807 Forrest Ave.
14. 731 Dartmouth Sq. N.   731 Dartmouth Sq.
15. 10943 Rednor Ave.   10943 Rednor Ave.
16. 6140 Saunders Pk.   6140 Saunders Pk.
17. 8811 Ingram Dr.   8811 Ingraham Dr.

PART II

1. 1212 Heyson Rd.   1212 Heyson St.
2. 465 N. N.Y. Blvd.   455 N. N.Y. Blvd.
3. 3217 Vernon Pl. N.W.   3217 Vernon Pl. N.W.
4. 6792 Holstein Ave.   6792 Holstine Ave.
5. 108-53 43rd Ave.   108-53 43rd Ave.
6. 344 Waint St.   344 Weightn St.
7. 317 S. Hollis Ave.   317 S. Holis Ave.
8. 44 Ries Pl.   44 Rees Pl.
9. 109-07 Lewis Blvd.   109-07 Lewis Blvd.
10. 4355 Kisena Ave.   4355 Kisena Ave.
11. 3043 Hobart St.   3044 Hobart St.
12. 188 Crescent Dr.   188 Crescent Dr.
13. 151-30 35th Ave.   151-30 53rd Ave.
14. 37 Newport Wk.   37 Newport Wk.
15. 1540 Atlantic Ave.   2540 Atlantic Ave.
16. 243 Northern Blvd.   234 Northern Blvd.
17. 986 Doughton Pl.   986 Douton Pl.

ADDRESS CHECKING TEST FIVE

DIRECTIONS: This is a test of your speed and accuracy in comparing addresses. For Part I of the test, blacken the proper space under A in the Answer Sheet if the two addresses are exactly alike in every way. Blacken B if they are not alike in every way. For Part II of the test, go back to number 1 on the Answer Sheet. But this time blacken the space under D if the two addresses are exactly alike in every way. Blacken the space under E if they are not exactly alike in every way. Allow exactly five minutes.

PART I

1.	2 Cavell Dr. N.	2 Cavel Dr. N.
2.	4521 S. Jackson Ave.	4521 S. Jackson Ave.
3.	10-9 177th St.	10-9 177th Ave.
4.	2724 N.W. Lake	2742 N.W. Lake
5.	372 Menahan Ave.	372 Menehan Ave.
6.	9904 Bushwick St.	9904 Bushwick St.
7.	43 Stuyvesant Pl.	43 Stuyvesant Pl.
8.	5473 S. 86th Ave.	5437 S. 86th Ave.
9.	388 N. Eastern Blvd.	388 N. Easton Blvd.
10.	1422 S. Lake Shore Dr.	1422 S. Lake Shore Dr.
11.	5133 S. Campbell St.	5133 S. Camel St.
12.	1311 Audubon Rd. E.	3133 Audubon Rd. E.
13.	3800 Field Bldg.	3800 Field Blvd.
14.	Anderson, Ia.	Andersen, Ia.
15.	1054 N.W. Euclid Pl.	1054 N.W. Euclid Pl.
16.	2383 W. Olive St.	2383 W. Olive St.
17.	7700 Weylin Dr.	7700 Waylin Dr.

PART II

1.	497 W. Madero Dr.	497 W. Manero Dr.
2.	7820 Ridge Bldg.	7820 Ridge Blvd.
3.	735 Ocean Ave.	735 Ocean Ave.
4.	4222 Surf Ave.	422 Surf Ave.
5.	29 Monroe Pl.	29 Monroe St.
6.	336 Blake Ave.	336 Blake St.
7.	2009 Mermaid Ave.	2009 Mermaid Rd.
8.	524 Brighton Beach Ave.	524 Brighton Ave.
9.	15554 Pitkin Ave.	1554 Pitkin Ave.
10.	266 Rochester Ave.	266 Rochester Ave.
11.	Chicago, Ill.	Chicago, Ind.
12.	1117 Greene Ave.	1117 Green Ave.
13.	101 53rd St.	101 53rd St.
14.	765 Fulton St.	765 Fulton Pl.
15.	510 Porter Ave.	510 Port Ave.
16.	320 Jay St.	320 J St.
17.	19 Fulton Pl.	19 Fulton Pk.

Correct Answers

	A	B	C	D	E
1		■			
2	■				
3		■			
4	■				
5		■			
6					■
7	■				
8	■				
9	■				
10	■			■	
11		■			
12		■			
13		■		■	
14		■			
15	■				
16	■				■
17		■			

Answer Sheet

	A	B	C	D	E
1					
2					
3					
4					
5					
6					
7					
8					
9					
10					
11					
12					
13					
14					
15					
16					
17					

ADDRESS CHECKING TEST SIX

DIRECTIONS: This is a test of your speed and accuracy in comparing addresses. For Part I of the test, blacken the proper space under A in the Answer Sheet if the two addresses are exactly alike in every way. Blacken B if they are not alike in every way. For Part II of the test, go back to number 1 on the Answer Sheet. But this time blacken the space under D if the two addresses are exactly alike in every way. Blacken the space under E if they are not exactly alike in every way. Allow exactly five minutes.

PART I

1. 623 Park Ave. — 623 Park Ave.
2. 653 Knickerbocker Ave. — 653 Knickerbocker Ave.
3. 93 Menahan St. — 93 Menahane St.
4. 9 Grady Pl. — 90 Grady Pl.
5. 263 E. Parkway — 263 Eastern Parkway
6. 210 Parkside Pl. — 201 Parkside Pl.
7. 1888 Hale Ave. — 1888 Hale Ave.
8. 2002 W. 6th St. — 2002 W. 6th St.
9. Halifax, N.D. — Halifax, N.F.
10. 905 St. Edwards — 950 St. Edwards
11. 766 Clursen Ave. — 766 Clurson Ave.
12. 324 N. President — 324 S. President
13. 1332 Gates Ave. — 1332 Gates Ave.
14. 542 W. Warren Pl. — 542 W. Waren Pl.
15. 1865 E. 22nd St. — 1685 E. 22nd St.
16. 1906 E. 52nd Ave. — 1906 E. 52nd Ave.
17. 1463 Broadway — 1463 Broadway

PART II

1. 3047 Falter Pl. — 3047 Falter Pl.
2. 365 Midwood Te. — 365 Milwood Te.
3. 7311 E. 5th St. — 1137 E. 5th St.
4. 1688 E. 28 St. — 1668 E. 28th St.
5. 460 Argyle Rd. — 460 Argyle Rd.
6. 3711 Ave. R S.W. — 3711 Ave. R N.E.
7. 94 Rutledge Lane — 49 Rutledge Lane
8. 5420 15th Ave. — 5420 15th Ave
9. 1308 Putnam Pl. — 1380 Putnam Pl.
10. 2195 Howard Ave. — 2195 Howard Ave.
11. 418 Baltic Dr. — 418 Baltic Dr.
12. 1269 W. 18th St. — 1269 W. 18th St.
13. 1610 Ave. A — 1016 Ave. A
14. 151 Bond Dr. — 151 Bond St.
15. 696 Stanlee Ave. — 696 Stanley Ave.
16. 45 Tenris Ct. — 45 Tenis Ct.
17. 6701 S. 6th Ave. — 6107 S. 6th Ave.

Correct Answers

	A	B	C	D	E
1	■			■	
2	■				■
3	■				■
4	■				■
5		■			■
6		■		■	
7	■				■
8	■			■	
9		■			■
10		■		■	
11		■			■
12		■		■	
13	■				■
14	■				■
15	■				■
16	■				■
17	■				■

Answer Sheet

	A	B	C	D	E
1					
2					
3					
4					
5					
6					
7					
8					
9					
10					
11					
12					
13					
14					
15					
16					
17					

ADDRESS CHECKING TEST SEVEN

DIRECTIONS: This is a test of your speed and accuracy in comparing addresses. For Part I of the test, blacken the proper space under A in the Answer Sheet if the two addresses are exactly alike in every way. Blacken B if they are not alike in every way. For Part II of the test, go back to number 1 on the Answer Sheet. But this time blacken the space under D if the two addresses are exactly alike in every way. Blacken the space under E if they are not exactly alike in every way. Allow exactly five minutes.

PART I

1.	474 Empire Blvd.	474 Empire Bldg.
2.	1193 Bedford Ave.	1193 Belfor Ave.
3.	77 Gold St.	77 Good St.
4.	443 Lincoln Pl.	443 Lincoln St.
5.	1806 Caton Ave.	1806 Caton Ave.
6.	510 McDonald Ave.	510 Mac Donald Ave.
7.	3303 Foster Ave.	330 Foster Ave.
8.	41 Harrison Ave.	41 Harison Ave.
9.	1623 Church Ave.	1623 Church St.
10.	35 Tennis Ct.	35 Tennis Ct.
11.	777 St. Marks Pl.	777 St. Marks Ave.
12.	22 Howard Pl.	22 Howard St.
13.	52 Hansen Pl.	52 Hanson Pl.
14.	311 Division Ave.	311 Division Ave.
15.	Woodridge, N.Y.	Woodbridge, N.J.
16.	188 City Hts.	18 City Hts.
17.	11 W. 42 St.	11 E. 42 St.

PART II

1.	53-09 97 Pl.	53-09 79 Pl.
2.	53 Myros Pl.	53 Myros Pl.
3.	207 Hart St.	207 Heart St.
4.	484 Tompkins Ave.	484 Tompkins Ave.
5.	2359 Coney Island Ave.	2359 Coney Ave.
6.	350 Hudson St.	350 Hudson St.
7.	57 Thames St.	57 Thomas St.
8.	268 Norman Ave.	268 Normandy Ave.
9.	322 Rockaway Ave.	322 Rockaway Pkway
10.	30 Rockefeller Plaza	30 Rockefeller Center
11.	632 St. Johns Pl.	632 St. Johns Pl.
12.	565 5 Ave.	565 5 Ave.
13.	1628 W. 6 St.	1628 E. 6 St.
14.	113 Malta St.	113 Malta St.
15.	549 Kingshighway	549 Kings Way
16.	1303 Ave. U	1303 Ave. U
17.	7314 21st St. N	7314 21st St. N

Correct Answers

	A	B	C	D	E
1		B			E
2			C		
3				D	
4				D	
5	A				
6		B			
7		B			
8		B			E
9					E
10	A				E
11		B			
12		B			
13		B			
14	A				
15		B			E
16		B			
17		B		C	

Answer Sheet

	A	B	C	D	E
1					
2					
3					
4					
5					
6					
7					
8					
9					
10					
11					
12					
13					
14					
15					
16					
17					

ADDRESS CHECKING TEST EIGHT

DIRECTIONS: This is a test of your speed and accuracy in comparing addresses. For Part I of the test, blacken the proper space under A in the Answer Sheet if the two addresses are exactly alike in every way. Blacken B if they are not alike in every way. For Part II of the test, go back to number I on the Answer Sheet. But this time blacken the space under D if the two addresses are exactly alike in every way. Blacken the space under E if they are not exactly alike in every way. Allow exactly five minutes.

PART I

1.	1009 E. Pkwy.	1090 E. Pkwy.
2.	2939 W. N.Y. St.	2939 W. N.Y. Ave.
3.	254 Quentin Rd.	254 Quentin Rd.
4.	3045 Brighton 12	3504 Brighton 12
5.	1728 E. 80th St.	1728 E. 80th St.
6.	757 Johnson Ave.	757 Johnston Ave.
7.	5017 Ave. N	5107 Ave. N
8.	9347 Cleveland Dr.	9347 Cleveland Dr.
9.	4 Wash Sq. N	4 Wash. Sq. S.
10.	418 Tecumseh	418 Tecumpseh
11.	1919 Sumner Ave.	2919 Sumner Ave.
12.	Bdwk & W. 31 St.	Bdwk. & 31st
13.	4778 W. Sterling	4778 N. Sterling
14.	237 Ovington Ave.	273 Ovington Ave.
15.	2242 Vandever	2242 Vandever
16.	3636 Gramercy Dr.	3636 Gramercy Dr.
17.	1278 E. 8th St.	1278 E. 8th Ave.

PART II

1.	134 N. Albetter St.	134 N. Albetter St.
2.	3389 W. Pinapple	3398 W. Pinapple
3.	9 Colby Ct.	9 Colby Ct.
4.	4669 West Way	4669 West St.
5.	2 Albrighton Te.	2 Allbrighton Te.
6.	395 Stratford Rd.	359 Stratford Rd.
7.	13 N.E. 6th Ave.	13 N.E. 6th Ave.
8.	1268 Decatur Pl.	1268 Decatur Pl.
9.	7006 Third Ave.	7060 Third Ave.
10.	308 Daltmas Blvd.	308 Dalmas Blvd.
11.	642 E. 55th St.	642 E. 55th St.
12.	4015 B Ave. S.	4051 B Ave. S.
13.	125 Bay 53rd	125 Bay 53rd
14.	12 Barnaby Ct.	12 Barnaby Pl.
15.	Buffalo, N.Y.	Buffalo, N.J.
16.	346 Glenmore Ave.	346 Glenmor Ave.
17.	967 Bergan St.	967 Bergan Ave.

Correct Answers

	A	B	C	D	E
1		■		■	
2	■				■
3	■			■	
4		■		■	
5	■				■
6		■		■	
7	■				■
8	■			■	
9		■			■
10		■			■
11		■		■	
12		■			■
13		■		■	
14		■			■
15	■				■
16	■				■
17		■			■

Answer Sheet

	A	B	C	D	E
1					
2					
3					
4					
5					
6					
7					
8					
9					
10					
11					
12					
13					
14					
15					
16					
17					

ADDRESS CHECKING TEST NINE

DIRECTIONS: This is a test of your speed and accuracy in comparing addresses. For Part I of the test, blacken the proper space under A in the Answer Sheet if the two addresses are exactly alike in every way. Blacken B if they are not alike in every way. For Part II of the test, go back to number 1 on the Answer Sheet. But this time blacken the space under D if the two addresses are exactly alike in every way. Blacken the space under E if they are not exactly alike in every way. Allow exactly five minutes.

PART I

1. 150 Prospect Pk. W. — 150 Prospect Pk. W.
2. 651 Elton St. — 651 Elton St.
3. 9605 Ave. B — 9605 Ave. B
4. 7411 3rd Ave. — 741 5th Ave.
5. Paris, France — Paris, N. Y.
6. 570 Kosciusko St. — 570 Koscusko St.
7. 4514 Ft. Hamilton Pk. — 4514 Ft. Hamilton Pk.
8. 453 Powell St. — 453 Powel St.
9. 1484 Sterling Pl. — 1484 Sterling Pl.
10. 557 Ave. Z — 557 Ave. C
11. 724 Marcy Ave. — 724 Marcy Pl.
12. 5614 14th Ave. — 5614 15th Ave.
13. 1018 Brighton 6 St. — 1018 Brighton 60 St.
14. 567 Ashford St. — 567 Ashfort St.
15. 310 Stagg St. — 310 Stagg St.
16. 117 Siegal St. — 117 Seigal St.
17. 465 Georgia Ave. — 456 George Ave.

PART II

1. 789 St. Marks Rd. — 798 St. Marks Rd.
2. 19 Lefferts Ave. — 19 Lefferts Ave.
3. 5018 Church St. — 5018 Church Ave.
4. 919 Park Row — 919 Park Row
5. 654 Dahill Rd. — 654 Dahil Rd.
6. 114 Reid Ave. — 114 Ried Ave.
7. 542 Evergreene Ave. — 452 Evergreen St.
8. 284 E. 31 St. — 284 W. 32 St.
9. 572 Livonia Ave. — 572 Livona Ave.
10. Boston, Mass. — Boston, Mass.
11. 1383 Dean St. — 1338 Dean St.
12. 323 Harriss Blvd. — 323 Harris Blvd.
13. 4359 Autumn Ave. — 4359 Autumn Ave.
14. 929 Ave. U S.W. — 929 Ave. U S.W.
15. 66 Livingston St. — 66 Livingstone St.
16. 5841 Patchen Pl. — 5841 Patchen Pl.
17. Chamber Ct. S.E. 4 — Chamber Ct. S.E. 4

Correct Answers

	A	B	C	D	E
1					●
2	●				
3	●				
4		●			
5	●				
6		●			
7	●				
8		●			
9	●				
10		●			
11	●				
12		●			
13		●			
14		●			
15	●				
16		●			
17		●			

Answer Sheet

	A	B	C	D	E
1					
2					
3					
4					
5					
6					
7					
8					
9					
10					
11					
12					
13					
14					
15					
16					
17					

ADDRESS CHECKING TEST TEN

DIRECTIONS: This is a test of your speed and accuracy in comparing addresses. For Part I of the test, blacken the proper space under A in the Answer Sheet if the two addresses are exactly alike in every way. Blacken B if they are not alike in every way. For Part II of the test, go back to number 1 on the Answer Sheet. But this time blacken the space under D if the two addresses are exactly alike in every way. Blacken the space under E if they are not exactly alike in every way. Allow exactly five minutes.

PART I

1. 8718 Ridge Dr. — 7818 Ridge Dr.
2. 3099 Emons Ave. — 3099 Emmons Ave.
3. 6701 Colonial Rd. — 6701 Colonial Rd.
4. Grosse Pt. Mich. — Gross Pt., Mass.
5. 7585 Ditmar Ave. — 7585 Diemar Ave.
6. 538 Ocean Dr. — 538 Ocean Rd.
7. 4904 14th Ave. — 4904 14th Ave.
8. 43 Andreas Pl. — 43 Andes Pl.
9. 2501 Summit Dr. — 2105 Summit Dr.
10. 1243 Mermaid St. — 1243 Mermaid St.
11. 180 S. Forrest Ave. — 180 S. Forest Ave.
12. 521 N. Albany St. — 521 N. Albany St.
13. 6868 Nostrand Ave. — 6888 Nostrand Ave.
14. 729 Minola St. — 729 Mineola St.
15. 1094 Hancock St. — 1049 Hancock St.
16. 2045 S.W. 62nd Ave. — 2045 S.W. 62nd Ave.
17. 1402 Ave. K N. — 1402 Ave. K N.

PART II

1. 981 N. Noonan Dr. E. — 981 N. Nooman Dr. W.
2. 131 Meserole Ave. — 131 Messerole Ave.
3. 26 Glenwood Rd. — 26 Glenwood Rd.
4. 1079 N. Blake St. — 1097 N. Blake St.
5. 2074 20th Lane — 2074 20th Lane
6. 1477 Carrol Ave. — 1477 Carol Ave.
7. 45 Tuckahoe Dr. — 54 Tuckahoe Dr.
8. 135 Ave. D W. — 135 Ave. D W.
9. 440 Liberty Ave. — 440 Liberty Pl.
10. 2040 21 Dr. — 2040 21 Rd.
11. 549 Herkimer St. — 549 Herkimore Rd.
12. 86 North Way — 86 North Lane
13. 128 Marin Ave. — 128 Marin Ave.
14. 1407 New York Ave. — 1407 East New York Ave.
15. 1182 Putnam Ave. — 1182 Putman Ave.
16. 106 Moffat Pl. — 106 Moffatt Pl.
17. 2175 Kimbel Rd. — 2175 Kimball Rd.

Correct Answers

	A	B	C	D	E
1	■				■
2	■				■
3		■		■	
4	■				■
5	■				
6		■			■
7	■				■
8	■			■	
9		■			■
10	■				■
11		■			■
12	■			■	
13		■		■	
14		■		■	
15		■			■
16	■				■
17	■				■

Answer Sheet

	A	B	C	D	E
1					
2					
3					
4					
5					
6					
7					
8					
9					
10					
11					
12					
13					
14					
15					
16					
17					

ADDRESS CHECKING TEST ELEVEN

DIRECTIONS: *This is a test of your speed and accuracy in comparing addresses. For Part I of the test, blacken the proper space under A in the Answer Sheet if the two addresses are exactly alike in every way. Blacken B if they are not alike in every way. For Part II of the test, go back to number 1 on the Answer Sheet. But this time blacken the space under D if the two addresses are exactly alike in every way. Blacken the space under E if they are not exactly alike in every way. Allow exactly five minutes.*

PART I

1.	240 Winthrop Ave.	240 Winthrop Ave.
2.	332 Macon St.	332 Malcolm St.
3.	3517 Beverly Rd.	3517 Beverley Rd
4.	182 Wilson Ave.	182 Willson Ave.
5.	50 Leffert Ave.	50 Leffert Ave.
6.	494 Seward Pk.	494 Seward Lane
7.	292 Montauk Ave.	292 Montalk Ave.
8.	3053 Bedford Ave.	2053 Bedford Ave.
9.	280 Parkside Ave.	280 Parkside Ave.
10.	419 Van Siclen Ave.	419 Van Sicklen Ave.
11.	766 Howard Ave.	766 Howard Ave.
12.	471 Ralph Ave.	417 Ralph Ave.
13.	8421 Glenwood Rd.	8421 Glenword Rd.
14.	Bayside, L.I.	Bayside, N.Y.
15.	718 Dun Ct.	718 Dun Ct.
16.	453 Sheffield St.	453 Shefield St.
17.	1440 50 St.	1440 55 St.

PART II

1.	160 Quincy St.	160 Quincy St.
2.	1001 Rutland Rd.	1001 Rutland Pl.
3.	5714 Farragut Pl.	5714 Farragut Pl.
4.	206 Albemarle Rd.	206 Albemarl Rd.
5.	1332 Throop Ave.	1332 Troop Ave.
6.	222 Franklin Rd.	222 Franklen Rd.
7.	April, Ga.	April, Va.
8.	84 S. Weirfield	84 S. Wierfield
9.	49 Bokee Ct.	49 Bokee Ct.
10.	4739 N. Marion St.	4739 N. Marion St.
11.	167 22nd Ave. E	167 27th Ave. E
12.	205 W. 77th Rd.	250 W. 77th Rd.
13.	1108 E. Chauncey Blvd.	1108 E. Chauncey Blvd.
14.	7 Union Plaza	7 Union Place
15.	3721 Filmore Ave.	3721 Filmoor Ave.
16.	919 Garfield Te.	919 Garfield Te.
17.	4316 Marino St.	4361 Marino St.

Correct Answers

	A	B	C	D	E
1	■			■	
2		■			■
3		■		■	
4		■			■
5	■				■
6		■		■	
7		■			
8		■			■
9	■			■	
10		■		■	
11	■				■
12	■				■
13	■			■	
14		■		■	
15	■				■
16		■			■
17		■			

Answer Sheet

	A	B	C	D	E
1					
2					
3					
4					
5					
6					
7					
8					
9					
10					
11					
12					
13					
14					
15					
16					
17					

ADDRESS CHECKING TEST TWELVE

DIRECTIONS: This is a test of your speed and accuracy in comparing addresses. For Part I of the test, blacken the proper space under A in the Answer Sheet if the two addresses are exactly alike in every way. Blacken B if they are not alike in every way. For Part II of the test, go back to number 1 on the Answer Sheet. But this time blacken the space under D if the two addresses are exactly alike in every way. Blacken the space under E if they are not exactly alike in every way. Allow exactly five minutes.

PART I

1. 356 Clifton Pl. N   356 Clifton Pl. N.
2. 9401 W. McDonald Ave.   9401 W. MacDonald Ave.
3. 2834 W. 15th St.   2843 W. 15th St.
4. 406 7th Ave. S.   406 7th Ave.
5. 4114 Purdue, La.   4114 Purdue, Ia
6. 723 S. Macon St.   723 S. Mason St.
7. 320 S. Webster St.   302 S. Webster St.
8. 577 Wnona Blvd.   577 Winona Blvd.
9. 8022 Washington St.   822 Washington St.
10. 5432 Ave. H N.W.   5432 Ave. H N.W.
11. 3374 Fifth Ave.   3374 Fitch Ave.
12. 62 W. Mataqua Pl.   62 W. Matakwa Pl.
13. 291 S.W. Adams St.   219 S.W. Adams St.
14. 585 N. Park Pl.   585 N. Park Pl.
15. 8604 23rd Ave.   8604 23rd Ave.
16. 244 W. Covert Sq.   244 W. Covert Sq.
17. 498 McLaren Pl.   498 Maclaren Pl.

PART II

1. 48 S. Rinaldi Rd.   48 S. Rinaldo Rd.
2. 82 Severn Dr. S.   82 Severn Dr. S.
3. 435 W. Hendricks   435 W. Hendrix
4. 20 Hubard Pl.   20 Hubbard Pl.
5. 51 Chamber St.   51 Chamber St.
6. 2015 Dorchester Rd.   2015 Dorchestor Rd.
7. 356 Miller Ave.   356 Mills Ave.
8. 45 Fleet Walk   45 Fleet Rd.
9. 1528 E. 9 St.   1528 E. 9 St.
10. 56 Monument Walk   56 Monument Rd.
11. 186 Hudson Blvd.   186 Hudson Bldg.
12. 53 Woodbine St.   53 Woodbine St.
13. 130 Martens Ave.   130 Martins Ave.
14. 3720 Nautilus Ave.   3270 Nautilus Ave.
15. 53 C Wyona Dr.   53 C Wyona Dr.
16. 511 Jaffry Ct.   511 Jaffrie Ct.
17. 76 Herzl St.   76 Herzel St.

Correct Answers

	A	B	C	D	E
1					●
2	●				
3	●				
4					●
5					●
6	●				
7	●				
8					●
9					●
10	●				
11	●				●
12					
13	●				
14	●				
15			●		
16					●
17		●			

Answer Sheet

	A	B	C	D	E
1					
2					
3					
4					
5					
6					
7					
8					
9					
10					
11					
12					
13					
14					
15					
16					
17					

ADDRESS CHECKING TEST THIRTEEN

DIRECTIONS: This is a test of your speed and accuracy in comparing addresses. For Part I of the test. blacken the proper space under A in the Answer Sheet if the two addresses are exactly alike in every way. Blacken B if they are not alike in every way. For Part II of the test. go back to number 1 on the Answer Sheet. But this time blacken the space under D if the two addresses are exactly alike in every way. Blacken the space under E if they are not exactly alike in every way. Allow exactly five minutes.

PART I

1.	375B 18 Lane	375B 18 Lane
2.	59 Stanhope St.	59 Standope St.
3.	279 Glenmore Ave.	279 Glenmor Ave.
4.	46 Tapscot St.	46 Tapscot St.
5.	728 Bristol St.	728 Bristol St.
6.	Portland, Ore.	Portland, Me.
7.	379 Irvington Ave.	379 Irving Ave.
8.	2042 Haring Pl.	2042 Hearing Pl.
9.	45 India Rd.	45 India Rd.
10.	210 Roebling Pl.	210 Robling Pl.
11.	23 O'Brien Pl.	23 O'Brein Pl.
12.	169 Ten Eyck Walk	169 Ten Eye Walk
13.	3210 Ave. H	3210 Ave. H
14.	3000 Emmons Ave.	3000 Emons Ave.
15.	Bloomington, Ill.	Bloomington, Ind.
16.	28 Covert Pl.	28 Convert Pl.
17.	179 Fountain Ave.	179 Fountain Ave.

PART II

1.	1793 Herkimer Ct.	1793 Herkimer Ct.
2.	4115 Snyder Ave.	4115 Snyder Ave.
3.	7316 Sea Cove, La.	7316 Sea Cove La.
4.	2201 Cortelyou Rd.	2201 Cortelyou Rd.
5.	763 Ridgwood Te.	768 Ridgewood Te.
6.	3919 De Quincey St.	3991 De Quincey St.
7.	3 N.E. Sackett Sq.	3 N.W. Sackett Sq.
8.	887 Jefferson Ave. S.	887 Jefferson Ave. S.
9.	498 W. 116 St.	498 W. 116 St.
10.	10 Bay Ridge Ave.	1 Bay Ridge Ave.
11.	5527 Albermarl Rd.	5527 Albermail Rd.
12.	1451 St. Nichols Ave.	1451 St. Nicholas Ave.
13.	5000 W. 13th St.	5000 W. 13th St.
14.	232 Ave. T N.	223 Ave. T N.
15.	7282 Monroe Ave.	7282 Munro Ave.
16.	525 E. 21st St.	525 E. 21st St.
17.	14 E. Bleeker St.	14 E. Bleecker St.

Correct Answers

Answer Sheet

ADDRESS CHECKING TEST FOURTEEN

DIRECTIONS: This is a test of your speed and accuracy in comparing addresses. For Part I of the test, blacken the proper space under A in the Answer Sheet if the two addresses are exactly alike in every way. Blacken B if they are not alike in every way. For Part II of the test, go back to number 1 on the Answer Sheet. But this time blacken the space under D if the two addresses are exactly alike in every way. Blacken the space under E if they are not exactly alike in every way. Allow exactly five minutes.

PART I

1.	707 Timothy Dr.	707 Timothy Dr.
2.	3510 S. Tapscot Ave.	3510 S. Tapscot Ave.
3.	1333 W. 51st St.	1330 W. 51st St.
4.	99 Dunhill Sq.	99 Dunhill Pl.
5.	75 East Division	75 East Division
6.	9324 St. Marks Ave.	9234 St. Marks Ave.
7.	624 N. Ashford St.	624 N. Ashford St.
8.	433 E. 91st Ave.	433 E. 91st Ave.
9.	3 Kings Hway.	3 Kings Hway.
10.	5901 Glenwood Rd.	5901 Glenwood Dr.
11.	2368 Jackson Blvd.	2638 Jackson Blvd.
12.	281 Corbin Bldg.	218 Corbin Bldg.
13.	8918 W. 16th Ave.	8918 W. 16th Ave.
14.	3223 Ave. K S.	3223 Ave. H S.
15.	8875 18th Ave.	8875 28th Ave.
16.	318 Dumont Ave.	318 Dumont Ave.
17.	364 Hinsdale St.	346 Hinsdale St.

PART II

1.	586 Columbus Ave.	586 Columbus Cir.
2.	35 Sutton Pl. So.	35 Sutton Pl. No.
3.	305 Broadway	305 Broadway
4.	935 St. Nicholas Ave.	935 St. Nicholas Ave.
5.	1495 Madison Ave.	149 Madison Ave.
6.	690 Riverside Dr.	690 Riverside Pl.
7.	Newark, N.Y.	Newark, N.J.
8.	30 W. 132 St.	30 W. 13 St.
9.	18 Jacobus Pl.	18 Jacoby Pl.
10.	198 Nagel Ave.	198 Nagle Ave.
11.	31 Washington Sq. W.	31 Washington Sq. W.
12.	78 Elwood Pl.	78 Elmwood Pl.
13.	261 5 Ave.	261 5 Ave.
14.	224 Lafayette St.	224 Lafayette St.
15.	1 Union Sq. W.	1 Union Sq. W.
16.	120 Vermilya Ave.	120 Vermilyia Ave.
17.	Middletown, N.Y.	Middletown, Conn.

Correct Answers

Answer Sheet

TEST XVIII. ADDRESS CHECKING

DIRECTIONS: This is a test of your speed and accuracy in comparing addresses. For Part I of the test, blacken the proper space under A in the Answer Sheet if the two addresses are exactly alike in every way. Blacken B if they are not alike in every way. For Part II of the test, go back to number 1 on the Answer Sheet. But this time blacken the space under D if the two addresses are exactly alike in every way. Blacken the space under E if they are not exactly alike in every way. Allow exactly five minutes.

PART I

1.	10 Mitchell Pl.	10 Mitchel Pl.
2.	154 Ave. D	154 Ave. B
3.	149 Elizabeth St.	149 Elizabeth St.
4.	70 Morningside Dr.	70 Morningside Dr.
5.	158 Dyckman St.	158 Dykman St.
6.	473 E. Houston St.	473 W. Houston St.
7.	76 Beaver St.	76 Beaver St.
8.	58 W. 58 St.	58 E. 58 St.
9.	83 Canon St.	83 Canal St.
10.	71 Waren St.	71 Warren St.
11.	Harrison, Pa.	Harrison, O.
12.	1474 Hindsal Sq.	1474 Hindsel Sq.
13.	2447 Pitkin St.	4247 Pitkin St.
14.	165 Woodruff Ave.	165 Woodruff Ave.
15.	892 E. Esplanade	829 E. Esplanade
16.	1241 44th St. N.W.	1241 44th St. N.W.
17.	728 Gerrison Dr.	728 Garrison Dr.

PART II

1.	9 Monument Wk.	9 Monument Pl.
2.	136 S. 3rd Ave.	136 S. 3rd Ave.
3.	393 Legion St.	939 Legion St.
4.	511 W. Williams	511 W. Williams
5.	3648 N. Griffin	3648 N. Griffin
6.	Wesley, O.	Wellesley, O.
7.	988 S. Portland Ave.	988 S. Portland Ave.
8.	4488 N. Becket Ave.	4488 N. Beckett Ave.
9.	2156 Linden Blvd.	2165 Linden Blvd.
10.	7219 Ionia Ave.	7219 Ionia Ave.
11.	1692 Walnut St.	1962 Walnut St.
12.	738 Christenberry, La.	738 Christenberry, La.
13.	454 Livonia Ave.	454 Livima Ave.
14.	6506 Rogers Pkwy.	6506 Rogers Pkwy.
15.	918 Audobon Rd.	918 Audubon Rd.
16.	76 Manhattan Ct.	76 Manhattan Ct.
17.	1513 W. 49th St.	1513 W. 49th St.

Correct Answers

	A	B	C	D	E
1		B			
2					E
3	A				
4	A				
5		B			
6		B			
7					E
8		B			
9		B			
10		B			
11		B			
12		B			
13		B			
14	A			D	
15	A				
16			C		
17		B			

Answer Sheet

	A	B	C	D	E
1					
2					
3					
4					
5					
6					
7					
8					
9					
10					
11					
12					
13					
14					
15					
16					
17					

TEST XIX. ADDRESS CHECKING

DIRECTIONS: This is a test of your speed and accuracy in comparing addresses. For Part I of the test, blacken the proper space under A in the Answer Sheet if the two addresses are exactly alike in every way. Blacken B if they are not alike in every way. For Part II of the test, go back to number 1 on the Answer Sheet. But this time blacken the space under D if the two addresses are exactly alike in every way. Blacken the space under E if they are not exactly alike in every way. Allow exactly five minutes.

PART I

1. 565 N. Wilson Ave. — 656 N. Wilson Ave.
2. 116 S. Haverymeyer — 116 S. Haverymcyer
3. 403 N.J. Ave. S. — 403 N.J. Ave. S
4. 1183 Saffrin Blvd. — 1183 Saffarin Blvd.
5. 194 Van Buren Ct. — 194 Van Buren Ct.
6. 2919 Owens Pl. S. — 2915 Owens Pl. S.
7. 1024 N. Riley St. — 1024 N. Riley Ave.
8. 3920 Cyprus Ave. — 3902 Cyprus Ave.
9. 59 W. Graham Ave. — 59 W. Graham Ave.
10. Waco, Texas — Waco, Tex.
11. Valley Forge, Pa. — Valley Forge, Pa.
12. 570 Grand Ave. — 570 Grande Ave.
13. Lowell, Mass. — Lowel, Mass.
14. 887 Anson Rd. — 887 Anson Rd.
15. 2051 Porter Pl. — 2051 Porter Pl.
16. Dover, N.H. — Dover
17. Hot Spring, Ark. — Hot Springs, Ark.
18. 37930 Dunbar Lane — 37039 Dunbar Lane

PART II

1. 7043 Layton Dr. — 7043 Layton Dr.
2. Williamsport, Pa. — Williamsport, Pa.
3. 1902 E. Sumac Ave. — 1092 Sumac Ave.
4. 118 Avon Ave. — 181 Avon Ave.
5. Hood River, Oreg. — Hoods River, Oreg.
6. Hazel Park, Mich. — Hazel Drive, Mich.
7. 4012 Austen Lane — 4012 Austen Lane
8. 91989 Winchester Lane — 19189 Winchestor Ave.
9. Elmwood, N.Y. — Elmwood, N.Y.
10. Pamlico, N.C. — Pimlico, N.C.
11. 3423 Kell St. — 3423 Kall St.
12. Haverhill, Mass. — Haverhill, Mass.
13. 160 Caleb St. — 160 Caleb St.
14. New Haven, Conn — New Haben, Conn.
15. 272 West End Ave. — 277 West End Ave.
16. Brewster, Maine — Brewer, Maine
17. 604 Sherman Ave. — 604 Sherman Ave.
18. Westport, Conn. — Westport, Conn.

TEST XX. ADDRESS CHECKING

DIRECTIONS: *This is a test of your speed and accuracy in comparing addresses. For Part I of the test, blacken the proper space under A in the Answer Sheet if the two addresses are exactly alike in every way. Blacken B if they are not alike in every way. For Part II of the test, go back to number 1 on the Answer Sheet. But this time blacken the space under D if the two addresses are exactly alike in every way. Blacken the space under E if they are not exactly alike in every way. Allow exactly five minutes.*

PART I

1. 1763 Bradley St.	1763 Bradly St.
2. Portsmouth, N.H.	Portsmouth, Va.
3. 130 Hicks St.	130 Hicks St.
4. Bristol, Conn.	Briston, Conn.
5. 702 Tyrol Lane	702 Tyrol Lane
6. Hickville, N.Y.	Hicksville, N.Y.
7. 465 S. Main St.	465 S. Main St.
8. Topeka, Kansas	Topeka Kansas
9. 323 Linden Blvd.	332 Linden Blvd.
10. Salt Lake City, Utah	Salt Lake, Utah
11. 1149 Cherry Grove	1149 Cheery Grove
12. Spokane, Wash.	Spokane, Wash.
13. 882 Vernon Blvd.	882 Vernan Blvd.
14. Boca Raton, Fla.	Boca Raton, Fla.
15. 775 Spruce Street	775 Spruce St.
16. Barrie, N.H.	Barrie, N.H.
17. 9055 Carter Rd.	9055 Carter Rd.
18. Englewood, N.J.	Englewood, N.J.

PART II

1. 6896 Tower Ave.	6869 Tower Ave.
2. Salem, Mass.	Salem, Mass.
3. 1202 Ogden	1220 Ogden
4. Albany, N.Y.	Albany, N.Y.
5. 3306 Dale Ave.	3306 Dale St.
6. Danbury, Conn.	Danbery, Conn.
7. Charlotte, N.C.	Charlotte, S.C.
8. Rockport, R.I.	Rockland, R.I.
9. 1421 White St.	14211 White St.
10. 2056 S. 10th St.	2056 S. 10th St.
11. Easton, Pa.	Eston, Pa.
12. 51510 Hamlen Pl.	5510 Hamlen Pl.
13. 7976 Stanton Rd.	7976 Stanton Rd.
14. 1711 Spring St.	1711 Spring St.
15. Troy, N.Y.	Troy, New York
16. Passaic, N.J.	Passaic, Md.
17. 282 N. Shore Dr.	282 N. Shore Dr.
18. 2765 Glenwood Ave.	2765 Glenwood Ave.

Correct Answers

	A	B	C	D	E
1		B			E
2	A		C		
3	A				
4	A			D	
5	A				
6		B			
7	A				
8	A				
9		B			
10		B			
11		B			
12	A				
13		B		D	
14	A				
15	A				E
16	A				E
17	A				
18	A	B			

Answer Sheet

	A	B	C	D	E
1					
2					
3					
4					
5					
6					
7					
8					
9					
10					
11					
12					
13					
14					
15					
16					
17					
18					

POST OFFICE CLERK-CARRIER

MEMORY FOR ADDRESSES

According to our information, your test will almost certainly be concerned with your clerical aptitude. This means that they will want to discover your chances of success in the job or in any clerical training they may find it necessary to give you. This section will familiarize you with clerical aptitude test questions. Read on.

HOW TO PROFIT FROM THE PRACTICE TESTS

On the following pages you are furnished practice tests consisting of questions like those on the actual exam. The time limit here is just about what you may expect. Take these tests as a series of dress rehearsals strengthening your ability to score high on this type of question. For each test use the Answer Sheet provided to mark down your answers. If the Answer Sheet is separated from the questions, tear it out so you can mark it more easily. As you finish each test, go back and check your answers to find your score, and to determine how well you did. This will help you discover where you need more practice.

DESCRIPTION OF THE TEST AND SAMPLE QUESTIONS

Here are some sample questions for you to do. Mark your answers on the Sample Answer Sheet, making sure to keep your mark inside the correct box. If you want to change an answer, erase the mark you don't want to count. Then mark your new answer. Use a No. 2 (medium) pencil.

Correct Answers are consolidated after the last question.

In this test you will be given 25 addresses to remember. The addresses are divided into five groups. Each group of five addresses is in a box such as those below. Each box has a letter—A, B, C, D, or E. You will have to learn which letter goes with each address. You will be given time to study in the examination room. In order to practice for this test, you need to be timed.

While you are doing the practice test, find out what is the best way for you to memorize which letter goes with each address. Some people learn best by studying the addresses in one box; then covering it and seeing whether they can say the addresses to themselves. If they can say them, they then try to learn the next box. If they cannot, they study the names in the first box again; and then try to say the names with the box covered. They do this for all the boxes. Other people learn best by studying across the page. Still others do best by memorizing everything at once. If you do not know your best way, try different ways and see which one is best for you. Do not try to memorize the names by writing them down because you won't be allowed to write them in the official examination.

Sample Questions

The test has five boxes labeled A, B, C, D, E. Each box contains five addresses. Three of the five addresses are groups of street addresses like 2100–2799 Mall, 4800–4999 Cliff and 1900–2299 Laurel, and two are names of places. They are different in each box. You will be given two lists of addresses. For each street address or name in the list, you are to decide in which lettered box (A, B, C, D, or E) it belongs and then mark that box on the answer sheet. For List 1, the boxes will be shown on the same page with the addresses. While you are working on List 2, you will not be able to look at the boxes. Then you will have to match the addresses with the correct box from memory. Try to memorize the location of as many addresses as you can.

A	B	C	D	E
2100–2799 Mall	3900–4399 Mall	4400–4599 Mall	3400–3899 Mall	2800–3399 Mall
Ceres	Cedar	Niles	Cicero	Delhi
4800–4999 Cliff	4000–4299 Cliff	3300–3999 Cliff	4500–4799 Cliff	4300–4499 Cliff
Natoma	Foster	Dexter	Pearl	Magnet
1900–2299 Laurel	2300–2999 Laurel	3200–3799 Laurel	3000–3199 Laurel	1500–1899 Laurel

Sample Questions:

1. 3300–3999 Cliff—This address is in box C. So you would **darken box C.**
2. Natoma—This name is in box A. So you would **darken box A.**
3. Foster
4. 1500–1899 Laurel
5. 3900–4399 Mall
6. Pearl
7. 3200–3799 Laurel

END OF TEST

CONSOLIDATE YOUR KEY ANSWERS HERE

Practice using Answer Sheets. Make ONE mark for each answer. Additional and stray marks may be counted as mistakes. In making corrections erase errors COMPLETELY. Make glossy black marks. To arrive at an accurate estimate of your ability and progress, cover the Correct Answers with a sheet of white paper while you are taking this test.

SAMPLE ANSWER SHEET

```
   A B C D E      A B C D E      A B C D E      A B C D E      A B C D E      A B C D E      A B C D E
1 [][][][][]  2 [][][][][]  3 [][][][][]  4 [][][][][]  5 [][][][][]  6 [][][][][]  7 [][][][][]
```

CORRECT ANSWERS TO SAMPLE QUESTIONS

Now compare your answers with the Correct Answers to Sample Questions. If your answers are not the same as the correct answers shown, go back and study the samples to see where you made a mistake.

1. C   2. A   3. B   4. E   5. B   6. D   7. C

TEST I.   MEMORIZING NAMES

MEMORIZING TIME: 3 Minutes

TESTING TIME: 3 Minutes. 88 Questions.

DIRECTIONS: This is a test of memory, speed, and accuracy in which you will be given names, numbers, or addresses to remember. They are divided into five groups, boxed and lettered A, B, C, D, E. For each question, mark the Answer Sheet to show the letter of the box in which the item belongs. If you are not sure of an answer you should guess. Try to remember the box-location of as many items as you can.

Correct Answers are consolidated after the last question.

A	B	C	D	E
Miller	Lovelock	Williams	Bruce	Hume
Ione	Reno	Fallon	Woolery	McLean
Jacobs	Ely	Avery	Jordan	Benton
Oreana	Austin	Rouse	Malone	Nevins

1. Woolery
2. Ely
3. Avery
4. Nevins
5. Miller

6. Fallon
7. Jordan
8. Lovelock
9. Austin
10. Jacobs

11. Benton
12. Malone
13. Ione
14. Oreana
15. McLean

16. Rouse
17. Hume
18. Reno
19. Williams
20. Bruce

21. Nevins
22. Austin
23. Lovelock
24. Fallon
25. Hume

26. Oreana
27. Ely
28. Jordan
29. McLean
30. Jacobs

31. Avery
32. Oreana
33. Rouse
34. Bruce
35. Woolery

36. Miller
37. Austin
38. Benton
39. Malone
40. Avery

41. Ione
42. Williams
43. McLean
44. Jordan
45. Ely

46. Nevins
47. Fallon
48. Reno
49. Lovelock
50. Woolery

51. Hume
52. Oreana
53. Jacobs
54. Rouse
55. Benton

56. Bruce
57. Malone
58. Miller
59. Austin
60. Benton

61. Ione
62. Nevins
63. Bruce
64. Williams
65. Reno

66. Hume
67. Rouse
68. McLean
69. Oreana
70. Ione

71. Malone
72. Benton
73. Jacobs
74. Austin
75. Lovelock

76. Jordan
77. Fallon
78. Miller
79. Nevins
80. Avery

81. Ely
82. Woolery
83. Jacobs
84. Jordan
85. Hume

86. Benton
87. Austin
88. Williams

STOP.

If you finish before the time is up, go back and check your answers for the questions on this page. Do not go to any other page until the time is up.

51108

CONSOLIDATE YOUR KEY ANSWERS HERE

Practice using Answer Sheets. Make ONE mark for each answer. Additional and stray marks may be counted as mistakes. In making corrections erase errors COMPLETELY. Make glossy black marks. To arrive at an accurate estimate of your ability and progress, cover the Correct Answers with a sheet of white paper while you are taking this test.

SAMPLE ANSWER SHEET

CORRECT ANSWERS TO THE FOREGOING PRACTICE QUESTIONS

Now compare your answers with these Correct Answers to the Practice Questions. If your answers differ from these, go back and study those questions to see where and how you made your mistakes.

1.D	12.D	23.B	34.D	45.B	56.D	67.C	78.A
2.B	13.A	24.C	35.D	46.E	57.D	68.E	79.E
3.C	14.A	25.E	36.A	47.C	58.A	69.A	80.C
4.E	15.E	26.A	37.B	48.B	59.B	70.A	81.B
5.A	16.C	27.B	38.E	49.B	60.E	71.D	82.D
6.C	17.E	28.D	39.D	50.D	61.A	72.E	83.A
7.D	18.B	29.E	40.C	51.E	62.E	73.A	84.D
8.B	19.C	30.A	41.A	52.A	63.D	74.B	85.E
9.B	20.D	31.C	42.C	53.A	64.C	75.B	86.E
10.A	21.E	32.A	43.E	54.C	65.B	76.D	87.B
11.E	22.B	33.C	44.D	55.E	66.E	77.C	88.C

TEST II. MEMORY FOR NAMES

TIME: 5 Minutes. 88 Questions.

DIRECTIONS: Having committed to memory the box-locations in the previous Memorizing test, you must now mark your Answer Sheet for each question to show the letter of the box in which the item belongs. Do not turn back to the lettered boxes in the previous Memorizing test. Answer as best you can from memory.

Correct Answers are consolidated after the last question.

1. Avery	21. Fallon	41. Hume	61. Avery	76. Miller
2. Jordan	22. Malone	42. Rouse	62. Oreana	77. Austin
3. Bruce	23. Avery	43. McLean	63. Rouse	78. Benton
4. Ione	24. Bruce	44. Oreana	64. Bruce	79. Malone
5. Fallon	25. Ione	45. Ione	65. Woolery	80. Avery
6. Austin	26. Austin	46. Ione	66. Fallon	81. Benton
7. Rouse	27. Jacobs	47. Nevins	67. Jordan	82. Malone
8. McLean	28. Williams	48. Bruce	68. Lovelock	83. Ione
9. Miller	29. Benton	49. Williams	69. Austin	84. Oreana
10. Benton	30. Miller	50. Reno	70. Jacobs	85. McLean
11. Williams	31. Nevins	51. Nevins	71. Hume	86. Nevins
12. Nevins	32. Rouse	52. Austin	72. Oreana	87. Fallon
13. McLean	33. Avery	53. Lovelock	73. Jacobs	88. Reno
14. Ely	34. Reno	54. Fallon	74. Rouse	
15. Jordan	35. Fallon	55. Hume	75. Benton	
16. Woolery	36. Malone	56. Bruce		
17. Reno	37. Benton	57. Malone		
18. Lovelock	38. Jacobs	58. Miller		
19. Oreana	39. Austin	59. Austin		
20. Hume	40. Lovelock	60. Benton		

STOP.

If you finish before the time is up, go back and rework the questions on this page only.

WHEN THE TIME IS UP, TURN TO THE NEXT PAGE.

CONSOLIDATE YOUR KEY ANSWERS HERE

Practice using Answer Sheets. Make ONE mark for each answer. Additional and stray marks may be counted as mistakes. In making corrections erase errors COMPLETELY. Make glossy black marks. To arrive at an accurate estimate of your ability and progress, Cover the Correct Answers with a sheet of white paper while you are taking this test.

SAMPLE ANSWER SHEET

CORRECT ANSWERS TO THE FOREGOING PRACTICE QUESTIONS

Now compare your answers with these Correct Answers to the Practice Questions. If your answers differ from these, go back and study those questions to see where and how you made your mistakes.

1.C	12.E	23.C	34.B	45.A	56.D	67.D	78.E
2.D	13.E	24.D	35.C	46.A	57.D	68.B	79.D
3.D	14.B	25.A	36.D	47.E	58.A	69.B	80.C
4.A	15.D	26.B	37.E	48.D	59.B	70.A	81.E
5.C	16.D	27.A	38.A	49.C	60.E	71.E	82.D
6.B	17.B	28.C	39.B	50.B	61.C	72.A	83.A
7.C	18.B	29.E	40.B	51.E	62.A	73.A	84.A
8.E	19.A	30.A	41.E	52.B	63.C	74.C	85.E
9.A	20.E	31.E	42.C	53.B	64.D	75.E	86.E
10.E	21.C	32.C	43.E	54.C	65.D	76.A	87.C
11.C	22.D	33.C	44.A	55.E	66.C	77.B	88.B

TEST III. MEMORIZING NAMES

MEMORIZING TIME: 5 Minutes

TESTING TIME: 5 Minutes. 88 Questions.

DIRECTIONS: This is a test of memory, speed, and accuracy in which you will be given names, numbers, or addresses to remember. They are divided into five groups, boxed and lettered A, B, C, D, E. For each question, mark the Answer Sheet to show the letter of the box in which the item belongs. If you are not sure of an answer you should guess. Try to remember the box-location of as many items as you can.

Correct Answers are consolidated after the last question.

A	B	C	D	E
Woodruff	Kirlin	Newland	Hansen	Charles
Drake	Brown	Cisco	Dryer	Tippet
Bradway	Wiggins	Volk	Forbes	Gentry
Snyder	Downer	Seward	Osborn	Ellison

1. Ellison
2. Wiggins
3. Brown
4. Drake
5. Hansen

6. Volk
7. Forbes
8. Snyder
9. Tippet
10. Cisco

11. Newland
12. Gentry
13. Woodruff
14. Dryer
15. Charles

16. Osborn
17. Seward
18. Bradway
19. Kirlin
20. Downer

21. Seward
22. Drake
23. Forbes
24. Cisco
25. Dryer

26. Ellison
27. Newland
28. Wiggins
29. Brown
30. Tippet

31. Snyder
32. Kirlin
33. Charles
34. Volk
35. Newland

36. Gentry
37. Drake
38. Dryer
39. Forbes
40. Bradway

41. Wiggins
42. Hansen
43. Osborn
44. Brown
45. Tippet

46. Downer
47. Seward
48. Woodruff
49. Ellison
50. Snyder

51. Kirlin
52. Gentry
53. Cisco
54. Newland
55. Charles

56. Bradway
57. Forbes
58. Drake
59. Osborn
60. Volk

61. Downer
62. Wiggins
63. Bradway
64. Gentry
65. Brown

66. Hansen
67. Cisco
68. Dryer
69. Kirlin
70. Seward

71. Snyder
72. Ellison
73. Drake
74. Forbes
75. Volk

76. Downer
77. Newland
78. Woodruff
79. Tippet
80. Osborn

81. Wiggins
82. Gentry
83. Gentry
84. Volk
85. Brown

86. Kirlin
87. Ellison
88. Snyder

STOP.

If you finish before the 5 minutes are up, go back and check your answers for the questions on this page.

CONSOLIDATE YOUR KEY ANSWERS HERE

Practice using Answer Sheets. Make ONE mark for each answer. Additional and stray marks may be counted as mistakes. In making corrections erase errors COMPLETELY. Make glossy black marks. To arrive at an accurate estimate of your ability and progress, cover the Correct Answers with a sheet of white paper while you are taking this test.

SAMPLE ANSWER SHEET

CORRECT ANSWERS TO THE FOREGOING PRACTICE QUESTIONS

Now compare your answers with these Correct Answers to the Practice Questions: If your answers differ from these, go back and study those questions to see where and how you made your mistakes.

1.E	12.E	23.D	34.C	45.E	56.A	67.C	78.A
2.B	13.A	24.C	35.C	46.B	57.D	68.D	79.E
3.B	14.D	25.D	36.E	47.C	58.A	69.B	80.D
4.A	15.E	26.E	37.A	48.A	59.D	70.C	81.B
5.D	16.D	27.C	38.D	49.E	60.C	71.A	82.E
6.C	17.C	28.B	39.D	50.A	61.B	72.E	83.E
7.D	18.A	29.B	40.A	51.B	62.B	73.A	84.C
8.A	19.B	30.E	41.B	52.E	63.A	74.D	85.B
9.E	20.B	31.A	42.D	53.C	64.E	75.C	86.B
10.C	21.C	32.B	43.D	54.C	65.B	76.B	87.E
11.C	22.A	33.E	44.B	55.E	66.D	77.C	88.A

TEST IV. MEMORY FOR NAMES

TIME: 5 Minutes. 88 Questions.

DIRECTIONS: Having committed to memory the box-locations in the previous Memorizing test, you must now mark your Answer Sheet for each question to show the letter of the box in which the item belongs. Do not turn back to the lettered boxes in the previous Memorizing test. Answer as best you can from memory.

Correct Answers are consolidated after the last question.

1. Cisco	21. Kirlin	41. Snyder	61. Ellison	76. Volk
2. Hansen	22. Gentry	42. Ellison	62. Wiggins	77. Forbes
3. Forbes	23. Hansen	43. Drake	63. Brown	78. Snyder
4. Charles	24. Charles	44. Forbes	64. Drake	79. Tippet
5. Snyder	25. Volk	45. Volk	65. Hansen	80. Cisco
6. Woodruff	26. Forbes	46. Downer	66. Osborn	81. Snyder
7. Seward	27. Snyder	47. Wiggins	67. Seward	82. Kirlin
8. Volk	28. Woodruff	48. Bradway	68. Bradway	83. Charles
9. Tippet	29. Tippet	49. Gentry	69. Kirlin	84. Volk
10. Forbes	30. Wiggins	50. Brown	70. Downer	85. Newland
11. Newland	31. Dryer	51. Newland	71. Seward	86. Bradway
12. Downer	32. Bradway	52. Gentry	72. Drake	87. Forbes
13. Osborn	33. Hansen	53. Woodruff	73. Forbes	88. Drake
14. Cisco	34. Drake	54. Dryer	74. Cisco	
15. Drake	35. Newland	55. Charles	75. Dryer	
16. Wiggins	36. Wiggins	56. Ellison		**STOP.**
17. Ellison	37. Gentry	57. Newland		
18. Dryer	38. Gentry	58. Wiggins		If you finish before the
19. Brown	39. Volk	59. Brown		5 minutes are up, go back
20. Bradway	40. Brown	60. Tippet		and check your answers.

At the end of the 5 minutes, compare your answers with those given in the Correct Answers for sample questions.

CONSOLIDATE YOUR KEY ANSWERS HERE

Practice using Answer Sheets. Make ONE mark for each answer. Additional and stray marks may be counted as mistakes. In making corrections erase errors COMPLETELY. Make glossy black marks. To arrive at an accurate estimate of your ability and progress, Cover the Correct Answers with a sheet of white paper while you are taking this test.

SAMPLE ANSWER SHEET

CORRECT ANSWERS TO THE FOREGOING PRACTICE QUESTIONS

Now compare your answers with these Correct Answers to the Practice Questions. If your answers differ from these, go back and study those questions to see where and how you made your mistakes.

1.C	12.B	23.D	34.A	45.C	56.E	67.C	78.A
2.D	13.D	24.E	35.C	46.B	57.C	68.A	79.E
3.D	14.C	25.C	36.B	47.B	58.B	69.B	80.C
4.E	15.A	26.D	37.E	48.A	59.B	70.B	81.A
5.A	16.B	27.A	38.E	49.E	60.E	71.C	82.B
6.A	17.E	28.A	39.C	50.B	61.E	72.A	83.E
7.C	18.D	29.E	40.B	51.C	62.B	73.D	84.C
8.C	19.B	30.B	41.A	52.E	63.B	74.C	85.C
9.E	20.A	31.D	42.E	53.A	64.A	75.D	86.A
10.D	21.B	32.A	43.A	54.D	65.D	76.C	87.D
11.C	22.E	33.D	44.D	55.E	66.D	77.D	88.A

TEST V.   MEMORIZING NAMES

MEMORIZING TIME: 3 Minutes

TESTING TIME: 3 Minutes. 88 Questions.

DIRECTIONS: This is a test of memory, speed, and accuracy in which you will be given names, numbers, or addresses to remember. They are divided into five groups, boxed and lettered A, B, C, D, E. For each question, mark the Answer Sheet to show the letter of the box in which the item belongs. If you are not sure of an answer you should guess. Try to remember the box-location of as many items as you can.

Correct Answers are consolidated after the last question.

A	B	C	D	E
Bellows Martin Wykoff Smith	Holmes Conrad Allee James	Cutler Syrus Pearson Mapps	Zubin Raker Friese Hutton	Danner Jonson Gage Ibler

1. Conrad	21. Cutler	41. Zubin	61. Bellows	76. Zubin
2. Ibler	22. Syrus	42. Martin	62. James	77. Allee
3. Wykoff	23. Ibler	43. Conrad	63. Jonson	78. Smith
4. Mapps	24. Wykoff	44. Danner	64. Martin	79. Ibler
5. Syrus	25. Hutton	45. Hutton	65. Friese	80. Pearson
6. Zubin	26. Bellows	46. Wykoff	66. Holmes	81. Bellows
7. Bellows	27. James	47. Raker	67. Syrus	82. Jonson
8. Gage	28. Danner	48. Bellows	68. Conrad	83. Holmes
9. Pearson	29. Zubin	49. Mapps	69. Mapps	84. Gage
10. Allee	30. Raker	50. Ibler	70. Hutton	85. Syrus
11. Cutler	31. Mapps	51. Smith	71. Wykoff	86. Danner
12. Danner	32. Allee	52. Gage	72. Raker	87. Friese
13. Friese	33. Jonson	53. Syrus	73. James	88. Smith
14. Holmes	34. Pearson	54. Friese	74. Gage	
15. Raker	35. Friese	55. Hutton	75. Danner	

STOP.

16. Hutton	36. Holmes	56. Raker	
17. Martin	37. Gage	57. Allee	
18. Jonson	38. Cutler	58. Conrad	
19. Smith	39. James	59. Danner	
20. James	40. Syrus	60. Pearson	

If you finish before the time is up, go back and check your answers for the questions on this page. Do not go to any other page until the time is up.

S1108

CONSOLIDATE YOUR KEY ANSWERS HERE

Practice using Answer Sheets. Make ONE mark for each answer. Additional and stray marks may be counted as mistakes. In making corrections erase errors COMPLETELY. Make glossy black marks. To arrive at an accurate estimate of your ability and progress, cover the Correct Answers with a sheet of white paper while you are taking this test.

SAMPLE ANSWER SHEET

CORRECT ANSWERS TO THE FOREGOING PRACTICE QUESTIONS

Now compare your answers with these Correct Answers to the Practice Questions. If your answers differ from these, go back and study those questions to see where and how you made your mistakes.

1.B	12.E	23.E	34.C	45.D	56.D	67.C	78.A
2.E	13.D	24.A	35.D	46.A	57.B	68.B	79.E
3.A	14.B	25.D	36.B	47.D	58.B	69.C	80.C
4.C	15.D	26.A	37.E	48.A	59.E	70.D	81.A
5.C	16.D	27.B	38.C	49.C	60.C	71.A	82.E
6.D	17.A	28.E	39.B	50.E	61.A	72.D	83.B
7.A	18.E	29.D	40.C	51.A	62.B	73.B	84.E
8.E	19.A	30.D	41.D	52.E	63.E	74.E	85.C
9.C	20.B	31.C	42.A	53.C	64.A	75.E	86.E
10.B	21.C	32.B	43.B	54.D	65.D	76.D	87.D
11.C	22.C	33.E	44.E	55.D	66.B	77.B	88.A

TEST VI. MEMORY FOR NAMES

TIME: 5 Minutes. 88 Questions.

DIRECTIONS: *Having committed to memory the box-locations in the previous Memorizing test, you must now mark your Answer Sheet for each question to show the letter of the box in which the item belongs. Do not turn back to the lettered boxes in the previous Memorizing test. Answer as best you can from memory.*

Correct Answers are consolidated after the last question.

1. Mapps	21. Mapps	41. Bellows	61. Smith	76. Wykoff
2. Raker	22. Zubin	42. Jonson	62. Gage	77. Raker
3. Smith	23. Martin	43. Holmes	63. Syrus	78. Bellows
4. Bellows	24. Raker	44. Gage	64. Friese	79. Mapps
5. Jonson	25. Danner	45. Syrus	65. Hutton	80. Ibler
6. James	26. Bellows	46. Zubin	66. Raker	81. Zubin
7. Ibler	27. Holmes	47. Allee	67. Allee	82. Martin
8. Zubin	28. Wykoff	48. Smith	68. Conrad	83. Conrad
9. Holmes	29. Ibler	49. Ibler	69. Danner	84. Danner
10. Wykoff	30. James	50. Pearson	70. Pearson	85. Hutton
11. Danner	31. Jonson	51. Wykoff	71. Bellows	86. Holmes
12. Smith	32. Pearson	52. Raker	72. James	87. Gage
13. Allee	33. Raker	53. James	73. Jonson	88. Cutler
14. Syrus	34. Smith	54. Gage	74. Martin	
15. Friese	35. Allee	55. Danner	75. Friese	
16. Raker	36. Danner	56. Holmes		
17. Hutton	37. Friese	57. Syrus		
18. Martin	38. Smith	58. Conrad		
19. Cutler	39. Ibler	59. Mapps		
20. Pearson	40. Conrad	60. Hutton		

STOP.

If you finish before the 5 minutes are up, go back and check your answers.

END OF TEST

Go on to do the following Test in this Examination, just as you would be expected to do on the actual exam.

CONSOLIDATE YOUR KEY ANSWERS HERE

Practice using Answer Sheets. Make ONE mark for each answer. Additional and stray marks may be counted as mistakes. In making corrections erase errors COMPLETELY. Make glossy black marks. To arrive at an accurate estimate of your ability and progress, Cover the Correct Answers with a sheet of white paper while you are taking this test.

SAMPLE ANSWER SHEET

CORRECT ANSWERS TO THE FOREGOING PRACTICE QUESTIONS

Now compare your answers with these Correct Answers to the Practice Questions. If your answers differ from these, go back and study those questions to see where and how you made your mistakes.

1.C	12.A	23.A	34.A	45.C	56.B	67.B	78.A
2.D	13.B	24.D	35.B	46.D	57.C	68.B	79.C
3.A	14.C	25.E	36.E	47.B	58.B	69.E	80.E
4.A	15.D	26.A	37.D	48.A	59.C	70.C	81.D
5.E	16.D	27.B	38.A	49.E	60.D	71.A	82.A
6.B	17.D	28.A	39.E	50.C	61.A	72.B	83.B
7.E	18.A	29.E	40.B	51.A	62.E	73.E	84.E
8.D	19.C	30.B	41.A	52.D	63.C	74.A	85.D
9.B	20.C	31.E	42.E	53.B	64.D	75.D	86.B
10.A	21.C	32.C	43.B	54.E	65.D	76.A	87.E
11.E	22.D	33.D	44.E	55.E	66.D	77.D	88.C

POST OFFICE CLERK-CARRIER

PART FOUR

Practice With Subjects

from Previous Exams

The examination for Post Office Clerk-Carrier has been administered in several different forms over the years. In the past a general examination was always included which consisted of testing in arithmetic, vocabulary, verbal analogies, reading comprehension and English usage. Recently the examination has been limited to two parts, address checking and memory for addresses. It is not known if future tests will again revert to the use of general testing. Therefore the sections for preparation for this part of the examination are still included in this book. If you use this section of the book to prepare for your examination it will be of enormous benefit to you whether or not general testing is used on the examination. Properly used, it will provide the "mental gymnastics" necessary to sharpen your mind for the actual examination. It will also provide you with the degree of patience necessary for successful examination participation and its contents will enhance your opportunities for promotion after being appointed to the position you are hoping to get.

In the past, the Post Office Clerk-Carrier exam included tests which measured reading comprehension and vocabulary. There was also a test of reasoning ability, called Number Series. The latest examination included only Address Checking and Memory for Addresses, as presented in the Verisimilar Examinations in this book.

The chapters in Part IV are intended to familiarize you with the kinds of questions asked on previous Postal Exams. We suggest that you study them so that you will be prepared to answer these questions if they should reappear on your exam.

TOP SCORES ON VOCABULARY TESTS

Although questions on vocabulary may not actually appear on your test, it is advisable to practice with the kind of material you have in this chapter. Words and their meanings are quite important in pushing up your score on tests of reading, comprehension, effective writing and correct usage. By broadening your vocabulary, you will definitely improve your marks in these and similar subjects.

INCREASE YOUR VOCABULARY

How is your vocabulary? Do you know the meanings of just about every word you come upon in your reading—or do you find several words that stump you? You must increase your vocabulary if you want to read with understanding. Following are steps that you can take in order to build up your word power:

(a) Read as much as you have the time for. Don't confine yourself to one type of reading either. Read all kinds of newspapers, magazines, books. Seek variety in what you read—different newspapers, several types of magazines, all types of books (novels, poetry, essays, plays, etc.). If you get into the habit of reading widely, your vocabulary will grow by leaps and bounds. You'll learn the meanings of words *by context.*

(b) Take vocabulary tests. There are many practice books which have word tests. We suggest one of these: *2300 Steps to Word Power* — (Arco Publishing Co.). These tests are fun to take—and they will build up your vocabulary fast.

(c) Listen to lectures, discussions, and talks by people who speak well. There are some worthwhile TV programs that have excellent speakers. Listen to such people—you'll learn a great many words.

(d) Use a dictionary. Whenever you don't know the meaning of a word, make a note of it. Then, when you get to a dictionary, look up the meaning of the word. Keep your own little notebook—call it "New Words." In a month or two, you will have added a great many words to your vocabulary. If you do not have a dictionary at home, you should buy one. A good dictionary is not expensive.

BASIC LETTER COMBINATIONS

One of the most efficient ways in which you can build up your vocabulary is by a systematic study of the basic word and letter combinations which make up the greater part of the English language.

Etymology is the science of the formation of words, and this somewhat frightening-sounding science can be of great help to you in learning new words and identifying words which may be unfamiliar to you. You will also find that the progress you make in studying the following pages will help to improve your spelling.

A great many of the words which we use every day have come into our language from the Latin and Greek. In the process of being absorbed into English, they appear as parts of words, many of which are related in meaning to each other.

For your convenience, this material is presented in easy-to-study form. Latin and Greek syllables and letter-combinations have been categorized into three groups:

1. *Prefixes:* letter combinations which appear at the beginning of a word.

2. *Suffixes:* letter combinations which appear at the end of a word.

3. *Roots or stems:* which carry the basic meaning and are combined with each other and with prefixes and suffixes to create other words with related meanings.

With the prefixes and suffixes, which you should study first, we have given examples of word formation with meanings, and additional examples. If you find any unfamiliar words among the samples, consult your dictionary to look up their meanings.

The list of roots or stems is accompanied by words in which the letter combinations appear. Here again, use the dictionary to look up any words which are not clear in your mind.

Remember that this section is not meant for easy reading. It is a guide to a program of study that will prove invaluable if you do your part. Do not try to swallow too much at one time. If you can put in a half-hour every day, your study will yield better results.

After you have done your preliminary work and have gotten a better idea of how words are formed in English, schedule the various vocabulary tests and quizzes we have provided in this chapter. They cover a wide variety of the vocabulary questions commonly encountered on examinations. They are short quizzes, not meant to be taken all at one time. Space them out. Adhere closely to the directions which differ for the different test types. Keep an honest record of your scores. Study your mistakes. Look them up in your dictionary. Concentrate closely on each quiz . . . and watch your scores improve.

HINTS FOR IMPROVING YOUR VOCABULARY

Vocabulary tests are really just tests of your knowledge of the meaning of words.

Would you like to increase your vocabulary so that you will do better on this kind of test?

Here are some things that you can do:

1. Some newspapers and magazines print quizzes, or little tests, on the meaning of words. Try these quizzes when you see them. Write down the words that you miss and try to learn what they mean.

2. Read newspapers and magazines and write down all the words that you don't know. Then look them up in a dictionary. The library has dictionaries.

3. Anytime you look up a word, write a sentence using it or try to use it when you talk.

4. Borrow a book to help build up your vocabulary from your library. Then do what the book tells you to do.

To increase your knowledge of words, remember to—

1. Read more.

2. Look up words you aren't sure of.

3. Use new words often so that they will become a part of your vocabulary.

ETYMOLOGY -
A KEY TO WORD RECOGNITION

PREFIXES

PREFIX	MEANING	EXAMPLE
ab, a	away from	absent, amoral
ad, ac, ag, at	to	advent, accrue, aggressive, attract
an	without	anarchy
ante	before	antedate
anti	against	antipathy
bene	well	beneficent
bi	two	bicameral
circum	around	circumspect
com, con, col	together	commit confound, collate
contra	against	contraband
de	from, down	descend
dis, di	apart	distract, divert
ex, e	out	exit, emit
extra	beyond	extracurricular
in, im, il, ir, un	not	inept, impossible, illicit
inter	between	interpose
intra, intro, in	within	intramural, introspective

PREFIX	MEANING	EXAMPLE
mal	bad	malcontent
mis	wrong	misnomer
non	not	nonentity
ob	against	obstacle
per	through	permeate
peri	around	periscope
poly	many	polytheism
post	after	post-mortem
pre	before	premonition
pro	forward	propose
re	again	review
se	apart	seduce
semi	half	semicircle
sub	under	subvert
super	above	superimpose
sui	self	suicide
trans	across	transpose
vice	instead of	vice-president

SUFFIXES

SUFFIX	MEANING	EXAMPLE
able, ible	capable of being	capable, reversible
age	state of	storage
ance	relating to	reliance
ary	relating to	dictionary
ate	act	confiscate
ation	action	radiation
cy	quality	democracy

SUFFIX	MEANING	EXAMPLE
ence	relating to	confidence
er	one who	adviser
ic	pertaining to	democratic
ious	full of	rebellious
ize	to make like	harmonize
ment	result	filament
ty	condition	sanity

LATIN AND GREEK STEMS

STEM	MEANING	EXAMPLE	STEM	MEANING	EXAMPLE
ag, ac	do	agenda, action	arch	chief, rule	archbishop
agr	farm	agriculture	astron	star	astronomy
aqua	water	aqueous	auto	self	automatic
cad, cas	fall	cadence, casual	biblio	book	bibliophile
cant	sing	chant	bio	life	biology
cap, cep	take	captive, accept	chrome	color	chromosome
capit	head	capital	chron	time	chronology
cede	go	precede	cosmo	world	cosmic
celer	speed	celerity	crat	rule	autocrat
cide, cis	kill, cut	suicide, incision	dent, dont	tooth	dental, indent
clud, clus	close	include, inclusion	eu	well, happy	eugenics
cur, curs	run	incur, incursion	gamos	marriage	monogamous
dict	say	diction	ge	earth	geology
duct	lead	induce	gen	origin, people	progenitor
fact, fect	make	factory, perfect	graph	write	graphic
fer, lat	carry	refer, dilate	gyn	women	gynecologist
fring, fract	break	infringe, fracture	homo	same	homogeneous
frater	brother	fraternal	hydr	water	dehydrate
fund, fus	pour	refund, confuse	logy	study of	psychology
greg	group	gregarious	meter	measure	thermometer
gress, grad	move forward	progress, degrade	micro	small	microscope
homo	man	homicide	mono	one	monotony
ject	throw	reject	onomy	science	astronomy
jud	right	judicial	onym	name	synonym
junct	join	conjunction	pathos	feeling	pathology
lect, leg	read, choose	collect, legend	philo	love	philosophy
loq, loc	speak	loquacious, interlocutory	phobia	fear	hydrophobia
manu	hand	manuscript	phone	sound	telephone
mand	order	remand	pseudo	false	pseudonym
mar	sea	maritime	psych	mind	psychic
mater	mother	maternal	scope	see	telescope
med	middle	intermediary	soph	wisdom	sophomore
min	lessen	diminution	tele	far off	telepathic
mis, mit	send	remit, dismiss	theo	god	theology
mort	death	mortician	thermo	heat	thermostat
mote, mov	move	remote, remove	sec	cut	dissect
naut	sailor	astronaut	sed	remain	sedentary
nom	name	nomenclature	sequ	follow	sequential
pater	father	paternity	spect	look	inspect
ped, pod	foot	pedal, podiatrist	spir	breathe	conspire
pend	hang	depend	stat	stand	status
plic	fold	implicate	tact, tang	touch	tactile, tangible
port	carry	portable	ten	hold	retentive
pos, pon	put	depose, component	term	end	terminal
reg, rect	rule	regicide, direct	vent	come	prevent
rupt	break	eruption	vict	conquer	evict
scrib, scrip	write	inscribe, conscription	vid, vis	see	video, revise
anthrop	man	anthropology	voc	call	convocation
			volv	roll	devolve

TEST I.   VOCABULARY: SYNONYMS

TIME: 8 Minutes. 24 Questions.

DIRECTIONS: In each of the sentences below, one word is in italics. Following each sentence are four or five lettered words or phrases. For each sentence, choose the letter preceding the word or phrase which most nearly corresponds in meaning with the italicized word.

1. *Simple* clothing should be worn to work. *Simple* means most nearly
   A) plain
   B) inexpensive
   C) nice
   D) comfortable
   E) old

2. Take your *finished* work to that area of the work floor. *Finished* means most nearly
   A) inspected
   B) assigned
   C) outgoing
   D) completed
   E) rejected

3. If we are not careful, the problem will *develop* further. *Develop* means most nearly
   A) continue
   B) appear
   C) be used
   D) grow
   E) be concerned

4. The mail handler was a *rapid* worker. *Rapid* means most nearly
   A) trained
   B) rash
   C) fast
   D) regular
   E) strong

5. The supply of envelopes is *abundant* for our use. *Abundant* means most nearly
   A) accessible
   B) plentiful
   C) concentrated
   D) divided
   E) scattered

6. The department is working on *experiments* in that area. *Experiments* means most nearly
   A) tests
   B) refinements
   C) statements
   D) plans
   E) patents

7. The members were concerned about two *fundamental* points. *Fundamental* means most nearly
   A) difficult
   B) serious
   C) emphasized
   D) essential
   E) final

8. The leader *asserted* that it was time to start. *Asserted* means most nearly
   A) believed
   B) decided
   C) declared
   D) agreed
   E) contradicted

9. All requests for supplies should be stated *exactly*. *Exactly* means most nearly
   A) briefly
   B) clearly
   C) promptly
   D) emphatically
   E) accurately

10. We had not meant to *alarm* them. *Alarm* means most nearly
    A) endanger
    B) insult
    C) accuse
    D) frighten
    E) confuse

11. The kind of car he bought was *costly*. *Costly* means most nearly
    A) custom made
    B) expensive
    C) desirable
    D) cheap
    E) scarce

12. The cause of the action was *revealed* before the meeting. *Revealed* means most nearly
    A) made known
    B) fully described
    C) carefully hidden
    D) guessed at
    E) seriously questioned

13. The material used to make mail sacks is *durable*. *Durable* means most nearly
    A) thick
    B) waterproof
    C) lasting
    D) elastic
    E) light

14. The *valiant* men and women were rewarded. *Valiant* means most nearly
    A) brave
    B) popular
    C) victorious
    D) loyal
    E) famous

15. The worker was affected by his *fatigue*. *Fatigue* means most nearly
    A) problem
    B) weariness
    C) relaxation
    D) sickness
    E) worry

16. The meeting was interrupted by an *urgent* call. *Urgent* means most nearly
    A) trivial
    B) annoying
    C) pressing
    D) surprising
    E) casual

17. The captain of the team will *participate in* the ceremony. *Participate in* means most nearly
    A) depend upon
    B) be recognized at
    C) be invited to
    D) supervise
    E) share in

18. Each office was asked to *restrict* the number of forms it used. *Restrict* means most nearly
    A) watch
    B) record
    C) limit
    D) replace
    E) provide

19. The pole was *rigid*. *Rigid* means most nearly
    A) broken
    B) pointed
    C) bent
    D) rough
    E) stiff

20. The supervisor *demonstrated* the sorting procedure. *Demonstrated* means most nearly
    A) changed
    B) controlled
    C) determined
    D) showed
    E) described

21. The effort was *futile*. *Futile* means most nearly
    A) wasteful
    B) useless
    C) foolish
    D) undesirable
    E) unfortunate

22. There was a pile of *sundry* items on the table. *Sundry* means most nearly
    A) miscellaneous
    B) valuable
    C) unusual
    D) necessary
    E) specific

23. The supervisor should not be *partial*. *Partial* means most nearly
    A) biased
    B) greedy
    C) irresponsible
    D) jealous
    E) suspicious

24. The retired postal worker led an *inactive* life. *Inactive* means most nearly
    A) restful
    B) idle
    C) peaceful
    D) ordinary
    E) weary

END OF TEST

Go on to do the following Test in this Examination, just as you would be expected to do on the actual exam.

CONSOLIDATE YOUR KEY ANSWERS HERE

Practice using Answer Sheets. Make ONE mark for each answer. Additional and stray marks may be counted as mistakes. In making corrections erase errors COMPLETELY. Make glossy black marks. To arrive at an accurate estimate of your ability and progress, cover the Correct Answers with a sheet of white paper while you are taking this test.

SAMPLE ANSWER SHEET

CORRECT ANSWERS TO SAMPLE QUESTIONS

Now compare your answers with the Correct Answers to Sample Questions. If your answers are not the same as the correct answers shown, go back and study the samples to see where you made a mistake.

1.A	4.C	7.D	10.D	13.C	16.C	19.E	22.A
2.D	5.B	8.C	11.B	14.A	17.E	20.D	23.A
3.D	6.A	9.E	12.A	15.B	18.C	21.B	24.B

Count how many you got right, and write that number on this line_____→ _____
(This is your Test Score.)

Meaning of Test Score

If your Test Score is *18 or over*, you have a Good score.
If your Test Score is from *15 to 17*, you have a Fair score.
If your Test Score is *14 or less*, you are not doing too well.

TEST II. VOCABULARY: SYNONYMS

TIME: 8 Minutes. 24 Questions.

DIRECTIONS: In each of the sentences below, one word is in italics. Following each sentence are four or five lettered words or phrases. For each sentence, choose the letter preceding the word or phrase which most nearly corresponds in meaning with the italicized word.

1. The officials *prevented* the action. *Prevented* means most nearly
   A) allowed
   B) urged
   C) hindered
   D) considered
   E) suggested

2. The postmaster's office expected to *report* the results next week. *Report* means most nearly
   A) decide
   B) tell
   C) approve
   D) study
   E) repeat

3. The conference room is now *vacant*. *Vacant* means most nearly
   A) empty
   B) quiet
   C) dark
   D) available
   E) lonely

4. Tapping on the desk can be an *irritating* habit. *Irritating* means most nearly
   A) nervous
   B) annoying
   C) noisy
   D) startling
   E) unsuitable

5. The package was *forwarded* by our office. *Forwarded* means most nearly
   A) returned
   B) canceled
   C) received
   D) detained
   E) sent

6. The postal service is *essential* in this country. *Essential* means most nearly
   A) inevitable
   B) needless
   C) economical
   D) indispensable
   E) established

7. The wheel turned at a *uniform* rate. *Uniform* means most nearly
   A) increasing
   B) unusual
   C) normal
   D) slow
   E) unchanging

8. Each carrier realized his *obligation*. *Obligation* means most nearly
   A) importance
   B) need
   C) duty
   D) kindness
   E) honor

9. The group was interested in the *origin* of the rumor. *Origin* means most nearly
   A) direction
   B) growth
   C) existence
   D) beginning
   E) end

10. Laws governing the *parole* of prisoners should be more flexible. *Parole* means most nearly
    A) conditional release
    B) withdrawal of privileges
    C) good behavior
    D) outside employment
    E) solitary confinement

11. That employee is *retiring* by nature. *Retiring* means most nearly
    A) complaining
    B) gruff
    C) neglected
    D) modest
    E) sluggish

12. The patron *verified* the contents of the package. *Verified* means most nearly
    A) justified
    B) explained
    C) confirmed
    D) guaranteed
    E) examined

13. The group was *repulsed* immediately. *Repulsed* means most nearly
    A) rebuffed
    B) excused
    C) mistreated
    D) loathed
    E) resented

14. The time was right for the committee to make a *decisive* statement. *Decisive* means most nearly
    A) official
    B) prompt
    C) judicial
    D) rational
    E) conclusive

S1258

15. Each person expects *compensation* for his work. *Compensation* means most nearly
A) fulfillment　　　D) approval
B) remuneration　　E) recommendation
C) appreciation

16. The department plans to increase the number of *novices* in the program. *Novices* means most nearly
A) volunteers　　　D) beginners
B) experts　　　　E) amateurs
C) trainers

17. The guests were overwhelmed by the *fabulous* decorations. *Fabulous* means most nearly
A) antiquated　　　D) immoderate
B) enormous　　　E) intricate
C) incredible

18. The duties of the job are mentioned *explicitly* in the handbook. *Explicitly* means most nearly
A) casually　　　　D) exclusively
B) informally　　　E) specifically
C) intelligibly

19. The school is supplying opportunities for *recreation*. *Recreation* means most nearly
A) diversion　　　D) learning
B) eating　　　　E) recess
C) resting

20. It was necessary to *recapitulate* the regulation. *Recapitulate* means most nearly
A) emphasize　　　D) interpret
B) withdraw　　　E) summarize
C) reinstate

21. The villagers *succumbed to* the enemy forces. *Succumbed to* means most nearly
A) aided　　　　　D) were checked by
B) opposed　　　　E) discouraged
C) yielded to

22. The shipments have been *accelerated*. *Accelerated* means most nearly
A) anxiously awaited
B) caused to move faster
C) delayed by traffic congestion
D) given careful handling
E) routed over shorter lines

23. He was not a good employee, because he was *indolent*. *Indolent* means most nearly
A) stupid　　　　D) lazy
B) indifferent　　E) incompetent
C) selfish

24. He had been cautioned not to be *vindictive*. *Vindictive* means most nearly
A) boastful　　　D) revengeful
B) impolite　　　E) aggressive
C) impulsive

CONSOLIDATE YOUR KEY ANSWERS HERE

Practice using Answer Sheets. Make ONE mark for each answer. Additional and stray marks may be counted as mistakes. In making corrections erase errors COMPLETELY. Make glossy black marks. To arrive at an accurate estimate of your ability and progress, cover the Correct Answers with a sheet of white paper while you are taking this test.

SAMPLE ANSWER SHEET

CORRECT ANSWERS TO SAMPLE QUESTIONS

Now compare your answers with the Correct Answers to Sample Questions. If your answers are not the same as the correct answers shown, go back and study the samples to see where you made a mistake.

1.C	4.B	7.E	10.A	13.A	16.D	19.A	22.B
2.B	5.E	8.C	11.D	14.E	17.C	20.E	23.D
3.A	6.D	9.D	12.C	15.B	18.E	21.C	24.D

TEST III. VOCABULARY: SYNONYMS

TIME: 11 Minutes. 32 Questions.

DIRECTIONS: In each of the sentences below, one word is in italics. Following each sentence are four or five lettered words or phrases. For each sentence, choose the letter preceding the word or phrase which most nearly corresponds in meaning with the italicized word.

1. He was asked to *speak* at the meeting. *Speak* means most nearly
   A) vote
   B) explain
   c) talk
   D) shout
   E) decide

2. They *discovered* the missing boxes in the morning. *Discovered* means most nearly
   A) sought
   B) found
   c) opened
   D) noticed
   E) inspected

3. The number of letters mailed by this office is *double* what it was last year. *Double* means most nearly
   A) twice
   B) different from
   c) more than
   D) almost
   E) the same as

4. The post office had to *purchase* the new equipment. *Purchase* means most nearly
   A) charge
   B) construct
   c) supply
   D) buy
   E) order

5. The shell was *hollow*. *Hollow* means most nearly
   A) smooth
   B) hard
   c) soft
   D) rough
   E) empty

6. The packages were kept in a *secure* place. *Secure* means most nearly
   A) distant
   B) safe
   c) convenient
   D) secret
   E) bad

7. It was *customary* for him to be at work on time. *Customary* means most nearly
   A) curious
   B) necessary
   c) difficult
   D) common
   E) important

8. An attempt was made to *unite* the groups. *Unite* means most nearly
   A) improve
   B) serve
   c) uphold
   D) advise
   E) combine

9. The leader *defended* his followers. *Defended* means most nearly
   A) praised
   B) liked
   c) informed
   D) protected
   E) delayed

10. The *aim* of the employees is to do their work well. *Aim* means most nearly
    A) hope
    B) purpose
    c) duty
    D) promise
    E) idea

11. The workers will *assemble* the sacks of mail before loading them on the truck. *Assemble* means most nearly
    A) bring together
    B) examine carefully
    c) locate
    D) fill
    E) mark

12. The mayor of the city sent a letter to each of the *merchants*. *Merchants* means most nearly
    A) producers
    B) advertisers
    c) bankers
    D) executives
    E) storekeepers

13. The clerk was *compelled* to concentrate on his job. *Compelled* means most nearly
    A) tempted
    B) persuaded
    c) forced
    D) unable
    E) content

14. The clerk *extended* his vacation. *Extended* means most nearly
    A) limited
    B) deserved
    c) enjoyed
    D) lengthened
    E) started

S1258

15. The *territory* is too large to see in one day. *Territory* means most nearly
    A) swamp   D) beach
    B) region   E) terminal
    C) city

16. The technicians *created* a new machine. *Created* means most nearly
    A) planned   D) tried
    B) copied   E) replaced
    C) invented

17. The *mended* mail sacks will be delivered. *Mended* means most nearly
    A) repaired   D) labelled
    B) torn   E) tied
    C) clean

18. The new post office building is *huge*. *Huge* means most nearly
    A) ugly   D) immense
    B) tall   E) narrow
    C) sturdy

19. He was asked to *mingle* with the other guests. *Mingle* means most nearly
    A) consult   D) mix
    B) visit   E) dance
    C) sing

20. The director of the program is *likewise* chairman of the committee. *Likewise* means most nearly
    A) also   D) however
    B) often   E) meanwhile
    C) thus

21. Doctors are determined to *conquer* the disease. *Conquer* means most nearly
    A) study   D) eliminate
    B) fight   E) trace
    C) overcome

22. The machine was *designed* for stamping envelopes. *Designed* means most nearly
    A) fine   D) approved
    B) used   E) intended
    C) essential

23. He *mourned* the loss of his friend. *Mourned* means most nearly
    A) resented   D) avenged
    B) grieved   E) faced
    C) remembered

24. The meeting will take place at the *usual* time. *Usual* means most nearly
    A) proper   D) best
    B) old   E) earliest
    C) customary

25. The employee was given *distinct* instructions. *Distinct* means most nearly
    A) clear   D) regular
    B) short   E) loud
    C) new

26. The worker will *bind* the pages together. *Bind* means most nearly
    A) press   D) return
    B) receive   E) fasten
    C) make

27. He *startled* the person standing next to him. *Startled* means most nearly
    A) alarmed   D) reassured
    B) touched   E) avoided
    C) scolded

28. He *deceived* them by claiming to be rich. *Deceived* means most nearly
    A) favored   D) imitated
    B) tricked   E) angered
    C) impressed

29. The flood brought *distress* to many families. *Distress* means most nearly
    A) shock   D) risk
    B) illness   E) hunger
    C) suffering

30. Some of the statements made at the meeting were *absurd*. *Absurd* means most nearly
    A) clever   D) foolish
    B) original   E) serious
    C) careless

31. The supervisor *implied* that the schedule would be changed. *Implied* means most nearly
    A) acknowledged   D) predicted
    B) imagined   E) insisted
    C) suggested

32. Each person works to earn his own *livelihood*. *Livelihood* means most nearly
    A) salary   D) education
    B) employment   E) maintenance
    C) fortune

END OF TEST

CONSOLIDATE YOUR KEY ANSWERS HERE

Practice using Answer Sheets. Make ONE mark for each answer. Additional and stray marks may be counted as mistakes. In making corrections erase errors COMPLETELY. Make glossy black marks. To arrive at an accurate estimate of your ability and progress, cover the Correct Answers with a sheet of white paper while you are taking this test.

SAMPLE ANSWER SHEET

CORRECT ANSWERS TO SAMPLE QUESTIONS

Now compare your answers with the Correct Answers to Sample Questions. If your answers are not the same as the correct answers shown, go back and study the samples to see where you made a mistake.

1.C	5.E	9.D	13.C	17.A	21.C	25.A	29.C
2.B	6.B	10.B	14.D	18.D	22.E	26.E	30.D
3.A	7.D	11.A	15.B	19.D	23.B	27.A	31.C
4.D	8.E	12.E	16.C	20.A	24.C	28.B	32.E

TEST IV. VOCABULARY: SYNONYMS

TIME: 6 Minutes. 20 Questions.

DIRECTIONS: In each of the sentences below, one word is in italics. Following each sentence are four or five lettered words or phrases. For each sentence, choose the letter preceding the word or phrase which most nearly corresponds in meaning with the italicized word.

1. The task *required* his attention. *Required* means most nearly
   A) held
   B) demanded
   C) aroused
   D) increased
   E) revived

2. Employees with previous training *assisted* the others. *Assisted* means most nearly
   A) instructed
   B) warned
   C) stimulated
   D) praised
   E) aided

3. He answered the question *hastily*. *Hastily* means most nearly
   A) incorrectly
   B) nervously
   C) indirectly
   D) bluntly
   E) quickly

4. The signs were *observable* to everyone. *Observable* means most nearly
   A) noticeable
   B) understandable
   C) acceptable
   D) agreeable
   E) available

5. The statements made in the article were *challenged*. *Challenged* means most nearly
   A) misunderstood
   B) disputed
   C) withdrawn
   D) expanded
   E) supported

6. A *trustworthy* messenger was needed to deliver the papers to the inspectors. *Trustworthy* means most nearly
   A) experienced
   B) cautious
   C) industrious
   D) capable
   E) dependable

7. They *endeavored* to keep the rate of production as high as it was when the machines were new. *Endeavor* means most nearly
   A) promised
   B) expected
   C) managed
   D) tried
   E) intended

8. The employee's *accomplishment* was unusually commendable. *Accomplishment* means most nearly
   A) solution
   B) achievement
   C) discovery
   D) proposal
   E) cooperation

9. She is *presumably* the only one who can help you. *Presumably* means most nearly
   A) undoubtedly
   B) practically
   C) probably
   D) reportedly
   E) possibly

10. It would be *advantageous* to begin this job first. *Advantageous* means most nearly
    A) proper
    B) profitable
    C) generous
    D) shrewd
    E) enterprising

11. The organization made a *deliberate* effort to conceal the facts. *Deliberate* means most nearly
    A) intentional
    B) impulsive
    C) desperate
    D) clever
    E) daring

12. The employee was *neglectful of* his responsibilities. *Neglectful of* means most nearly
    A) unworthy of
    B) inattentive to
    C) impatient about
    D) unhappy over
    E) unfit for

13. The foreman gave *specific* orders. *Specific* means most nearly
    A) precise
    B) brief
    C) urgent
    D) fundamental
    E) adequate

14. The procedure to be followed has been *sanctioned*. *Sanctioned* means most nearly
    A) publicly announced
    B) criticized
    C) officially authorized
    D) standardized
    E) carefully planned

15. He contradicted the statement *emphatically*. *Emphatically* means most nearly
    A) eagerly
    B) immediately
    c) positively
    D) reluctantly
    E) repeatedly

16. The trainees were given *minute* directions regarding the work. *Minute* means most nearly
    A) easy
    B) timely
    c) recorded
    D) numerous
    E) detailed

17. The news will bring a prompt *reaction*. *Reaction* means most nearly
    A) response
    B) outburst
    c) admission
    D) recommendation
    E) investigation

18. Only two of the members *participated* in the event. *Participated* means most nearly
    A) advanced
    B) took sides
    c) interfered
    D) took part
    E) argued

19. The facts he presented were *undeniable*. *Undeniable* means most nearly
    A) indefensible
    B) logical
    c) contestable
    D) justifiable
    E) indisputable

20. Attendance at safety lectures is *obligatory*. *Obligatory* means most nearly
    A) optional
    B) important
    c) inconvenient
    D) compulsory
    E) advisable

END OF TEST

Go on to do the following Test in this Examination, just as you would be expected to do on the actual exam.

CONSOLIDATE YOUR KEY ANSWERS HERE

Practice using Answer Sheets. Make ONE mark for each answer. Additional and stray marks may be counted as mistakes. In making corrections erase errors COMPLETELY. Make glossy black marks. To arrive at an accurate estimate of your ability and progress, cover the Correct Answers with a sheet of white paper while you are taking this test.

SAMPLE ANSWER SHEET

CORRECT ANSWERS TO SAMPLE QUESTIONS

Now compare your answers with the Correct Answers to Sample Questions. If your answers are not the same as the correct answers shown, go back and study the samples to see where you made a mistake.

1.B	4.A	7.D	10.B	13.A	16.E	19.E
2.E	5.B	8.B	11.A	14.C	17.A	20.D
3.E	6.E	9.C	12.B	15.C	18.D	

TEST V. VOCABULARY: SYNONYMS

TIME: 8 Minutes. 24 Questions.

DIRECTIONS: In each of the sentences below, one word is in italics. Following each sentence are four or five lettered words or phrases. For each sentence, choose the letter preceding the word or phrase which most nearly corresponds in meaning with the italicized word.

Correct Answers for this Test are consolidated after the last question.

1. The *power* of that organization cannot be ignored any longer. *Power* means most nearly
   A) size
   B) courage
   C) success
   D) force
   E) ambition

2. The employees reached the *shore* several days later. *Shore* means most nearly
   A) ocean
   B) reef
   C) island
   D) water
   E) coast

3. The *instructor* was enthusiastic. *Instructor* means most nearly
   A) expert
   B) foreman
   C) teacher
   D) beginner
   E) assistant

4. A *responsible* employee is an asset to any business. *Responsible* means most nearly
   A) considerate
   B) trustworthy
   C) smart
   D) experienced
   E) resourceful

5. He was a good clerk because he was *alert*. *Alert* means most nearly
   A) watchful
   B) busy
   C) honest
   D) helpful
   E) faithful

6. The machine was *revolving* rapidly. *Revolving* means most nearly
   A) working
   B) inclining
   C) vibrating
   D) turning
   E) producing

7. The canceling machine did not *function* yesterday. *Function* means most nearly
   A) finish
   B) stop
   C) overheat
   D) vibrate
   E) operate

8. The supervisor did not *comprehend* the clerk's excuse. *Comprehend* means most nearly
   A) hear
   B) understand
   C) suspect
   D) consider
   E) accept

9. His conduct was *becoming*. *Becoming* means most nearly
   A) improved
   B) heroic
   C) deliberate
   D) suitable
   E) patient

10. The men were not aware of the *hazard*. *Hazard* means most nearly
    A) peril
    B) choice
    C) decision
    D) contest
    E) damage

11. A *flexible* policy was developed to handle the situation. *Flexible* means most nearly
    A) pliable
    B) weak
    C) rigid
    D) uniform
    E) active

12. The clerk suggested an *innovation*. *Innovation* means most nearly
    A) conventional practice
    B) improvement
    C) inadequate change
    D) new method
    E) preliminary trial

13. Many parents *indulge* their children too much. *Indulge* means most nearly
    A) admire
    B) humor
    C) flatter
    D) coax
    E) discipline

S1258

14. The men were *commended* for their actions during the emergency. *Commended* means most nearly
    A) blamed
    B) reprimanded
    C) promoted
    D) encouraged
    E) praised

15. Two men were *designated* by the postmaster. *Designated* means most nearly
    A) dismissed
    B) assisted
    C) instructed
    D) named
    E) rebuked

16. The package will be *conveyed* by the employees. *Conveyed* means most nearly
    A) carried
    B) wrapped
    C) exchanged
    D) refused
    E) guarded

17. It seems *feasible* to start the physical fitness training now. *Feasible* means most nearly
    A) praiseworthy
    B) justifiable
    C) practicable
    D) beneficial
    E) profitable

18. He was a *notorious* rebel. *Notorious* means most nearly
    A) condemned
    B) unpleasant
    C) vexatious
    D) pretentious
    E) well-known

19. The main speaker appeared to be a *pompous* person. *Pompous* means most nearly
    A) narrow-minded
    B) insincere
    C) talkative
    D) self-important
    E) rude

20. The office was surprised that he had *disregarded* his duty. *Disregarded* means most nearly
    A) contemplated
    B) discerned
    C) neglected
    D) resisted
    E) renounced

21. The collector described the *blemish* on the new stamp. *Blemish* means most nearly
    A) color
    B) flaw
    C) design
    D) imprint
    E) figure

22. The *ardor* of the patriot was contagious. *Ardor* means most nearly
    A) anger
    B) desire
    C) zeal
    D) happiness
    E) daring

23. All the employees *vied* for that award. *Vied* means most nearly
    A) contended
    B) cooperated
    C) petitioned
    D) persevered
    E) prepared

24. Immediately after hearing the bad news, the group was in a state of *ferment*. *Ferment* means most nearly
    A) lawlessness
    B) indecision
    C) disintegration
    D) reorganization
    E) agitation

END OF TEST

Go on to do the following Test in this Examination, just as you would be expected to do on the actual exam.

CONSOLIDATE YOUR KEY ANSWERS HERE

SAMPLE ANSWER SHEET

CORRECT ANSWERS TO SAMPLE QUESTIONS

1.D	4.B	7.E	10.A	13.B	16.A	19.D	22.C
2.E	5.A	8.B	11.A	14.E	17.C	20.C	23.A
3.C	6.D	9.D	12.D	15.D	18.E	21.B	24.E

READING COMPREHENSION TESTS

Even though this course of study has been carefully planned to help you get in shape by the day your test comes, you'll have to do a little planning on your own to be successful. And you'll also need a few pointers proven effective for many other good students.

HELPFUL HINTS FOR THE READING COMPREHENSION PART OF THE EXAMINATION

1. Do as many of the reading comprehension exercises in this book as you have time for. Such exercises appear in the two Sample Tests (page 18 and page 62) and also in the pages that follow. In these pages, you will find paragraphs of various types and of various levels of difficulty.

2. Use the following sources for getting additional practice in comprehending what you read:
    a. Editorial pages of various newspapers — you'll find many interesting editorials.
    b. Book reviews (also drama and movie reviews).
    c. Magazine articles.

For each selection that you read, do the following:
    a. Jot down the main idea of the article.
    b. Look up the meanings of words that you don't know or that you aren't sure of.

3. Refer to the book, *Scoring High on Reading Tests* (Arco Publishing, 219 Park Avenue South, New York, N. Y. 10003), for a complete treatment of reading comprehension.

Spot The Topic Sentence To Get The Main Thought

An analysis of paragraphs shows that they all have a unity of construction that is fundamental for all writing. There is a central idea in every paragraph, called a topic sentence from which all other sentences grow. The topic sentence may occur at the beginning, in the middle, or at the end of a paragraph. The development of the topic sentence may take the form of presenting details, of showing a comparison or a contrast, of listing examples, or of citing causes or results. Whatever the method used, you must remember that the topic sentence is the clue for the main idea or central thought of the whole paragraph. It is similar to the headline or lead in a newspaper article. It gives you at a glance the theme or subject matter of the article. The supporting ideas are merely a detailed development of the thought of the topic sentence.

When you get to the reading comprehension questions on the test, these hints may be helpful:

A 10-Point Check List To Insure Success In Reading Comprehension

(1) Read over the entire paragraph carefully to get the general sense. Look for a topic sentence.

(2) Then look at the questions asked.

(3) Go back over the paragraph to get the exact answers. Sometimes the question cannot be answered on the basis of the stated facts. You may be required to make a deduction from the facts given, to interpret or analyze the facts, or to draw a conclusion regarding the facts or the author. If you understand what you read, you should have little difficulty with any reading comprehension question.

(4) Read rapidly.

(5) Underline words and phrases in the paragraph that seem important to you.

(6) Check for "false-impressions."

(7) Eliminate your personal opinions.

(8) Rule out subordinate ideas.

(9) Re-read the paragraph several times, if necessary.

(10) Beware of negatives and all-inclusive statements. Watch particularly words like always, never, all, only, every, absolutely, completely, none, entirely.

TEST I. READING INTERPRETATION

TIME: 10 Minutes. 12 Questions.

HERE'S HOW YOU SHOULD ANSWER THESE READING QUESTIONS. Each one is made up of a paragraph, followed by four or five statements based on the paragraph. You may never have seen the paragraph before, but you must now read it carefully so that you understand it. Then read the statements following. Any one of them might be right. You have to choose the one that is most correct. Try to pick the one that's most complete, most accurate . . . the one that is best supported by and necessarily flows from the paragraph. Be sure that it contains nothing false so far as the paragraph itself is concerned. After you've thought it out, write the capital letter preceding your best choice in the margin next to the question. When you've answered all the questions, score yourself faithfully by checking with our answers that follow the last question.

1. "Iron is used in making our bridges and skyscrapers, subways and steamships, railroads and automobiles, and nearly all kinds of machinery—besides millions of small articles varying from the farmer's scythe to the woman's needle."

The paragraph best supports the statement that iron
A) is the most abundant of the metals
B) has many different uses
C) is the strongest of all metals
D) is the only material used in building skyscrapers and bridges
E) is the most durable of the metals

2. "Some fire-resistant buildings, although wholly constructed of materials that will not burn, may be completely gutted by the spread of fire through their contents by way of hallways and other openings. They may even suffer serious structural damage by the collapse of metal beams and columns."

The paragraph best supports the statement that some fire-resistant buildings
A) suffer less damage from fire than from collapse of metal supports
B) can be damaged seriously by fire
C) have specially constructed halls and doors
D) afford less protection to their contents than would ordinary buildings
E) will burn readily

3. "Life is too short for one person to do very many things well. The person who determines fairly early what he can do that he likes to do, and who goes at it hard and stays with it, is likely to do the best work and find the most peace of mind."

The paragraph best supports the statement that the reason the average man does not master many different jobs is that he
A) desires peace of mind
B) seldom has more than a few interests
C) is unable to organize his ideas
D) lacks the necessary time
E) has a natural tendency to specialize

4. "Both the high school and the college should take the responsibility for preparing the student to get a job. Since the ability to write a good application letter is one of the first steps toward this goal, every teacher should be willing to do what he can to help the student learn to write such letters."

The paragraph best supports the statement that
A) inability to write a good letter often reduces one's job prospects
B) the major responsibility of the school is to obtain jobs for its students
C) success is largely a matter of the kind of work the student applies for first
D) every teacher should teach a course in the writing of application letters
E) letter writing is more important than most subjects taught in high schools and colleges

5. " 'White collar' is a term used to describe one of the largest groups of workers in American industry and trade. It distinguishes those who work with the pencil and the mind from those who depend on their hands and the machine. It suggests occupations in which physical exertion and handling of materials are not primary features of the job."

The paragraph best supports the statement that "white collar" workers are
A) the most powerful labor group because of their numbers
B) not so strong physically as those who work with their hands
C) those who supervise workers handling materials
D) all whose work is entirely indoors
E) not likely to use machines so much as are other groups of workers

6. "The location of a railway line is necessarily a compromise between the desire to build the line with as little expense as possible and the desire to construct it so that its route will cover that over which trade and commerce are likely to flow."

The paragraph best supports the statement that the route selected for a railway line
A) should be the one over which the line can be built most cheaply
B) determines the location of commercial centers
C) should always cover the shortest possible distance between its terminals
D) cannot always be the one involving the lowest construction costs
E) is determined chiefly by the kind of production in the area

7. "A survey to determine the subjects that have helped students most in their jobs shows that typewriting leads all other subjects in the business group. It also leads among the subjects college students consider most valuable and would take again if they were to return to high school."

The paragraph best supports the statement that
A) the ability to type is an asset in business and in school
B) students who return to night school take typing
C) students with a knowledge of typing do superior work in college
D) every person should know how to type
E) success in business is assured those who can type

8. "It is a common assumption that city directories are prepared and published by the cities concerned. However, the directory business is as much a private business as is the publishing of dictionaries and encyclopedias. The companies financing the publication make their profits through the sales of the directories themselves and through the advertising in them."

The paragraph best supports the statement that
A) the publication of a city directory is a commercial enterprise
B) the size of a city directory limits the space devoted to advertising
C) many city directories are published by dictionary and encyclopedia concerns
D) city directories are sold at cost to local residents and businessmen
E) the preparation of a city directory, but not the printing, is a responsibility of the local government

9. "Since duplicating machines are being changed constantly, the person who is in the market for such a machine should not purchase offhand the kind with which he is most familiar or the one recommended by the first salesman who calls on him. Instead he should analyze his particular equipment situation and then investigate all the possibilities."

The paragraph best supports the statement that, when duplicating equipment is being purchased,
A) the purchaser should choose equipment that he can use with the least extra training
B) the latest models should always be bought
C) the needs of the purchaser's office should determine the selection
D) the buyer should have his needs analyzed by an office-equipment salesman
E) the recommendations of salesmen should usually be ignored

10. "There has been a slump in first-aid training in the industries, and yet one should not fall into the error of thinking there is less interest in first aid in industry. The falling off has been in the number of new employees needing such training. It appears that in industries interested in first-aid training there is now actually a higher percentage so trained than there ever was before."

The paragraph best supports the statement that first-aid training is
A) a means of avoiding the more serious effects of accidents
B) being abandoned because of expense
C) helpful in every line of work
D) of great importance to employees
E) sometimes given new workers in industry

11. "There exists a false but popular idea that a clue is a mysterious fact which most people overlook but which some very keen investigator easily discovers and recognizes as having, in itself, a remarkable meaning. The clue is most often an ordinary fact which an observant person picks up—something which gains its significance when, after a long series of careful investigations, it is connected with a network of other clues."

The paragraph best supports the statement that to be of value clues must be

A) discovered by skilled investigators
B) found under mysterious circumstances
C) connected with other facts
D) discovered soon after the crime
E) observed many times

12. "It is wise to choose a duplicating machine that will do the work required with the greatest efficiency and at the least cost. Users with a large volume of business need speedy machines that cost little to operate and are well made."

The paragraph best supports the statement that
A) most users of duplicating machines prefer low operating cost to efficiency
B) a well-built machine will outlast a cheap one
C) a duplicating machine is not efficient unless it is sturdy
D) a duplicating machine should be both efficient and economical
E) in duplicating machines speed is more usual than low operating cost

END OF TEST

Go on to do the following Test in this Examination, just as you would be expected to do on the actual exam.

CONSOLIDATE YOUR KEY ANSWERS HERE

Practice using Answer Sheets. Make ONE mark for each answer. Additional and stray marks may be counted as mistakes. In making corrections erase errors COMPLETELY. Make glossy black marks. To arrive at an accurate estimate of your ability and progress, cover the Correct Answers with a sheet of white paper while you are taking this test.

SAMPLE ANSWER SHEET

CORRECT ANSWERS TO THE FOREGOING PRACTICE QUESTIONS

Now compare your answers with these Correct Answers to the Practice Questions. If your answers differ from these, go back and study those questions to see where and how you made your mistakes.

1. B	2. B	3. D	4. A	5. E	6. D
7. A	8. A	9. C	10. E	11. C	12. D

TEST II. READING INTERPRETATION

TIME: 8 Minutes. 10 Questions.

This test of reading interpretation consists of a number of brief passages. One question is based on each passage. A question consists of an incomplete statement about the passage. The statement is followed by five choices lettered (A) (B) (C) (D) (E). For each question, mark your answer sheet with the letter of that choice which best conveys the meaning of the passage, and which best completes the statement.

Correct Answers are consolidated after the last question.

1. "Any business not provided with capable substitutes to fill all important positions is a weak business. Therefore a foreman should train each man not only to perform his own particular duties but also to do those of two or three positions."

The paragraph best supports the statement that
A) dependence on substitutes is a sign of a weak organization
B) training will improve the strongest organization
C) the foreman should be the most expert at any particular job under him
D) every employee can be trained to perform efficiently work other than his own
E) vacancies in vital positions should be provided for in advance

2. "The coloration of textile fabrics composed of cotton and wool generally requires two processes, as the process used in dyeing wool is seldom capable of fixing the color upon cotton. The usual method is to immerse the fabric in the requisite baths to dye the wool and then to treat the partially dyed material in the manner found suitable for cotton."

The paragraph best supports the statement that the dyeing of textile fabrics composed of cotton and wool
A) is less complicated than the dyeing of wool alone
B) is more successful when the material contains more cotton than wool
C) is not satisfactory when solid colors are desired
D) is restricted to two colors for any one fabric
E) is usually based upon the methods required for dyeing the different materials

3. "The Federal investigator must direct his whole effort toward success in his work. If he wishes to succeed in each investigation, his work will be by no means easy, smooth, or peaceful; on the contrary, he will have to devote himself completely and continuously to a task that requires all his ability."

The paragraph best supports the statement that an investigator's success depends most upon
A) ambition to advance rapidly in the service
B) persistence in the face of difficulty
C) training and experience
D) willingness to obey orders without delay
E) the number of investigations which he conducts

4. "Honest people in one nation find it difficult to understand the viewpoint of honest people in another. State departments and their ministers exist for the purpose of explaining the viewpoints of one nation in terms understood by another. Some of their most important work lies in this direction."

The paragraph best supports the statement that
A) people of different nations may not consider matters in the same light
B) it is unusual for many people to share similar ideas
C) suspicion prevents understanding between nations
D) the chief work of state departments is to guide relations between nations united by a common cause
E) the people of one nation must sympathize with the viewpoints of others

5. "Economy once in a while is just not enough. I expect to find it at every level of responsibility, from cabinet member to the newest and youngest recruit. Controlling waste is

something like bailing a boat; you have to keep at it. I have no intention of easing up on my insistence on getting a dollar of value for each dollar we spend."

The paragraph best supports the statement that
A) we need not be concerned about items which cost less than a dollar
B) it is advisable to buy the cheaper of two items
c) the responsibility of economy is greater at high levels than at low levels
D) economy becomes easy with practice
E) economy is a continuing responsibility

6. "On all permit imprint mail the charge for postage has been printed by the mailer before he presents it for mailing and pays the postage. Such mail of any class is mailable only at the post office that issued a permit covering it. Since the postage receipts for such mail represent only the amount of permit imprint mail detected and verified, employees in receiving, handling, and outgoing sections must be alert constantly to route such mail to the weighing section before it is handled or dispatched."

The paragraph best supports the statement that, at post offices where permit mail is received for dispatch,
A) dispatching units make a final check on the amount of postage payable on permit imprint mail
B) employees are to check the postage chargeable on mail received under permit
c) neither more nor less postage is to be collected than the amount printed on permit imprint mail
D) the weighing section is primarily responsible for failure to collect postage on such mail
E) unusual measures are taken to prevent unstamped mail from being accepted

7. "Education should not stop when the individual has been prepared to make a livelihood and to live in modern society. Living would be mere existence were there no appreciation and enjoyment of the riches of art, literature, and science."

The paragraph best supports the statement that true education
A) is focused on the routine problems of life
B) prepares one for full enjoyment of life
c) deals chiefly with art, literature and science
D) is not possible for one who does not enjoy scientific literature
E) disregards practical ends

8. "Insured and c.o.d. air and surface mail is accepted with the understanding that the sender guarantees any necessary forwarding or return postage. When such mail is forwarded or returned, it shall be rated up for collection of postage; except that insured or

c.o.d. air mail weighing 8 ounces or less and subject to the 10 cents an ounce rate shall be forwarded by air if delivery will be advanced, and returned by surface means, without additional postage."

The paragraph best supports the statement that the return postage for undeliverable insured mail
A) is included in the original prepayment on air mail parcels
B) is computed but not collected before dispatching surface parcel post mail to sender
c) is not computed or charged for any air mail that is returned by surface transportation
D) is included in the amount collected when the sender mails parcel post
E) is collected before dispatching for return if any amount due has been guaranteed

9. "All undeliverable first-class mail, except first-class parcels and parcel post paid with first-class postage, which cannot be returned to the sender, is sent to a dead-letter branch. Undeliverable matter of the third- and fourth-classes of obvious value for which the sender does not furnish return postage and undeliverable first-class parcels and parcel-post matter bearing postage of the first-class, which cannot be returned, is sent to a dead parcel-post branch."

The paragraph best supports the statement that matter that is sent to a dead parcel-post branch includes all undeliverable
A) mail, except first-class letter mail, that appears to be valuable
B) mail, except that of the first-class, on which the sender failed to prepay the original mailing costs
c) parcels on which the mailer prepaid the first-class rate of postage
D) third- and fourth-class matter on which the required return postage has not been paid
E) parcels on which first-class postage has been prepaid, when the sender's address is not known

10. "Civilization started to move rapidly when man freed himself of the shackles that restricted his search for truth."

The paragraph best supports the statement that the progress of civilization
A) came as a result of man's dislike for obstacles
B) did not begin until restrictions on learning were removed
c) has been aided by man's efforts to find the truth
D) is based on continually increasing efforts
E) continues at a constantly increasing rate

CONSOLIDATE YOUR KEY ANSWERS HERE

Practice using Answer Sheets. Make ONE mark for each answer. Additional and stray marks may be counted as mistakes. In making corrections erase errors COMPLETELY. Make glossy black marks. To arrive at an accurate estimate of your ability and progress, cover the Correct Answers with a sheet of white paper while you are taking this test.

SAMPLE ANSWER SHEET

CORRECT ANSWERS TO THE FOREGOING PRACTICE QUESTIONS

Now compare your answers with these Correct Answers to the Practice Questions. If your answers differ from these, go back and study those questions to see where and how you made your mistakes.

1.E	2.E	3.B	4.A	5.E
6.B	7.B	8.B	9.E	10.C

TEST III. READING INTERPRETATION

TIME: 8 Minutes. 10 Questions.

DIRECTIONS: *Below each of the following passages, you will find questions or incomplete statements about the passage. Each statement or question is followed by lettered words or expressions. Select the word or expression that most satisfactorily completes each statement or answers each question in accordance with the meaning of the passage. Write the letter of that word or expression on your answer paper.*

Correct Answers are consolidated after the last question.

1. "A city directory, where available, interleaved with suitable blank leaves and subdivided into a number of volumes equal to the maximum number of employees assigned to directory work at one time, shall be used to give directory service. Where a city directory is not published, a telephone directory, if available, may be used. Dual use of a city directory and a telephone directory shall be confined to firm, insured, c.o.d., special handling, and special delivery mail."

The paragraph best supports the statement that the use of a city directory
A) at times may be supplemented by the use of a telephone directory
B) is of little value unless postal directory service is kept current
c) is less productive than is the use of a telephone directory
D) is to be confined to insured, c.o.d., and special delivery mail
E) provides more accurate information than does the use of a telephone directory

2. "Taxes are deducted each pay period from the amount of salaries or wages, including payments for overtime and night differential, paid to employees of the postal service in excess of the withholding exemptions allowed under the Internal Revenue Act. The amount of tax to be withheld from each payment of wages to any employee, except fourth-class postmasters, will be determined from the current official table of pay and withholding exemptions published by the Post Office Department."

The paragraph best supports the statement that the salaries of most postal employees
A) are paid in amounts depending upon the exemptions fixed by the Department

B) do not include overtime or night differential payments
c) are determined by provisions of the Internal Revenue Act
D) include taxable overtime or night differential payments that are due each pay period
E) are subject to tax deductions if the salaries are greater than exemptions

3. "Telegrams should be clear, concise, and brief. Omit all unnecessary words. The parts of speech most often used in telegrams are nouns, verbs, adjectives, and adverbs. If possible, do without pronouns, prepositions, articles, and copulative verbs. Use simple sentences, rather than complex and compound."

The paragraph best supports the statement that in writing telegrams one should always use
A) common and simple words
B) only nouns, verbs, adjectives, and adverbs
c) incomplete sentences
D) only words essential to the meaning
E) the present tense of verbs

4. "The Suggestion System is conducted to give thorough and understanding study to ideas presented by postal employees for promoting the welfare of postal personnel and for improving mail handling and other postal business; and to encourage and reward postal employees who think out, develop, and present acceptable ideas and plans. Through this system the talent and ability of postal employees are to be used for improving postal service and reducing expenses."

The paragraph best supports the statement that one purpose of the Suggestion System is to
A) maintain a unit of experienced employees to plan and develop improvements

b) obtain ideas that will help postal employees improve their work

c) offer promotions to postal employees who suggest useful changes in service

d) provide pay raises for employees who increase their output

e) reduce postal operating expenses by limiting postal service

5. "Metered mail must bear the correct date of mailing in the meter impression. When metered mail bearing the wrong date or time is presented for mailing, it shall be run through the canceling machine or otherwise postmarked to show the proper date and time, and then dispatched. The irregularity shall be called to the attention of the mailer. If the irregularity is repeated, the mail may be refused."

The paragraph best supports the statement that, if a first mailing of metered mail bears a wrong date or time,

A) no action shall be taken by the postal service

B) the mailing privileges of the sender may be canceled

C) the mailer will not be permitted to submit additional improperly prepared mail

D) the mailer will be notified of the error before the mail is dispatched

E) the postal service accepts the responsibility for correction

6. "Through advertising, manufacturers exercise a high degree of control over consumers' desires. However, the manufacturer assumes enormous risks in attempting to predict what consumers will want and in producing goods in quantity and distributing them in advance of final selection by the consumers."

The paragraph best supports the statement that manufacturers

A) can eliminate the risk of overproduction by advertising

B) completely control buyers' needs and desires

C) must depend upon the final consumers for the success of their undertakings

D) distribute goods directly to the consumers

E) can predict with great accuracy the success of any product they put on the market

7. "In the business districts of cities, collections from street letter boxes are made at stated hours, and collectors are required to observe these hours exactly. Any businessman using these boxes can rely with certainty upon the time of the next collection."

The paragraph best supports the statement that

A) mail collections are both efficient and inexpensive

b) mail collections in business districts are more frequent during the day than at night

c) mail collectors are required to observe safety regulations exactly

d) mail collections are made often in business districts

e) mail is collected in business districts on a regular schedule

8. "The function of business is to increase the wealth of the country and the value and happiness of life. It does this by supplying the material needs of men and women. When the nation's business is successfully carried on, it renders public service of the highest value."

The paragraph best supports the statement that

A) all businesses which render public service are successful

B) human happiness is enhanced only by the increase of material wants

C) the value of life is increased only by the increase of wealth

D) the material needs of men and women are supplied by well-conducted business

E) business is the only field of activity which increases happiness

9. "In almost every community, fortunately, there are certain men and women known to be public-spirited. Others, however, may be selfish and act only as their private interests seem to require."

The paragraph best supports the statement that those citizens who disregard others are

A) fortunate

B) needed

C) found only in small communities

D) not known

E) not public-spirited

10. "Whenever two groups of people whose interests at the moment conflict meet to discuss a solution of that conflict, there is laid a basis for an interchange of facts and ideas which increases the total range of knowledge of both parties and tends to break down the barrier which their restricted field of information has helped to create."

The paragraph best supports the statement that conflicts between two parties may be brought closer to a settlement through

A) frank acknowledgement of error

B) the exchange of accusations

C) gaining a wider knowledge of facts

D) submitting the dispute to an impartial judge

E) limiting discussion to plans acceptable to both groups

END OF TEST

CONSOLIDATE YOUR KEY ANSWERS HERE

Practice using Answer Sheets. Make ONE mark for each answer. Additional and stray marks may be counted as mistakes. In making corrections erase errors COMPLETELY. Make glossy black marks. To arrive at an accurate estimate of your ability and progress, cover the Correct Answers with a sheet of white paper while you are taking this test.

SAMPLE ANSWER SHEET

CORRECT ANSWERS TO THE FOREGOING PRACTICE QUESTIONS

Now compare your answers with these Correct Answers to the Practice Questions. If your answers differ from these, go back and study those questions to see where and how you made your mistakes.

1.A	2.E	3.D	4.B	5.E
6.C	7.E	8.D	9.E	10.C

Count how many you got right, and write that number on this line→ _____
(This is your Test Score.)

Meaning of Test Score

If your Test Score is *8 or over*, you have a Good score.
If your Test Score is *6 or 7*, you have a Fair score.
If your Test Score is *5 or less*, you are not doing too well.

TEAR OUT ALONG THIS LINE AND MARK YOUR ANSWERS AS INSTRUCTED IN THE TEXT

TEST IV. READING INTERPRETATION

TIME: 8 Minutes. 10 Questions.

This test of reading interpretation consists of a number of brief passages. One question is based on each passage. A question consists of an incomplete statement about the passage. The statement is followed by five choices lettered (A) (B) (C) (D) (E). For each question, mark your answer sheet with the letter of that choice which best conveys the meaning of the passage, and which best completes the statement.

Correct Answers are consolidated after the last question.

1. "Carriers shall be careful to deliver mail to the persons for whom it is intended or to someone authorized to receive it. In case of doubt they shall make inquiry to ascertain the owner. Failing in this, they shall return the mail to the post office for disposition."

   The paragraph best supports the statement that, if a carrier has an ordinary letter for delivery, he must
   A) ask the neighbors to identify the addressee before delivering the letter
   B) deliver it only to the address placed on the letter by the sender
   c) never return the letter to the post office if he has definite knowledge of an addressee's address
   D) not deliver the letter if more than one unidentified person claims to be the addressee
   E) return it to the post office if the addressee is not at home

2. "Letter carriers, whether assigned to delivery or collection duty, and special-delivery messengers shall receive all prepaid matter bearing a special-delivery stamp, or the equivalent thereof, which may be handed to them on their trips or runs, and shall keep such matter separate from other mail, and turn it in immediately upon their arrival at the post office."

   The paragraph best supports the statement that a letter carrier on delivery duty shall accept from a patron
   A) mail bearing a special-delivery stamp or unstamped mail and money for the stamp
   B) all prepaid mail handed to him and turn it in promptly at the post office
   c) special-delivery mail fully prepaid by stamps, and deliver it to the post office

   D) mail for which he receives a special-delivery fee, and keep it separate from ordinary mail
   E) special-delivery mail for posting, but make no deliveries of special-delivery mail

3. "Formerly it was only unskilled labor which was shifted from place to place in the wake of industrial booms. Since so many business concerns have become nationwide in the fields they cover, the white-collar workers have been in a similar state of flux."

   The paragraph best supports the statement that the growth of big business has resulted in
   A) a shifting supply of unskilled labor
   B) an increased tendency toward movement of workers
   c) an increased proportion of white-collar jobs
   D) the stabilization of industrial booms
   E) the use of fewer workers to do equal work

4. "Collections are made by all delivery-carriers in connection with their regular delivery trips, except in the larger post offices, where it has been found necessary to maintain a collection service in business sections during delivery hours. Under ordinary conditions no mounted collection is needed in strictly residential territory during the time delivery carriers are at work."

   The paragraph best supports the statement that at small post offices that have delivery service mail collections
   A) are not made on many residential routes by mounted carriers
   B) ordinarily are not made on residential routes during delivery periods
   c) are made in all business and residential districts by carriers on delivery routes

D) usually are made by mounted collectors when the amount of mail is large

E) are made only by delivery carriers in business districts

5. "In accordance with the ancient principle that a sovereign state may not be sued without its consent, a special Court of Claims has been established in each of several States of the United States. In this court, claims may be brought against the State. However, the State legislature must make the necessary appropriation before the claim awarded by the court can be paid."

The paragraph best supports the statement that a
A) sovereign state cannot be sued by its citizens
B) claim against a State can only be brought with the approval of the State legislature
C) sovereign state can only be sued by a Court of Claims
D) Court of Claims does not have the authority to enforce payment of approved claims
E) resident or business firm of any State has the right to bring suit against that State

6. "What constitutes skill in any line of work is not always easy to determine; economy of time must be carefully distinguished from economy of energy, as the quickest method may require the greatest expenditure of muscular effort, and may not be essential or at all desirable."

The paragraph best supports the statement that
A) the most efficiently executed task is not always the one done in the shortest time
B) energy and time cannot both be conserved in performing a single task
C) if a task requires muscular energy it is not being performed economically
D) skill in performing a task should not be acquired at the expense of time
E) a task is well done when it is performed in the shortest time

7. "When a number of letters are deposited in a letter box without stamps affixed and a sum of money is found in the box which is not sufficient to pay one full rate of postage on all of the letters, they shall, if mailed by the same person and if he is known and resides within the delivery limit of the mailing office, be returned to him, together with the money. The letters shall be treated as 'Held for postage' if the sender is unknown or resides beyond the delivery limit of the mailing office."

The paragraph best supports the statement that, when unstamped letters and money are placed in a mail box by the sender,

A) the letters are held for postage if sender is unknown and the money is insufficient to pay one full rate on each letter
B) the letters for which sufficient postage is paid are dispatched, and the others are held
C) the letters will be returned if the amount of money is insufficient for full postage and the sender lives in another city
D) only a full return address on the envelope will insure prompt dispatch of the letters
E) the postal service is not obliged to dispatch such mail even if the money covers full postage

8. "When a card money order is presented for payment, the paying employee shall examine it to see that it is properly drawn and stamped by the issuing post office, and assure himself that it is not issued on a form reported stolen, and that it is signed and presented by the payee or remitter or by a person authorized by either to receive payment. Payment must not be refused if one year or more has elasped since the last day of the month in which the order was issued."

The paragraph best supports the statement that payment for an otherwise correct card money order will not be refused if the order
A) was issued by a post office that has since been discontinued
B) bears the stamp of a post office other than the one that issued the order
C) bears a date more than a year earlier than the date payment is requested
D) is presented for payment by a person whose signature is unfamiliar to the paying clerk
E) is signed by a person other than the payee or a person authorized by the remitter

9. "If a parcel originating in another country proves to be undeliverable in the United States owing to the removal of the addressee to a known address in the country where the parcel was mailed, and if the parcel does not bear the sender's instructions for delivery to a second address or for abandonment, it shall be marked 'Parti (removed)' followed by an indication of the forwarding address of the addressee, and treated for return to the country of origin."

The paragraph best supports the statement that if the sender has not authorized other delivery or abandonment of an undeliverable parcel, but addressee's new address in sender's country is known, the
A) parcel should be marked and forwarded to the address
B) sender's instructions should be followed, by returning the parcel to him

c) parcel should be prepared to permit return to and forwarding in the sender's country

D) return of the parcel should be planned and accomplished promptly

E) postal service in the country of origin should inquire how to dispose of the parcel

10. "The post office of delivery shall require the addressee, or his authorized representative, to open a bad-order registered article, whether repaired with sealing stamps or reenclosed, in the presence of the delivering employee, the envelope being cut at the end so as to preserve the sealing intact. If any of the contents is missing, the envelope (letter and penalty, if any) or wrapper shall be obtained from the addressee, with his endorsement as to shortage of contents, and sent to the proper inspector in charge with a report of the facts."

The paragraph best supports the statement that a bad-order registered article

A) should be repaired or reenclosed and sent with a report to the inspector in charge

B) must be delivered to the addressee only and opened by him in the presence of the delivering employee

c) is not likely to be received by the addressee with its contents intact

D) should be checked as to contents, upon delivery, in the presence of the delivering employee

E) will not be intact upon delivery if the sealing stamps have been tampered with

END OF TEST

Go on to do the following Test in this Examination, just as you would be expected to do on the actual exam.

CONSOLIDATE YOUR KEY ANSWERS HERE

Practice using Answer Sheets. Make ONE mark for each answer. Additional and stray marks may be counted as mistakes. In making corrections erase errors COMPLETELY. Make glossy black marks. To arrive at an accurate estimate of your ability and progress, cover the Correct Answers with a sheet of white paper while you are taking this test.

SAMPLE ANSWER SHEET

CORRECT ANSWERS TO THE FOREGOING PRACTICE QUESTIONS

Now compare your answers with these Correct Answers to the Practice Questions. If your answers differ from these, go back and study those questions to see where and how you made your mistakes.

1.D	2.C	3.B	4.C	5.D
6.A	7.A	8.C	9.C	10.D

Count how many you got right, and write that number on this line————→ _____
(This is your Test Score.)

Meaning of Test Score

If your Test Score is *8 or over*, you have a Good score.

If your Test Score is *6 or 7*, you have a Fair score.

If your Test Score is *5 or less*, you are not doing too well.

Practice Using Answer Sheets

Alter numbers to match the practice and drill questions in each part of the book.
Make only ONE mark for each answer. Additional and stray marks may be counted as mistakes.
In making corrections, erase errors COMPLETELY. Make glossy black marks.

1	A B C D E	1	A B C D E	1	A B C D E	1	A B C D E	1	A B C D E
2	A B C D E	2	A B C D E	2	A B C D E	2	A B C D E	2	A B C D E
3	A B C D E	3	A B C D E	3	A B C D E	3	A B C D E	3	A B C D E
4	A B C D E	4	A B C D E	4	A B C D E	4	A B C D E	4	A B C D E
5	A B C D E	5	A B C D E	5	A B C D E	5	A B C D E	5	A B C D E
6	A B C D E	6	A B C D E	6	A B C D E	6	A B C D E	6	A B C D E
7	A B C D E	7	A B C D E	7	A B C D E	7	A B C D E	7	A B C D E
8	A B C D E	8	A B C D E	8	A B C D E	8	A B C D E	8	A B C D E
9	A B C D E	9	A B C D E	9	A B C D E	9	A B C D E	9	A B C D E
0	A B C D E	0	A B C D E	0	A B C D E	0	A B C D E	0	A B C D E

1	A B C D E	1	A B C D E	1	A B C D E	1	A B C D E	1	A B C D E
2	A B C D E	2	A B C D E	2	A B C D E	2	A B C D E	2	A B C D E
3	A B C D E	3	A B C D E	3	A B C D E	3	A B C D E	3	A B C D E
4	A B C D E	4	A B C D E	4	A B C D E	4	A B C D E	4	A B C D E
5	A B C D E	5	A B C D E	5	A B C D E	5	A B C D E	5	A B C D E
6	A B C D E	6	A B C D E	6	A B C D E	6	A B C D E	6	A B C D E
7	A B C D E	7	A B C D E	7	A B C D E	7	A B C D E	7	A B C D E
8	A B C D E	8	A B C D E	8	A B C D E	8	A B C D E	8	A B C D E
9	A B C D E	9	A B C D E	9	A B C D E	9	A B C D E	9	A B C D E
0	A B C D E	0	A B C D E	0	A B C D E	0	A B C D E	0	A B C D E

1	A B C D E	7	A B C D E	13	A B C D E	19	A B C D E	25	A B C D E
2	A B C D E	8	A B C D E	14	A B C D E	20	A B C D E	26	A B C D E
3	A B C D E	9	A B C D E	15	A B C D E	21	A B C D E	27	A B C D E
4	A B C D E	10	A B C D E	16	A B C D E	22	A B C D E	28	A B C D E
5	A B C D E	11	A B C D E	17	A B C D E	23	A B C D E	29	A B C D E
6	A B C D E	12	A B C D E	18	A B C D E	24	A B C D E	30	A B C D E

POST OFFICE CLERK-CARRIER

INTERPRETING POSTAL INSTRUCTIONS

This kind of question, which is almost certain to appear on your test, demands that your new-found skill in interpreting reading passages be applied to Post Office instructions, rules, and readings. They are usually taken from the Postal Manual. You are NOT required to memorize any of this material. Your ability to understand what you read is what is being tested here. As you practice for the real thing by answering our practice questions you'll be helping yourself in still another way. You'll be getting to know the technical language and the postal words that might ordinarily unsettle you were they encountered without warning on your test.

HERE'S HOW YOU SHOULD ANSWER THESE POSTAL READING QUESTIONS.

Each one is made up of a paragraph, followed by four or five statements based on the paragraph. You may never have seen the paragraph before, but you must now read it carefully so that you understand it. Then read the statements following. Any one of them might be right. You have to choose the *one* that's *most* correct. Try to pick the one that's most complete, most accurate . . . the one that is best supported by and necessarily flows from the paragraph. Be sure that it contains nothing false so far as the paragraph itself is concerned. After you've thought it out, write the capital letter preceding your best choice in the margin next to the question. When you've answered all the questions, score yourself faithfully by checking with our answers that follow the last question. But please don't look at those answers until you've written your own. You just won't be helping yourself if you do that. Besides, you'll have ample opportunity to do the questions again, and to check with our answers, in the event that your first try results in a low score. If you'd really like to get into the swing of the thing while practicing, you might want to answer on facsimiles of the kind of answer sheets provided on machine-scored examinations. For practice purposes we have provided several such facsimiles throughout this book. Tear one out if you wish, and mark your answers on it . . . just as you would do on an actual exam. In machine-scored examinations you should record all your answers on the answer sheet provided. Don't make the mistake of putting answers on the test booklet itself. It's best NOT to mark your booklet unless you are sure that it is permitted. And it's most important that you learn to mark your answers clearly and in the right place.

TEST-TYPE QUESTIONS TO PROVIDE
PRACTICE FOR YOUR EXAM.

1. (READING) "If you are in doubt as to whether any matter is properly mailable, you should ask the postmaster. Even though the Post Office Department has not expressly declared any matter to be nonmailable, the sender of such matter may be held fully liable for violation of law if he does actually send non-mailable matter through the mails."

Of the following, the most accurate statement made concerning the above paragraph is:
(A) non-mailable matter is not always clearly defined
(B) ignorance of what constitutes non-mailable matter relieves the sender of all responsibility
(C) though doubt may exist about the mailability of any matter, the sender is fully liable for law violation if such matter should be non-mailable
(D) the Post Office Department is not explicit in its position on the violation of the non-mailable matter law
(E) no one may send doubtful matter through the mails.

2. (READING) "First-class mail, except postal and post cards, is returned to the sender, if known, without additional charge. Only postal and post cards that bear the sender's guarantee to pay return postage are returned, and postage at the card rate is collected on delivery to the sender. Mail paid at the drop-letter rate is returned to the sender at the same post office without additional charge. If the sender is at another post office, additional postage for the difference between the amount prepaid and total postage computed at the first-class rate is collected on delivery. Any postage due because of failure to fully prepay postage at the time of mailing will be collected from the sender when the undeliverable mail is returned."

According to the above paragraph, which of the following statements is true?
(A) no first-class mail should be sent without a return address
(B) all first-class, undeliverable mail is returned to sender, if known
(C) the sender is subject to any charge which is deemed necessary for the return of undeliverable mail

(D) all first-class mail, with the exception of postal and post cards, is returned to sender without additional charge, regardless of where mailed
(E) post cards may be returned to sender if it bears his guarantee to pay return postage.

3. "Mail chutes and receiving boxes may be placed, subject to the approval of the postmaster, in public buildings, railroad stations, hotels, and office buildings of not less than four stories in height, and apartment houses with not less than 40 residential apartments. Mail chutes must conform to the requirements in the pamphlet containing mail-chute rules, regulations, and specifications, copies of which may be secured through the postmaster."

Which of the following statements is most accurate in regard to the above paragraph?
(A) subject to the approval of the postmaster, mail chutes may be placed in public buildings of not less than four stories
(B) a railroad station less than four stories in height is not entitled to a mail chute
(C) mail chutes and receiving boxes may be placed in dwellings with at least 40 residential apartments
(D) all office buildings may have mail chutes placed in them
(E) height requirements apply to every building in which the placing of mail chutes is being considered.

4. "Post office boxes (which term includes post office drawers) are for the convenience of the public in the delivery of mail. The service affords patrons privacy, eliminates the necessity of waiting in line at delivery windows, and permits them to obtain mail after regular post office hours where the lobby is kept open. Postmasters will not disclose the names of box holders to any person outside the Postal Service."

According to this paragraph, a post office box is
(A) available only to certain groups
(B) opened only during regular post office hours

(C) opened only in the presence of a postal employee

(D) used to speed mail delivery

(E) primarily for the privacy and convenience of the public.

5. "The Post Office Department has a monopoly over the transportation of letters for others over post routes. This monopoly was created prior to the adoption of the Constitution and has existed, with varying provisions, continuously from that time to the present. This subchapter defines the types of matters which constitute letters and hence which are subject to the monopoly. It sets forth the types of transportation covered under the monopoly. It also prescribes exceptions to the monopoly."

This introduction prepares you for a subchapter on

(A) monopoly vs. the Constitution

(B) definitions of types of matters which constitute letters, and other aspects covered under, and exceptions to the monopoly

(C) how the Post Office Department defends its monopoly

(D) why the monopoly was created prior to the Constitution

(E) the need for varying provisions of the monopoly.

6. "Commercial papers are not classed as letters since they are valued as evidence of rights of the holder rather than for any information they may carry when shipped from one person to another. Such commercial papers include contracts, stock certificates, promissory notes, bonds and other negotiable securities, insurance policies, title policies, abstracts of title, mortgages, deeds, leases and articles of incorporation."

The best reason for not classifying commercial papers as letters is that

(A) they do not convey information

(B) they are seldom addressed to individuals

(C) they are valued as legal documents

(D) their value is not primarily that of carrying information

(E) they are letter substitutes.

7. "Letters may be transmitted by private hands without compensation. A person or firm engaged in the transportation of goods or persons for hire cannot be considered 'private hands without compensation.' The phrase just quoted denotes transportation of a letter which does not take place in the course of business of the person or firm carrying the letter."

About which of the following points is the above paragraph most specific?

(A) by whom letters may be transmitted

(B) what "private hands without compensation" cannot be

(C) what "private hands without compensation" really means

(D) defining what is meant by "in the course of business"

(E) that the person carrying the letter must be hired by a firm to be "private hands without compensation."

8. "When the COD remittance is to be sent to someone other than the actual mailer, the name and address of the person to whom the money is to be sent must appear in the proper spaces on the address side of the COD tag. The name and address of the actual mailer must be placed on the back of the delivery office portion of the tag. The name and address of the person to whom the money is to be paid must be shown as sender on the COD parcel itself, together with directions as to return, if undeliverable."

The reason, in the paragraph on the preceding page, for showing on the package the name of the person to whom the money is to be remitted as sender, even though that person is not the actual mailer, is

(A) that the person receiving remittance must be protected

(B) that the person to whom remittance is entitled should receive the parcel if it is undeliverable

(C) that the mailer, and not the person receiving remittance, may otherwise be liable

(D) not given

(E) that all packages must be plainly marked.

9. "No attempt is made to keep maps current on items other than postal data. Copies furnished are prints of the original maps that are revised from time to time as changes in the line of travel are authorized. It is not possible to keep all originals up to date at all times, and no assurance can be given that any map purchased will show the latest changes in service."

The accuracy of the maps referred to above

(A) is doubtful, because of frequent revisions

(B) is certain, because they are issued by an official agency

(C) can be assured by the Post Office

(D) cannot be questioned, since they are duplicates of originals

(E) rests on the fact that they reflect the latest changes in service.

10. "Combustible liquids having a flash point of 150° F. or lower but above 80° F. (Tag, open tester) may be sent to foreign countries generally in quantities not exceeding one quart in any one parcel, except that paints, varnishes, turpentine and similar substances may be sent in quantities of less than one gallon in any one parcel. Each parcel containing a combustible liquid must be marked by the sender to indicate that the flash point is above 80° F."

Which of the following statements does the above paragraph best support?
(A) combustible liquids may be sent to any foreign country in quantities not exceeding one quart
(B) there are no exceptions to quantitative restrictions on combustible liquids
(C) the flash point of combustible liquids determines the quantity allotted to a parcel
(D) parcels containing combustible liquids with a flash point above 80 degrees F. must be so marked
(E) turpentine and related substances may be sent in larger quantities because of their uniform flash point.

11. "Special-handling service is available for fourth-class mail only including that which is insured or sent COD. It provides the most expeditious handling, dispatch, and transportation available, but does not provide special delivery. Special-handling parcels are delivered as parcel post is ordinarily delivered, on regular scheduled trips. The special-handling fee must be paid on all parcels that must be given special attention in handling, transportation, and delivery, such as parcels containing baby chicks or other baby poultry, package bees carried outside mail bags, baby alligators, etc."

The major advantage of special handling is that it
(A) protects perishable items, such as baby chicks
(B) expedites fourth-class mail in every way short of special delivery
(C) provides COD parcels with assured delivery
(D) provides an extra source of income for the Post Office
(E) discourages the mailing of matter which is difficult to handle.

12. "Air mail weighing 8 ounces or less, on which the rate for one ounce is prepaid, is dispatched to its destination, and any unpaid portion is collected on delivery. Airmail weighing more than 8 ounces is dispatched by air if it bears at least 50 percent of the full amount of air postage. If it bears less than 50 percent of the full amount of air postage, the piece is returned to sender. If prepaid postage is enough for surface transportation and the piece would be delayed by return, it is sent on as surface mail."

The position taken by the Post Office Department on air mail which does not bear full postage is
(A) that such mail is not entitled to delivery
(B) that at least three-fourths of required postage is enough
(C) that if it weighs less than 8 ounces, it may go for half-postage, and the balance collected on delivery
(D) that any piece over 8 ounces may be delivered, even though half the amount of air postage is unpaid
(E) lenient, since it allows delivery under many conditions.

13. "News agents must furnish postmasters evidence that copies of publications offered for mailing are entitled to second-class postage rates, and that they are sent to actual subscribers or to other news agents for the purpose of sale. A printed notice of second-class entry in the copies is sufficient evidence that a publication is entitled to be mailed at second-class rates. The addresses on bulk packages must show that the packages are sent to other news agents."

Evidence that a publication is entitled to second-class rates is considered sufficient by
(A) a contract made with the postmaster
(B) a printed notice of second-class entry in the copies of publication
(C) a label on bulk packages containing the publication
(D) proof of subscribers
(E) the opinion of the postmaster.

14. "The responsibility of the Postal Service for registered mail ends with its proper delivery. Mail for delivery by carriers is taken on the first trip after it is received unless the addressee has requested the postmaster to hold his mail at the Post Office. You may obtain the name and address of the sender, and you may look at registered mail while it is held by the postal employee, before accepting delivery and signing the delivery receipt. Identification will be required if the applicant for registered mail is unknown. The mail will not be given to the addressee until the delivery receipt is obtained by the postal employee."

Registered mail is considered properly delivered when
(A) it has been deposited in the receiving box of the addressee
(B) the addressee has taken it from the postal employee's hands
(C) the delivery receipt has been given to the postal employee
(D) identification has been acquired from the applicant
(E) the addressee has requested the postmaster to hold his mail at the Post Office.

15. "You may not obtain registration if: a. Articles are placed in street letter boxes or in mail drops in Post Offices, even though the articles bear sufficient stamps to cover all charges. The articles will be dispatched with the registered mail but a registration receipt will not be issued, and liability for the loss or rifling of or damage to such mail will not be accepted by the Postal Service. b. Articles are addressed to the Post Offices to which they cannot be transported with safety."

Articles deposited in mail drops, and bearing sufficient stamps for all registration charges, are
(A) entitled to all services rendered registered mail
(B) subject to inspection before being accepted as registered
(C) returned to sender if not properly presented in accordance with registration procedure
(D) dispatched with registered mail without issuance of receipt or liability for loss accepted
(E) often subject to rifling or damage.

16. "Any matter addressed to a person using a fictitious, false or assumed name, title, or address in conducting, promoting, or carrying on or assisting therein, through the mails, any business scheme or device is in violation of law. The recipient must appear at the post office of receipt and be identified. If the addressee fails to appear and be identified, after notification, or if the fictitious character of such mail is satisfactorily established, it is forwarded to the dead letter office as fictitious matter."

The first passage in the above paragraph defines fictitious matter. Such matter is most nearly
(A) that which is addressed to a false name in carrying on a business scheme in violation of law
(B) that which bears an assumed return address
(C) that which contains fraudulent material

(D) that which promotes a fictitious device
(E) that which is unclassified and forwarded to the dead letter office.

17. "A postmaster or other postal employee will comply with a summons requiring his appearance in court. He will not testify in regard to reports of Post Office Inspectors or other records of the Post Office Inspection Service. A postmaster or other postal employee will not testify as to names and address of post office patrons, mail matter, postal savings accounts, or money orders unless he is specifically directed to do so by the court after first calling attention of the court to this regulation."

In compliance with the above instructions, a post office employee is
(A) never to testify in court concerning postal business
(B) relied upon in court cases to uphold the actions of fellow employees
(C) permitted to testify if directed to do so by the court after it has been advised of the above regulation
(D) directed to answer all questions except those concerning records of the Post Office Inspection Service
(E) prevented from going beyond the requirement of answering a summons.

18. "When mail of a higher class is enclosed with mail of a lower class, the rate of postage on the entire piece or package is that of the higher class. Persons knowingly concealing or enclosing matter of a higher class in that of a lower class to avoid payment of the correct postage are liable to a fine of not more than $100.

It is clear from the above that
(A) matter of mixed classes is undesirable
(B) in a piece containing mixed classes, the rate for the higher class applies to the entire piece
(C) a piece containing mixed classes makes the sender liable to a fine of $100 or less
(D) persons sending pieces containing mixed classes are avoiding payment of correct postage
(E) higher class postage is the only answer to questionable envelopes.

19. "Two or more persons or firms, or a person acting as the agent of two or more persons or firms, may not mail in one envelope to a mutual customer the bills, statements of account, or other letters of the persons or firms. No two firms that are distinct entities may send their letters in one envelope even though they are affiliated or jointly owned."

It is not permissible, from the above, for
(A) a single firm to render more than one invoice in a single wrapper
(B) anyone to enclose two letters in one envelope
(C) two firms, whether affiliated or not, to enclose their bills in one envelope
(D) any firm to use one envelope when two are called for
(E) mutual customers of two or more firms to request their bills in one envelope.

20. "Sealed mail while in the custody of the Post Office Department is accorded absolute secrecy. No persons in the Postal Service, except those employed for that purpose in dead-mail offices may break or permit the breaking of the seal of any mailed matter, without a legal warrant, even though it may contain criminal or otherwise unmailable matter, or furnish evidence of the conviction of a crime."

From the above, sealed mail may be opened when in the custody of the Post Office Department
(A) by persons in search of criminal evidence
(B) by any Postal Inspector
(C) when suspicion is aroused as to its mailability
(D) only by those employed for that purpose in dead-mail offices
(E) by anyone with a legal warrant.

21. "The editor, publisher, business manager, or owner must file, in duplicate, not later than October 1 of each year on Form 3526 a sworn statement showing the ownership and management of their publication. The statement must be published in the second issue of the publication printed next after the statement has been filed. Copies of Form 3526 are furnished by the local postmaster. The two copies of Form 3526 and one copy of the issue in which the statement is published must be filed with the postmaster at the office where the publication has original second-class mail privileges."

To comply with the above regulation, a publisher must
(A) file a copy of Form 3526, and an issue of his publication containing statement of ownership, this issue being the second one printed after original filing date
(B) notify the postmaster not later than October 1 of each year that he intends to file, and then submit the second subsequent issue bearing statement of ownership

(C) swear to ownership and management of the publication, and print statement of same in publication
(D) contact post office where publication has original second-class privileges, and file what is necessary at their direction
(E) file two copies Form 3526 to post office where privilege was originally obtained before October 1 of each year, and print statement of ownership in second issue subsequent to filing date, and file with same post office.

22. "Franked mail is forwarded like any other mail, but when once delivered to the addressee it may not be remailed. A package of franked pieces may be sent by a person entitled to the franking privilege, to one addressee, who, on receiving and opening the package may on behalf of such person, place addresses on the franked articles and mail them."

The above paragraph does *not* say that
(A) franked pieces may be forwarded to someone else for mailing
(B) once delivered, franked mail may not be remailed
(C) someone other than a person entitled to the franking privilege may address franked mail
(D) only addressees receiving packages of franked mail are extended the franking privilege
(E) franked mail is forwarded like any other mail.

23. (READING) "The person who presents a money order for payment must be identified if unknown to the postmaster. Personal identification should be by someone known to be financially responsible and such person should understand that he is assuming responsibility for correct payment. Paying clerks should not accept as conclusive evidence of identity letters, receipted bills, bank deposit books, social security account number cards, chauffeur's licenses, or temporary driver's permits. Letters, bills and bank books are frequently stolen with the money orders. It is comparatively easy in many states for any person to obtain a driver's permit or chauffeur's license under an assumed name, and postal employees should be especially careful when this type of identification is offered by persons presenting money order for payment. Thieves even employ photographs, pocket card cases and printed business cards bearing fictitious names corresponding with forged orders made out on regular money-order forms stolen from post offices."

According to this section of the P. L. & R., money orders should not be paid to a person unknown to the postmaster unless:

(A) the person presents a driver's or chauffeur's license with his photograph
(B) the person shows receipted bills bearing his name
(C) he has a social security account number
(D) another person of known financial responsibility vouches for him.

24. The word CONCLUSIVE as used here means most nearly:
(A) Collusive   (C) Convincing
(B) Fraudulent   (D) Legally binding.

25. The purpose of this section is apparently to:
(A) protest against the ease with which some states give driver's licenses to persons with criminal records
(B) warn the public to be careful and not lose money order blanks
(C) help postal employees detect criminals who steal money order blanks
(D) advise postal employees to exercise extreme care in cashing money orders presented by unknown persons.

26. (READING) "Every letter carrier having in his possession a mail key shall attach it securely to his clothing by means of a safety chain. He shall be held strictly responsible for the safety and proper use of the key, and he shall not permit it to be examined or handled by any person not authorized to do so. At the end of the day's work carriers shall deliver their keys to the person designated by the postmaster to receive them, except that carriers who make early morning collections and carriers engaged in late collections who end their tour of duty in the field, at a distance from the post office, may be permitted to retain their keys overnight."

The purpose of the above ruling is probably intended to:

(A) reduce the loss of mail keys
(B) prevent mail keys from falling into the hands of unauthorized persons
(C) make certain that each postal employee is provided with a safety chain
(D) limit overtime work by postal employees.

27. Letter carriers may retain their keys overnight if they:
(A) have the key attached to a safety chain
(B) live at a distance from the post office
(C) do not permit it to be handled by unauthorized persons
(D) make early morning or late collections and end their tour of duty in the field at a distance from the post office.

28. (READING) "A letter carrier or substitute carrier shall not be removed except for just cause upon written charges filed with the First Assistant Postmaster General, Division of Post Office Service, of which he shall be given due notice and allowed full opportunity for defense. The charges shall specifically set forth alleged delinquency or misconduct giving date and place of the occurrence."

The section would appear to be intended to:
(A) protect carriers from arbitrary removal from their position
(B) give the First Assistant Postmaster General the power to dismiss carriers and substitutes
(C) prevent carriers and substitutes from resigning without the permission of the First Assistant Postmaster General
(D) remove misconduct as a reason for dismissing a postal carrier or substitute.

29. Which of the following statements regarding charges filed with the First Assistant Postmaster General against a letter carrier or substitute is not true.
(A) charges must be in writing
(B) charges must be approved by the letter carrier or substitute
(C) charges must give time and place of the alleged offense
(D) charges must state the nature of the alleged offense.

30. (READING) "Every postmaster, before entering upon the duties of his office shall give bond, with good and approved security, and in such penalty as the Postmaster General shall deem sufficient, conditioned for the faithful discharge of all duties and trusts imposed on him either by law or the rules and regulations of the department. On the death, resignation or removal of a postmaster, his bond shall be delivered to the General Accounting Office. The bond of any married woman who may be appointed postmaster shall be binding upon her and her sureties and she shall be liable for misconduct in office as if she were sole."

According to this section, a married woman serving as Postmaster:
(A) is not required to give a bond upon taking office
(B) may allow her husband to assume responsibilities for her actions in office
(C) is fully responsible for her discharge of duties as postmaster
(D) may not be removed from office for misconduct.

31. The purpose of this section of the Postal Manual is apparently to:
(A) limit the number of married women Postmasters
(B) require Postmasters to purchase government saving bonds
(C) protect against misconduct on the part of postmasters which may cause financial loss to the government
(D) protect the families of Postmasters in case of their deaths while in office.

Correct Answers

(Please don't look at these until after you've written your own.)

1.	C	9.	A	17.	C	25.	D
2.	E	10.	D	18.	B	26.	B
3.	C	11.	B	19.	C	27.	D
4.	E	12.	E	20.	D	28.	A
5.	B	13.	B	21.	E	29.	B
6.	D	14.	C	22.	D	30.	C
7.	B	15.	D	23.	D	31.	C
8.	D	16.	A	24.	C		

POST OFFICE CLERK-CARRIER

SERIES REASONING TESTS

Questions such as those below test your ability to see relationship between the elements of a series. These questions are sometimes referred to as series or progressions, and in them you are asked to determine the rule that binds the elements together and then select or arrange the following elements according to that rule.

HOW TO PROFIT FROM THE PRACTICE TESTS

On the following pages you are furnished practice tests consisting of questions like those on the actual exam. The time limit here is just about what you may expect. Take these tests as a series of dress rehearsals strengthening your ability to score high on this type of question. For each test use the Answer Sheet provided to mark down your answers. If the Answer Sheet is separated from the questions, tear it out so you can mark it more easily. As you finish each test, go back and check your answers to find your score, and to determine how well you did. This will help you discover where you need more practice.

DESCRIPTION OF THE TEST AND SAMPLE QUESTIONS

Here are some sample questions for you to do. Mark your answers on the Sample Answer Sheet, making sure to keep your mark inside the correct box. If you want to change an answer, erase the mark you don't want to count. Then mark your new answer. Use a No. 2 (medium) pencil.

NUMBER SERIES QUESTIONS ANALYZED AND EXPLAINED

DIRECTIONS: *Each question consists of a series of letters or numbers (or both) which follow some definite order. Study each series to determine what the order is. Then look at the answer choices. Select the one answer that will complete the set in accordance with the pattern established.*

Each of the first three sample questions gives a series of six numbers. Each series of numbers is made up according to a certain rule or order. You are to find what the next number in the series would be.

① 2 4 6 8 10 12
  (A) 14   (B) 16
  (C) 18   (D) 20
     (E) none of these

In question 1, the rule is to add 2 to each number (2 + 2 = 4; 4 + 2 = 6; etc.). The next number in the series is 14 (12 + 2 = 14). Since 14 is lettered (A), (A) is your correct answer.

② 7 8 6 7 5 6
  (A) 2   (B) 3
  (C) 4   (D) 5
     (E) none of these

In question 2, the rule is to add 1 to the first number, subtract 2 from the next, add 1, subtract 2, and so on. The next number in the series is 4, letter (C) is your correct answer.

③ 3 6 9 12 15 18
  (A) 39   (B) 40
  (C) 45   (D) 59
     (E) none of these

In question 3, the rule is to add 3, making 21 the next number in the series. The correct answer to question 3 is *none of these*, since 39, 40, 45, and 59, are all incorrect; (E) is the correct answer.

DIRECTIONS: *This test measures your ability to think with numbers instead of words. In each problem you are given a series of numbers that are changing according to a rule. The series is followed on the right by five pairs of numbers, lettered (A) (B) (C) (D) (E). These are the suggested answers. Study each problem to determine what the pattern is so that you can figure out a rule which would make one of the lettered sets the next two numbers in the series. Mark the Answer Sheet with the letter of the one pair that completes the series in accordance with the pattern established.*

④ 1 1 2 1 3 1 4 1
  (A) 1 5   (B) 4 1
  (C) 5 1   (D) 5 5
     (E) 6 1

The series consists of 1's alternating with numbers in ascending numerical order. The next two numbers would be 5 and 1: therefore (C) is the correct answer.

⑤ 2 8 3 7 5 6 8 5
  (A) 10 6   (B) 11 3
  (C) 11 4   (D) 12 4
     (E) 12 6

This series consists of a subseries for which the rule is to add 1, add 2, add 3, and add 4, alternating with another subseries in descending numerical order. The next number in the first subseries would be 8 + 4, or 12; and the next number in the descending series would be 4. Therefore (D) is correct.

The problems do not use hard arithmetic. The task is merely to see how the numbers are related to each other. The sample questions will explain several types in detail so that you may become familiar with what you have to do.

⑥ 1 2 3 4 5 6 7 . . . . A) 1 2   B) 5 6   C) 8 9   D) 4 5   E) 7 8
How are these numbers changing? The numbers in this series are increasing by 1 or the rule is "add 1." If you apply this rule to the series, what would the next two numbers be? $7+1=8+1=9$. Therefore, the correct answer is 8 and 9, and you would select c) 8 9 as your answer.

⑦ 15 14 13 12 11 10 9 . . . . A) 2 1   B) 17 16   C) 8 9   D) 8 7   E) 9 8
The numbers in this series are decreasing by 1 or the rule is "subtract 1." If you apply that rule, what would the next two numbers be? $9-1=8-1=7$. The correct answer is 8 and 7, and you would select D) 8 7 as your answer.

⑧ 20 20 21 21 22 22 23 . . . . A) 23 23   B) 23 24   c) 19 19   D) 22 23   E) 21 22
In this series each number is repeated and then increased by 1. The rule is "repeat, add 1, repeat, add 1, etc." The series would be $20^{+0}\ 20^{+1}\ 21^{+0}\ 21^{+1}\ 22^{+0}\ 22^{+1}\ 23^{+0}\ 23^{+1}\ 24$. The correct answer is 23 and 24, and you should have darkened B on the Sample Answer Sheet for question ⑧

⑨ 17 3 17 4 17 5 17 . . . . A) 6 17   B) 6 7   c) 17 6   D) 5 6   E) 17 7
If you can't find a single rule for all the numbers in a series, see if there are really two series in the problem. This series is the number 17 separated by numbers increasing by 1, starting with 3. If the series were continued for two more numbers, it would read 17 3 17 4 17 5 17 6 17. The correct answer is 6 and 17, and you should have darkened A on the Sample Answer Sheet for question ⑨

⑩ 1 2 4 5 7 8 10 . . . . A) 11 12   B) 12 14   c) 10 13   D) 12 13   E) 11 13
The rule in this series is not easy to see until you actually set down how the numbers are changing: $1^{+1}\ 2^{+2}\ 4^{+1}\ 5^{+2}\ 7^{+1}\ 8^{+2}\ 10$. The numbers in this series are increasing first by 1 (that is plus 1) and then by 2 (that is plus 2). If the series were continued for two more numbers, it would read: 1 2 4 5 7 8 10 (plus 1) which is *11* (plus 2) which is *13*. Therefore the correct answer is 11 and 13, and you should have darkened E on the Sample Answer Sheet for question ⑩

Now read and work sample questions ⑪ through ⑮ and mark your answers on the Sample Answer Sheet on this page.

⑪ 21 21 20 20 19 19 18 . . . . . . A) 18 18   B) 18 17   c) 17 18   D) 17 17   E) 18 19
⑫ 1 22 1 23 1 24 1 . . . . A) 2 61   B) 25 26   c) 25 1   D) 1 26   E) 1 25
⑬ 1 20 3 19 5 18 7 . . . . A) 8 9   B) 8 17   c) 17 10   D) 17 9   E) 9 18
⑭ 4 7 10 13 16 19 22 . . . . A) 23 26   B) 25 27   c) 25 26   D) 25 28   E) 24 27
⑮ 30 2 28 4 26 6 24 . . . . A) 23 9   B) 26 8   c) 8 9   D) 26 22   E) 8 22

Explanations for questions ⑪ through ⑮
⑪ Each number in the series repeats itself and then decreases by 1 or minus 1; *21* (repeat) *21* (minus 1) which makes *20* (repeat) *20* (minus 1) which makes *19* (repeat) *19* (minus 1) which makes *18* (repeat) *?* (minus 1) *?*

⑫ The number *1* is separated by numbers which begin with *22* and increase by 1; *1 22 1* (increase 22 by 1) which makes *23 1* (increase 23 by 1) which makes *24 1* (increase 24 by 1) which makes *?*

(13) This is best explained by two alternating series—one series starts with *1* and increases by 2 or plus 2; the other series starts with *20* and decreases by 1 or minus 1.

$$1 \uparrow 3 \uparrow 5 \uparrow 7 \uparrow ?$$
$$20 \quad 19 \quad 18 \quad ?$$

(14) This series of numbers increases by 3 (plus 3) beginning with the first number —*4* (plus 3) *7* (plus 3) *10* (plus 3) *13* (plus 3) *16* (plus 3) *19* (plus 3) *22* (plus 3) ? (plus 3) ?

(15) Look for two alternating series—one series starts with *30* and decreases by 2 (minus 2); the other series starts with *2* and increases by 2 (plus 2).

$$30 \uparrow 28 \uparrow 26 \uparrow 24 \uparrow ?$$
$$2 \quad 4 \quad 6 \quad ?$$

Now try questions (16) to (23). Mark your answers on the Sample Answer Sheet.

		A)	B)	C)	D)	E)
(16)	5 6 20 7 8 19 9	10 18	18 17	10 17	18 19	10 11
(17)	9 10 1 11 12 2 13	2 14	3 14	14 3	14 15	14 1
(18)	4 6 9 11 14 16 19	21 24	22 25	20 22	21 23	22 24
(19)	8 8 1 10 10 3 12	13 13	12 5	12 4	13 5	4 12
(20)	14 1 2 15 3 4 16	5 16	6 7	5 17	5 6	17 5
(21)	10 12 50 15 17 50 20	50 21	21 50	50 22	22 50	22 24
(22)	1 2 3 50 4 5 6 51 7 8	9 10	9 52	51 10	10 52	10 50
(23)	20 21 23 24 27 28 32 33 38 39 .	45 46	45 52	44 45	44 49	40 46

Hints for questions (16) through (23)

(16) Alternating series: $5\ 6 \uparrow 7\ 8 \uparrow 9\ ? \uparrow$
$\qquad\qquad\qquad 20 \qquad 19 \qquad ?$

(17) Alternating series: $9\ 10 \uparrow 11\ 12 \uparrow 13\ ? \uparrow$
$\qquad\qquad\qquad\quad 1 \qquad 2 \qquad ?$

(18) Increases alternately by 2 (plus 2) then 3 (plus 3) —*4* (plus 2) *6* (plus 3) *9* (plus 2) *11* (plus 3) *14* (plus 2) *16* (plus 3) *19* (plus 2) ? (plus 3) ?

(19) Alternating series: $8\ 8 \uparrow 10\ 10 \uparrow 12\ ? \uparrow$
$\qquad\qquad\qquad\quad 1 \qquad\quad 3 \qquad ?$

(20) Alternating series: $14 \uparrow \uparrow 15 \uparrow \uparrow 16 \uparrow \uparrow$
$\qquad\qquad\qquad\quad 1\ 2 \quad 3\ 4 \quad ?\ ?$

(21) Alternating series: $10\ 12 \uparrow 15\ 17 \uparrow 20\ ? \uparrow$
$\qquad\qquad\qquad\quad 50 \qquad 50 \qquad ?$

(22) Alternating series: $1\ 2\ 3 \uparrow 4\ 5\ 6 \uparrow 7\ 8\ ? \uparrow$
$\qquad\qquad\qquad\quad 50 \qquad 51 \qquad ?$

(23) Increases alternately by (plus 1), (plus 2), (plus 1), (plus 3), (plus 1), (plus 4), etc. —*20* (plus 1) *21* (plus 2) *23* (plus 1) *24* (plus 3) *27* (plus 1) *28* (plus 4) *32* (plus 1) *33* (plus 5) *38* (plus 1) *39* (plus 6) ? (plus 1) ?

							(a)	**(b)**	**(c)**	**(d)**	**(e)**
㉔	3	6	9	12	15	18	19	20	21	22	23

In example ㉔ above, each number is three larger than the preceding number. Therefore, to complete the series, choice (c), number 21, is the next number in the series.

							(a)	**(b)**	**(c)**	**(d)**	**(e)**
㉕	20	18	16	14	12	10	6	8	10	12	14

In series ㉕ above, each number is two less than the preceding number. Accordingly the correct answer is 8, choice (b).

Now do example Y ㉖ below and indicate the correct answer on your answer sheet.

							(a)	**(b)**	**(c)**	**(d)**	**(e)**
㉖	10	11	13	14	16	17	18	19	20	21	22

In example ㉖ the correct rule is add 1 then add 2, add 1 then add 2, etc. Therefore, the correct answer is 19, choice (b).

Now do example ㉗ and indicate your answer on the answer sheet.

							(a)	**(b)**	**(c)**	**(d)**	**(e)**
㉗	4	6	9	13	18	24	27	28	29	30	31

The rule is add 2, then add 3, then add 4, etc. Therefore, the correct answer is 31, choice (e).

CONSOLIDATE YOUR KEY ANSWERS HERE

Practice using Answer Sheets. Make ONE mark for each answer. Additional and stray marks may be counted as mistakes. In making corrections erase errors COMPLETELY. Make glossy black marks. To arrive at an accurate estimate of your ability and progress, cover the Correct Answers with a sheet of white paper while you are taking this test.

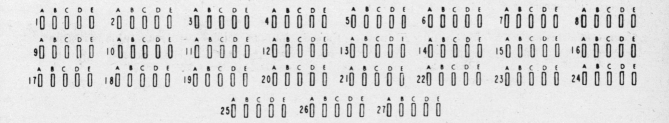

CORRECT ANSWERS TO SAMPLE QUESTIONS

Now compare your answers with the Correct Answers to Sample Questions. If your answers are not the same as the correct answers shown, go back and study the samples to see where you made a mistake.

1.A	5.D	9.A	13.D	17.C	21.D	25.B
2.C	6.C	10.E	14.D	18.A	22.B	26.B
3.E	7.D	11.B	15.E	19.B	23.A	27.E
4.C	8.B	12.C	16.A	20.D	24.C	

Hints for Answering Number Series Questions

- Do the ones that are easiest for you first. Then go back and work on the others.
  Enough time is allowed for you to do all the questions, providing you don't stay too long on the ones you have trouble answering.
- Sound out the series to yourself. You may hear the rule: 2 4 6 8 10 12 14 . . . What are the next two numbers?
- Look at the series carefully. You may see the rule: 9 2 9 4 9 6 9 . . . What are the next two numbers?
- If you can't hear it or see it, you may have to figure it out by writing down how the numbers are changing: 6 8 16 18 26 28 36 . . . What are the next two numbers?
  $6^{+2} 8^{+8} 16^{+2} 18^{+8} 26^{+2} 28^{+8} 36$ . . . What are the next two numbers if this is $+2 +8$?
  $36+2=38+8=46$ or 38 46. You would mark the letter of the answer that goes with 38 46.
- If none of the answers given fit the rule you have figured out, try again. Try to figure out a rule that makes one of the five answers a correct one.

DON'T SPEND TOO MUCH TIME ON ANY ONE QUESTION. SKIP IT AND COME BACK. A FRESH LOOK SOMETIMES HELPS.

TEST I. NUMBER SERIES

TIME: 10 Minutes. 25 Questions.

DIRECTIONS: Each question consists of a series of letters or numbers (or both) which follow some definite order. Study each series to determine what the order is. Then look at the answer choices. Select the one answer that will complete the set in accordance with the pattern established.

DIRECTIONS: Explanations of the key points behind each question are given at the end of the test. They follow the key answers which we have consolidated, facilitating comparison of your answers with ours.

1. 8 12 17 24 28 33
   (A) 36   (D) 39
   (B) 37   (E) 40
   (C) 38

2. 3 12 6 24 12 48
   (A) 24   (D) 40
   (B) 32   (E) 64
   (C) 36

3. 7 11 16 22 26 31
   (A) 32   (D) 37
   (B) 34   (E) 39
   (C) 36

4. 24 12 36 24 48 36
   (A) 40   (D) 58
   (B) 50   (E) 60
   (C) 52

5. 15 13 11 14 17 15
   (A) 11   (D) 14
   (B) 12   (E) 16
   (C) 13

6. 8 7 10 5 4 7
   (A) 6   (D) 2
   (B) 4   (E) 1
   (C) 3

7. 15 11 7 14 10 6
   (A) 4   (D) 10
   (B) 6   (E) 12
   (C) 8

8. 7 4 12 9 27 24
   (A) 11   (D) 72
   (B) 36   (E) 96
   (C) 48

9. 5 3 9 7 21 19
   (A) 9   (D) 64
   (B) 36   (E) 72
   (C) 57

10. 11 8 16 17 14 28
    (A) 20   (D) 38
    (B) 29   (E) 40
    (C) 32

11. 64 32 16 8 4 2
    (A) ⅛   (D) 1
    (B) ¼   (E) 0
    (C) ½

12. 48 24 20 10 6 3
    (A) 2   (D) —1
    (B) 1   (E) —2
    (C) 0

13. 77 76 74 71 67 62
    (A) 60   (D) 57
    (B) 59   (E) 56
    (C) 58

14. 4 2 8 4 12 6
    (A) 8   (D) 11
    (B) 9   (E) 12
    (C) 10

15. 1 6 36 3 18 108
    (A) 7   (D) 10
    (B) 8   (E) 11
    (C) 9

16. 2 6 12 36 72 216
    (A) 288   (D) 476
    (B) 376   (E) 648
    (C) 432

17. .05 .1 .3 1.2 6 36
(A) 48
(B) 72
(C) 164
(D) 216
(E) 252

18. 7 6½ 6¼ 5¾ 5½ 5
(A) 4¾
(B) 4½
(C) 4¼
(D) 4
(E) 3¾

19. 1 2 4 8 16 32
(A) 48
(B) 56
(C) 64
(D) 80
(E) 96

20. 4 9 16 25 36 49
(A) 51
(B) 53
(C) 54
(D) 60
(E) 64

21. 17 19 22 26 31 37
(A) 40
(B) 41
(C) 42
(D) 43
(E) 44

22. ¹⁄₁₆ ¼ ½ 2 4 16
(A) 24
(B) 32
(C) 48
(D) 64
(E) 80

23. 1 2 3 2 3 4
(A) 3
(B) 4
(C) 5
(D) 6
(E) 7

24. 3 9 14 18 21 23
(A) 24
(B) 25
(C) 26
(D) 27
(E) 28

25. 90 45 50 25 30 15
(A) 16
(B) 18
(C) 20
(D) 10
(E) 5

CONSOLIDATE YOUR KEY ANSWERS HERE

Practice using Answer Sheets. Make ONE mark for each answer. Additional and stray marks may be counted as mistakes. In making corrections erase errors COMPLETELY. Make glossy black marks. To arrive at an accurate estimate of your ability and progress, cover the Correct Answers with a sheet of white paper while you are taking this test.

SAMPLE ANSWER SHEET

CORRECT KEY ANSWERS TO THE PRACTICE QUESTIONS

Check our key answers with your own. You'll probably find very few errors. In any case, check your understanding of all questions by studying the following explanatory answers. They illuminate the subject matter. Here you will find concise clarifications of basic points behind the key answers.

1.E	5.C	9.C	13.E	17.E	21.E	25.C
2.A	6.D	10.B	14.E	18.A	22.B	
3.D	7.E	11.D	15.C	19.C	23.A	
4.E	8.D	12.D	16.C	20.E	24.A	

NOW, CHECK YOUR METHODS WITH OUR SIMPLIFIED PROBLEM SOLUTIONS, WHICH FOLLOW DIRECTLY

TEAR OUT ALONG THIS LINE AND MARK YOUR ANSWERS AS INSTRUCTED IN THE TEXT

TEST I: NUMBER SERIES

EXPLANATORY ANSWERS CLARIFYING CARDINAL POINTS

The core of the Question and Answer Method . . . getting help when and where you need it. Even if you were able to write correct key answers for the preceding questions, the following explanations illuminate fundamental facts, ideas, and principles which just might crop up in the form of questions on future tests.

1. **(E)** To obtain the terms in the series, take the first term—then add 4, add 5, add 7; repeat the cycle.

2. **(A)** Multiply by 4, divide by 2; repeat the cycle.

3. **(D)** Add 4, add 5, add 6; repeat the cycle.

4. **(E)** Subtract 12, add 24; repeat the cycle.

5. **(C)** Subtract 2, subtract 2, add 3, add 3; repeat the cycle.

6. **(D)** Subtract 1, add 3, subtract 5; repeat the cycle.

7. **(E)** Subtract 4, subtract 4, multiply by 2; repeat the cycle.

8. **(D)** Subtract 3, multiply by 3; repeat the cycle.

9. **(C)** Subtract 2, multiply by 3; repeat the cycle.

10. **(B)** Subtract 3, multiply by 2, add 1; repeat the cycle.

11. **(D)** Divide by 2; repeat.

12. **(D)** Divide by 2, subtract 4; repeat the cycle.

13. **(E)** Subtract 1, subtract 2, subtract 3, subtract 4 . . . (subtract one more each time).

14. **(E)** Divide by 2, multiply by $\underline{4}$; divide by 2, multiply by $\underline{3}$; divide by 2, multiply by $\underline{2}$; etc. (repeat, subtracting one from the underlined number each time).

15. **(C)** Multiply by 6, multiply by 6, divide by 12; repeat the cycle.

16. **(C)** Multiply by 3, multiply by 2; repeat the cycle.

17. **(E)** Multiply by $\underline{2}$; multiply by $\underline{3}$; multiply by $\underline{4}$; etc. (repeat, adding one to the underlined number each time).

18. **(A)** Subtract ½, subtract ¼; repeat cycle.

19. **(C)** Multiply by 2; repeat.

20. **(E)** Add $\underline{5}$; add $\underline{7}$; add $\underline{9}$; etc. (repeat, adding two to the underlined number each time).

21. **(E)** Add $\underline{2}$; add $\underline{3}$; add $\underline{4}$; etc. (repeat, adding one to the underlined number each time).

22. **(B)** Multiply by 4, multiply by 2; repeat the cycle.

23. **(A)** Add 1, add 1, subtract 1; repeat the cycle.

24. **(A)** Add $\underline{6}$; add $\underline{5}$; add $\underline{4}$; etc. (repeat, subtracting one from the underlined number each time).

25. **(C)** Divide by 2, add 5; repeat the cycle.

END OF TEST

Go on to do the following Test in this Examination, just as you would be expected to do on the actual exam.

TEST II. NUMBER SERIES

TIME: 10 Minutes. 25 Questions.

DIRECTIONS: Each question consists of a series of letters or numbers (or both) which follow some definite order. Study each series to determine what the order is. Then look at the answer choices. Select the one answer that will complete the set in accordance with the pattern established.

DIRECTIONS: Explanations of the key points behind each question are given at the end of the test. They follow the key answers which we have consolidated, facilitating comparison of your answers with ours.

1. 19 24 20 25 21 26
   - (A) 18
   - (B) 22
   - (C) 23
   - (D) 27
   - (E) 28

2. 25 25 22 22 19 19
   - (A) 18
   - (B) 17
   - (C) 16
   - (D) 15
   - (E) 14

3. 10 2 8 2 6 2
   - (A) 1
   - (B) 2
   - (C) 3
   - (D) 4
   - (E) 5

4. 8 9 11 14 18 23
   - (A) 25
   - (B) 26
   - (C) 27
   - (D) 28
   - (E) 29

5. 11 14 12 15 13 16
   - (A) 14
   - (B) 15
   - (C) 16
   - (D) 17
   - (E) 18

6. 14 2 12 4 10 6
   - (A) 5
   - (B) 6
   - (C) 7
   - (D) 8
   - (E) 9

7. 7 16 9 15 11 14
   - (A) 12
   - (B) 13
   - (C) 17
   - (D) 18
   - (E) 19

8. 40 42 39 44 38 46
   - (A) 37
   - (B) 38
   - (C) 41
   - (D) 43
   - (E) 45

9. 3 18 4 24 5 30
   - (A) 2
   - (B) 6
   - (C) 8
   - (D) 36
   - (E) 40

10. 18 20 10 12 4 6
    - (A) 0
    - (B) 2
    - (C) 5
    - (D) 8
    - (E) 12

11. 3 3 4 8 10 30
    - (A) 30
    - (B) 33
    - (C) 46
    - (D) 60
    - (E) 90

12. 7 6 8 5 3 7
    - (A) 1
    - (B) 4
    - (C) 5
    - (D) 9
    - (E) 12

13. 9 9 18 21 25 20
    - (A) 10
    - (B) 14
    - (C) 18
    - (D) 25
    - (E) 30

14. 18 20 22 20 18 20
    - (A) 18
    - (B) 20
    - (C) 22
    - (D) 24
    - (E) 26

15. 30 28 25 29 34 28
    - (A) 21
    - (B) 26
    - (C) 27
    - (D) 31
    - (E) 32

16. 4 8 16 32 64 128
    - (A) 228
    - (B) 130
    - (C) 256
    - (D) 264
    - (E) 280

17. 8 16 24 32 40 48
    (A) 64   (D) 62
    (B) 72   (E) 56
    (C) 96

18. 4 4 8 8 16 16
    (A) 54   (D) 32
    (B) 48   (E) 24
    (C) 16

19. 6 18 36 108 216 648
    (A) 1946   (D) 1056
    (B) 1944   (E) 960
    (C) 1296

20. 13 11 14 12 15 13
    (A) 16   (D) 17
    (B) 11   (E) 18
    (C) 15

21. 2 6 18 54 162 486
    (A) 1556   (D) 1458
    (B) 496   (E) 1600
    (C) 1286

22. 4 20 35 49 62 74
    (A) 82   (D) 94
    (B) 85   (E) 96
    (C) 93

23. 10 15 12 17 14 19
    (A) 16   (D) 15
    (B) 24   (E) 18
    (C) 21

24. 4 10 8 14 12 18
    (A) 16   (D) 22
    (B) 20   (E) 26
    (C) 24

25. 10 18 15 23 20 28
    (A) 23   (D) .36
    (B) 24   (E) 30
    (C) 25

CONSOLIDATE YOUR KEY ANSWERS HERE

Practice using Answer Sheets. Make ONE mark for each answer. Additional and stray marks may be counted as mistakes. In making corrections erase errors COMPLETELY. Make glossy black marks. To arrive at an accurate estimate of your ability and progress, cover the Correct Answers with a sheet of white paper while you are taking this test.

SAMPLE ANSWER SHEET

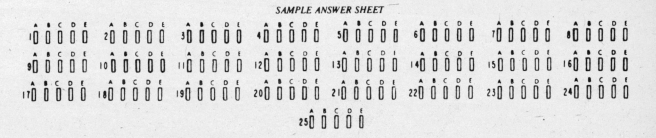

CORRECT KEY ANSWERS TO THE PRACTICE QUESTIONS

Check our key answers with your own. You'll probably find very few errors. In any case, check your understanding of all questions by studying the following explanatory answers. They illuminate the subject matter, Here you will find concise clarifications of basic points behind the key answers.

1. B	5. A	9. B	13. B	17. E	21. D	25. C
2. C	6. D	10. A	14. C	18. D	22. B	
3. D	7. B	11. B	15. A	19. C	23. A	
4. E	8. A	12. A	16. C	20. A	24. A	

EXPLANATORY ANSWERS CLARIFYING CARDINAL POINTS

The core of the Question and Answer Method ... getting help when and where you need it. Even if you were able to write correct key answers for the preceding questions, the following explanations illuminate fundamental facts, ideas, and principles which just might crop up in the form of questions on future tests.

1. **(B)** Add 5, subtract 4; repeat the cycle.

2. **(C)** No change, subtract 3; repeat the cycle.

3. **(D)** Every even-numbered term is 2, while every odd-numbered term is a member of the series 10, 8, 6, 4, . . .

4. **(E)** Add 1; add 2; add 3; etc. (repeat, adding one to the underlined number each time).

5. **(A)** Add 3, subtract 2; repeat the cycle.

6. **(D)** Odd-numbered terms are 14, 12, 10 . . . Even numbered terms are 2, 4, 6 . . . Subtract 2 from the odd-numbered term; add 2 to the even-numbered term. Repeat the cycle.

7. **(B)** Add 2 to the odd-numbered terms; subtract 1 from the even-numbered terms.

8. **(A)** Subtract 1 from the odd-numbered terms; add 2 to the even-numbered terms.

9. **(B)** Add 1 to the odd-numbered terms; add 6 to the even-numbered terms.

10. **(A)** Add 2, subtract 10; add 2, subtract 8; etc. (repeat, subtracting 2 from the underlined number each time).

11. **(B)** Multiply by 1, add 1; multiply by 2, add 2; multiply by 3, add 3; etc. (repeat, adding one to the underlined number each time).

12. **(A)** Subtract 1, add 2, subtract 3; subtract 2, add 4, subtract 6; etc. (repeat, multiplying the underlined numbers in the cycle by 2 each time.

13. **(B)** Multiply by 1, multiply by 2; add 3, add 4; subtract 5, subtract 6; etc. (The operations in each cycle are the same, and the number involved is increased by one each time).

14. **(C)** The series is simply 18, 20, 22, 20; repeat the cycle.

15. **(A)** Subtract 2, subtract 3; add 4, add 5; subtract 6, subtract 7; etc. (repeat, with the operations changed for each cycle, and the numbers increasing by 1 for each operation).

16. **(C)** Multiply by 2; repeat.

17. **(E)** Add 8; repeat.

18. **(D)** Multiply by 1, multiply by 2; repeat the cycle.

19. **(C)** Multiply by 3, multiply by 2; repeat the cycle.

20. **(A)** Subtract 2, add 3; repeat the cycle.

21. **(D)** Multiply by 3; repeat.

22. **(B)** Add 16; add 15; add 14; etc.

23. **(A)** Add 5, subtract 3; repeat the cycle.

24. **(A)** Add 6, subtract 2; repeat the cycle.

25. **(C)** Add 8, subtract 3; repeat the cycle.

END OF TEST

Go on to do the following Test in this Examination, just as you would be expected to do on the actual exam.

TEST III. NUMBER SERIES

TIME: 20 Minutes. 24 Questions.

DIRECTIONS: This test measures your ability to think with numbers instead of words. In each problem you are given a series of numbers that are changing according to a rule. The series is followed on the right by five pairs of numbers, lettered (A) (B) (C) (D) (E). These are the suggested answers. Study each problem to determine what the pattern is so that you can figure out a rule which would make one of the lettered sets the next two numbers in the series. Mark the Answer Sheet with the letter of the one pair that completes the series in accordance with the pattern established.

Correct Answers are consolidated after the last question.

1. 8 9 10 8 9 10 8............ A) 8 9   B) 9 10   C) 9 8   D) 10 8   E) 8 10
2. 3 4 4 3 5 5 3.............. A) 3 3   B) 6 3   C) 3 6   D) 6 6   E) 6 7
3. 7 7 3 7 7 4 7.............. A) 7 7   B) 7 8   C) 5 7   D) 8 7   E) 7 5
4. 18 18 19 20 20 21 22...... A) 22 23   B) 23 24   C) 23 23   D) 22 22   E) 21 22
5. 2 6 10 3 7 11 4.......... A) 12 16   B) 5 9   C) 8 5   D) 12 5   E) 8 12
6. 11 8 15 12 19 16 23........ A) 27 20   B) 24 20   C) 27 24   D) 20 24   E) 20 27
7. 16 8 15 9 14 10 13......... A) 12 11   B) 13 12   C) 11 13   D) 11 12   E) 11 14
8. 4 5 13 6 7 12 8............ A) 9 11   B) 13 9   C) 9 13   D) 11 9   E) 11 10

9. 3 8 4 9 5 10 6 11 7........ A) 7 11   B) 7 8   C) 11 8   D) 12 7   E) 12 8
10. 18 14 19 17 20 20 21...... A) 22 24   B) 14 19   C) 24 21   D) 21 23   E) 23 22
11. 6 9 10 7 11 12 8........... A) 9 10   B) 9 13   C) 16 14   D) 13 14   E) 14 15
12. 7 5 3 9 7 5 11............. A) 13 12   B) 7 5   C) 9 7   D) 13 7   E) 9 9
13. 7 9 18 10 12 18 13........ A) 18 14   B) 15 18   C) 14 15   D) 15 14   E) 14 18
14. 2 6 4 8 6 10 8............. A) 12 10   B) 6 10   C) 10 12   D) 12 16   E) 6 4
15. 7 9 12 14 17 19 22........ A) 25 27   B) 23 24   C) 23 25   D) 24 27   E) 26 27
16. 3 23 5 25 7 27 9........... A) 10 11   B) 27 29   C) 29 11   D) 11 28   E) 28 10

17. 18 17 16 14 13 12 10...... A) 9 8   B) 6 7   C) 8 6   D) 8 7   E) 10 9
18. 5 7 8 10 11 13 14 16...... A) 18 19   B) 17 18   C) 18 20   D) 17 19   E) 19 20
19. 28 27 25 24 22 21 19...... A) 18 16   B) 17 16   C) 18 17   D) 17 15   E) 20 18
20. 2 2 4 6 6 8 10.............. A) 12 12   B) 12 14   C) 10 10   D) 10 8   E) 10 12
21. 2 7 3 8 4 9 5.............. A) 6 7   B) 10 6   C) 6 10   D) 10 11   E) 5 10
22. 19 18 16 21 20 18 23...... A) 20 25   B) 25 20   C) 22 25   D) 22 20   E) 25 22
23. 3 5 7 7 4 6 8 8 5 7 9...... A) 9 6   B) 6 6   C) 6 9   D) 10 8   E) 8 10
24. 15 26 24 16 21 19 17 16 14 18.. A) 17 15   B) 11 9   C) 15 14   D) 17 16   E) 11 10

END OF TEST

Go on to do the following Test in this Examination, just as you would be expected to do on the actual exam.

CONSOLIDATE YOUR KEY ANSWERS HERE

Practice using Answer Sheets. Make ONE mark for each answer. Additional and stray marks may be counted as mistakes. In making corrections erase errors COMPLETELY. Make glossy black marks. To arrive at an accurate estimate of your ability and progress, cover the Correct Answers with a sheet of white paper while you are taking this test.

SAMPLE ANSWER SHEET

	A	B	C	D	E			A	B	C	D	E			A	B	C	D	E
1	‖	‖	‖	‖	‖		2	‖	‖	‖	‖	‖		3	‖	‖	‖	‖	‖

(Sample answer grid, items 1–24, each with bubbles A B C D E)

CORRECT ANSWERS TO THE FOREGOING PRACTICE QUESTIONS

Now compare your answers with these Correct Answers to the Practice Questions. If your answers differ from these, go back and study those questions to see where and how you made your mistakes.

1.B	4.A	7.D	10.E	13.B	16.C	19.A	22.D
2.D	5.E	8.A	11.D	14.A	17.A	20.E	23.A
3.E	6.E	9.E	12.C	15.D	18.D	21.B	24.B

TEAR OUT ALONG THIS LINE AND MARK YOUR ANSWERS AS INSTRUCTED IN THE TEXT

TEST IV. NUMBER SERIES

TIME: 20 Minutes. 24 Questions.

DIRECTIONS: This test measures your ability to think with numbers instead of words. In each problem you are given a series of numbers that are changing according to a rule. The series is followed on the right by five pairs of numbers, lettered (A) (B) (C) (D) (E). These are the suggested answers. Study each problem to determine what the pattern is so that you can figure out a rule which would make one of the lettered sets the next two numbers in the series. Mark the Answer Sheet with the letter of the one pair that completes the series in accordance with the pattern established.

Correct Answers are consolidated after the last question.

Do first those questions that you can do easily. Then go back and do the ones that you skipped.

1. 10 11 12 10 11 12 10...... A) 10 11   B) 12 10   C) 11 10   D) 11 12   E) 10 12
2. 4 6 7 4 6 7 4.............. A) 6 7   B) 4 7   C) 7 6   D) 7 4   E) 6 8
3. 7 7 3 7 7 4 7.............. A) 4 5   B) 4 7   C) 5 7   D) 7 5   E) 7 7
4. 3 4 10 5 6 10 7............ A) 10 8   B) 9 8   C) 8 14   D) 8 9   E) 8 10
5. 6 6 7 7 8 8 9............. A) 10 11   B) 10 10   C) 9 10   D) 9 9   E) 10 9
6. 3 8 9 4 9 10 5............. A) 6 10   B) 10 11   C) 9 10   D) 11 6   E) 10 6
7. 2 4 3 6 4 8 5.............. A) 6 10   B) 10 7   C) 10 6   D) 9 6   E) 6 7
8. 11 5 9 7 7 9 5............. A) 11 3   B) 7 9   C) 7 11   D) 9 7   E) 3 7

9. 12 10 8 8 6 7 4............ A) 2 2   B) 6 4   C) 6 2   D) 4 6   E) 2 6
10. 20 22 22 19 21 21 18....... A) 22 22   B) 19 19   C) 20 20   D) 20 17   E) 19 17
11. 5 7 6 10 7 13 8............ A) 16 9   B) 16 10   C) 9 15   D) 10 15   E) 15 9
12. 13 10 11 15 12 13 17...... A) 18 14   B) 18 15   C) 15 16   D) 14 15   E) 15 18
13. 30 27 24 21 18 15 12...... A) 9 3   B) 9 6   C) 6 3   D) 12 9   E) 8 5
14. 3 7 10 5 8 10 7............ A) 10 11   B) 10 5   C) 10 9   D) 10 10   E) 9 10
15. 12 4 13 6 14 8 15......... A) 10 17   B) 17 10   C) 10 12   D) 16 10   E) 10 16
16. 21 8 18 20 7 17 19........ A) 16 18   B) 18 6   C) 6 16   D) 5 15   E) 6 18

17. 14 16 16 18 20 20 22...... A) 22 24   B) 26 28   C) 24 26   D) 24 24   E) 24 28
18. 5 6 8 9 12 13 17.......... A) 18 23   B) 13 18   C) 18 22   D) 23 24   E) 18 19
19. 1 3 5 5 2 4 6 6 3......... A) 7 4   B) 5 5   C) 1 3   D) 5 7   E) 7 7
20. 12 24 15 25 18 26 21...... A) 27 22   B) 24 22   C) 29 24   D) 27 27   E) 27 24
21. 17 15 21 18 10 16 19...... A) 20 5   B) 5 11   C) 11 11   D) 11 20   E) 15 14
22. 12 16 10 14 8 12 6........ A) 10 14   B) 10 8   C) 10 4   D) 4 10   E) 4 2
23. 13 4 5 13 6 7 13.......... A) 13 8   B) 8 13   C) 8 9   D) 8 8   E) 7 8
24. 10 10 9 11 11 10 12....... A) 13 14   B) 12 11   C) 13 13   D) 12 12   E) 12 13

END OF TEST

Go on to do the following Test in this Examination, just as you would be expected to do on the actual exam.

CONSOLIDATE YOUR KEY ANSWERS HERE

Practice using Answer Sheets. Make ONE mark for each answer. Additional and stray marks may be counted as mistakes. In making corrections erase errors COMPLETELY. Make glossy black marks. To arrive at an accurate estimate of your ability and progress, cover the Correct Answers with a sheet of white paper while you are taking this test.

SAMPLE ANSWER SHEET

CORRECT ANSWERS TO THE FOREGOING PRACTICE QUESTIONS

Now compare your answers with these Correct Answers to the Practice Questions. If your answers differ from these, go back and study those questions to see where and how you made your mistakes.

1.D	4.E	7.C	10.C	13.B	16.C	19.D	22.C
2.A	5.C	8.A	11.A	14.E	17.D	20.E	23.C
3.D	6.B	9.E	12.D	15.E	18.A	21.B	24.B

Count how many you got right, and write that number on this line————————→ _____
(This is your Test Score.)

Meaning of Test Score

If your Test Score is *17 or more*, you have a Good score.
If your Test Score is *from 12 to 16*, you have a Fair score.
If your Test Score is *11 or less*, you are not doing too well.

TEAR OUT ALONG THIS LINE AND MARK YOUR ANSWERS AS INSTRUCTED IN THE TEXT

PART FIVE

Postal Information

5

UNITED STATES POSTAL SERVICE

The major purpose of the United States Postal Service (USPS) is to provide postal services promptly, reliably, and efficiently, to individuals and businesses in all areas of the Nation.

The Postal Service was created as an independent establishment of the executive branch by section 2 of the Postal Reorganization Act, approved August 12, 1970 (84 Stat. 719; 39 U.S.C. 101 et seq.). The United States Postal Service commenced operations on July 1, 1971.

The Postal Service is an enormous service organization handling approximately 90 billion pieces of mail yearly. The 700,000 people who make the Postal Service work are headed by the Postmaster General and the Deputy Postmaster General, the principal officers of the Service under a Board of Governors, composed of nine Governors appointed by the President with the advice and consent of the Senate for overlapping 9-year terms. The Postmaster General and the Deputy Postmaster General are named by the Board of Governors, and both serve on the Board of Governors.

In addition to the national headquarters, there are five Regional organizations, to which the 85 Districts report. The Districts are divided into 321 Sectional Center Manager Areas which are composed of the nearly 32,000 post offices throughout the United States.

CUSTOMER SERVICES

In order to expand and improve service to the public, the Postal Service is engaged in customer cooperation activities, including the development of programs for both the general public and major customers. The Consumer Advocate, a postal ombudsman, represents the interest of the individual mail customer in matters involving the Postal Service by bringing complaints and suggestions to the attention of top postal management and solving the problems of individual customers.

MAIL PROCESSING

In its mail processing activities, the Postal Service is concerned with expedited mail movement within the postal system, and is responsible for the construction and mechanization of facilities to this end.

SUPPORT

Postal Service activities designed to facilitate postal operations include design and maintenance of the postal rate structure, developing mail classification standards, and liaison with international postal organizations.

EMPLOYEE AND LABOR RELATIONS

The Postal Service is the only Federal agency whose employment policies are governed by a process of collective bargaining. Labor contract negotiations, affecting all bargaining unit personnel, as well as personnel matters involving employees not covered by collective bargaining agreements, are administered by the Employee and Labor Relations Group.

EXECUTIVE FUNCTIONS

As a Federal agency, the Postal Service maintains active liaison with national and local elected officials through its Executive Functions Group. All philatelic affairs are likewise administered by this Group.

INSPECTION SERVICE

Through its Inspection Service activities, the Postal Service protects the mails, postal funds, and property; investigates internal conditions and needs which may affect its security and effectiveness; apprehends those who violate the postal laws; and inspects and audits financial and nonfinancial operations. There is a regional Chief Inspector in each of the five postal regions.

POSTAL REGIONS

There are five Regional Postmasters General, each managing postal activities in his geographical area. The five Regions are the Eastern, New York Metropolitan, Southern, Central, and Western, with headquarters at Philadelphia, New York City, Memphis, Chicago, and San Francisco, respectively.

Sources of Information

Inquiries for the following information should be directed to the specified office, U.S. Postal Service, Washington, D.C. 20260.

CONSUMER INFORMATION

Contact the Consumer Advocate. Information on specific products and services is available from Customer Services. Information on past and present schemes used to defraud the public is available through the Regional Chief Inspector of any Postal Region.

READING ROOMS

Located in 11th Floor, Penthouse North, Library Division.

CONTRACTS AND SMALL BUSINESS ACTIVITIES

Contact the Administration Department.

SPEAKERS

Contact the Assistant Postmaster General, Communications, to schedule speakers and to coordinate Postal Service participation in meetings of national organizations and associations.

Speakers for meetings which are regional or local in nature are scheduled by the appropriate Regional Postmaster General's office or the Regional Chief Inspector's office.

PHILATELIC INFORMATION

Contact the Office of Philatelic Affairs.

PHILATELIC SALES

Contact the Philatelic Sales Unit, Washington, D.C. 20036.

FILMS

Contact the Communications Department for films available for loan to the public.

EMPLOYMENT

General information about jobs such as clerk, letter carrier, etc. may be obtained by contacting the nearest post office.

Individuals, generally college graduates interested in engineering, management, finance, personnel work, or in employment as physicists, mathematicians, and operations research analysts, may obtain information by contacting the Employee and Labor Relations Group.

Information about Inspection Service employment may be obtained from the Assistant Postmaster General, Inspection Service.

PUBLICATIONS

Pamphlets on *How to Address Mail, Mailing Permits, Domestic Postage Rates and Fees,* and many others may be obtained free of charge from the Postal Service.

Postal Regulations are contained in the *Postal Service Manual* and other publications of the Postal Service. This publication and others, such as the *Postal Contracting Manual, International Mail* (Publication 42), *Instructions for Mailers, Postal Laws* (Publication 11), *Directory of Post Offices,* and *National ZIP Code Directory,* may be purchased from the Superintendent of Documents, Government Printing Office, Washington, D.C. 20402.

For further information, contact the Communications Department, U.S. Postal Service, Washington, D.C. 20260. Phone, 202–961–7500.

BEGINNING POSTAL JOBS

A great deal depends on your examination score, as you know. And this book will help you achieve your highest possible score. You'll get plenty of practice with relevant test subjects and questions. But first we want you to pick up a few facts about the test which may make things easier for you. Forgive us if some of these facts seem self-evident. Our experience has shown that this kind of information is sometimes overlooked . . . to the candidate's detriment.

As a new employee, you will be introduced to various assignments. There is a right and a wrong way of doing almost any job. The Post Office, with many years of practical experience in job methods, has developed and established tested methods for the efficient performance of your tasks. You will receive on-the-job training in these basic tasks on the work floor. The following explanations present the processes and operations involved in actual work situations:

Outgoing Mails Section

Outgoing mails are mails mostly addressed for delivery to out-of-town post offices. Station and Street collected mails are usually forwarded to large terminal stations for processing in the outgoing mails section. The bulk of the work in outgoing sections is concerned with culling, facing or batching, canceling, primary and secondary (side-table) distribution, and dispatching.

Culling

Mail coming into the station from various sources, such as street collection boxes and large business mailings, must first be "culled" before it can be further processed.

The culling of mail means to pick out of the large mass of mail, certain kinds of mail that should not go onto the facing or batching table. These kinds of mail are usually parcels, bundles of metered or stamped letters, large quantities of loose uniform letters or cards, oversized envelopes (flats), bulky letters ("slugs"), airmail and special delivery letters, newspapers and periodicals, and quantities of circulars.

These kinds of mail are placed on their proper takeaway conveyors (Mail-Flo System) or in proper carts for further processing. The remaining letters are now ready for facing or batching.

S1800

Batching Mail

In the large terminal stations, where the Mark II automatic facer-canceler machines are in use, mail is mostly "batched" rather than "faced". Several letters at a time, from a pile of letters on a table, are drawn by hand into a slot on the side of the table. A belt on the bottom of the slot carries them to a stacker, stacking them positioned on the long edges. They are then placed in trays and moved to the facer-canceler machines on a roller conveyor for postmarking.

While performing this operation, hold out bulky letters, (slugs), thin paper airmail, and special delivery mail, for processing elsewhere.

Facing

Sometimes the letter mail is "dumped" onto large facing tables. Then the letters are inserted one at a time into the slot, <u>with the stamp in the lower left corner and facing you.</u> Use BOTH HANDS SEPARATELY in this operation, feeding mail directly into the slot. Do not feed letters from one hand with the other.

While performing this operation, bulky letters (slugs), thin paper airmail, and special delivery mail are held out by you and placed where required.

USE **2** HANDS

Postmarking

When running a canceling machine or using a hand stamp, watch the postmark. The impression must be clear, sharp, and legible. Postmarks are changed every twelve hours on first-class mail.

The postmark must show plainly the city and station, the date, and the part of the day such as A.M. or P.M.. The stamps on letters must be canceled to prevent re-use. A clear impression is particularly important when backstamping special delivery matter, on which the time for each half-hour is shown. Extreme care must be exercised in postmarking philatelic matter.

Primary Separation

Clerks will receive on-the-job training at the primary case. The primary separation is the first sorting or "box-up" operation.

A separate copy of the primary separation will be issued to you by your Station Superintendent. This must be studied and memorized by all employees assigned to primary separation, since you will be tested on it.

When distributing mail on the primary, watch for airmail and special delivery letters, and separate them to the "Airmail" and "Specials" boxes, according to primary scheme instructions. It should be noted that there are separate boxes for shortpaid letters, and letters without postmarks, as well as for airmail and specials. "Hard" pieces (illegibly addressed mail), hotel keys, and incompletely addressed matter, as well as shortpaid mail, are separated to the shortpaid box on the primary separation.

To distribute mail, take a handful of letters in the left hand from the ledge and distribute with the right hand. (This applies to both "Righties" and "Lefties"). The letters are placed into the correct box under the label on your case with the stamps toward you and to your right. The distribution into the case boxes is made in accordance with the primary separation issued to you.

Separate zoned and unzoned where indicated. With experience you will become familiar with the directs, the Long Island, the hold-outs, etc. Learning the first three digits of Zip Code Numbers of near-by post offices will also be helpful.

When boxing up do not place either foot on any part of the conveyors below the cases. It is dangerous and awkward, the interferes with proper productivity on the case. With a little practice, you should be able to separate with ease as many pieces per hour as is normally required.

Removing Mail From Boxes

If you work at a primary separation case in a station which has the Mail-Flo-System in operation, you will be required to remove mail from the proper boxes in answer to a "call" over the loudspeakers. This is done by taking the mail out of the separation "called" and placing it on the moving cleated belt under the case, stamps down and toward you.

If you are in a station which does <u>not</u> have the <u>Mail-Flo-System</u> in operation you may be assigned to the job of "sweeping" (or "skinning"). This means that you will be required to remove the mail from a particular separation <u>box</u> of <u>every</u> primary <u>case</u> in the area assigned to you; - <u>for</u> <u>example</u> - if it is the "Ohio" box, you go to every case, in sequence, and remove the mail from each box labeled "Ohio" (under the label) without disturbing the person at the case. You then bring the mail to a designated section, hamper or tray.

You must be very accurate and certain that you take the proper mail out of the proper box.

Secondary Separation

The difference between a primary separation and a secondary separation is that on a primary case, mail is separated broadly to any post office area in the United States or the world, whereas on a secondary separation case mail can be separated specifically only within a particular state, area or country.

Tying Bundles Of Letters

There are two methods of tying used in the post office-mechanical and manual. Where necessary, you will be given instruction in the use of the tying machine and also how to tie manually. In both methods, you must tie a bundle of letters lengthwise, first, and crosswise, next. The objective is always to produce a tight, secure, and neat bundle.

BASIC POSTAL PROCEDURES

Most people who take exams are busy people. They cannot afford to waste time searching in libraries and elsewhere for the precise study material required. If you're such a person, this chapter should help. It presents a workable plan for broadening your background and strengthening your ability in this probable test subject.

Outgoing Parcel Post

Parcel Post is received at parcel post windows, and in bulk at station and terminal platforms. The stamps on this matter are usually canceled with steel roller cancelers.

Separating outgoing parcel post is not difficult and consists simply of sorting this mail in accordance with the separation charts set up in each station.

Insured and C.O.D. parcels are sacked with ordinary parcels. Special delivery and special handling parcels are NOT included with ordinary parcel post matter. They are sacked out separately, the labels are endorsed "Special Delivery" or "Special Handling," and a tag identifying them as such is attached to each sack. Registered, first class, or air parcel post pieces found inadvertently mixed in with ordinary parcel post must be held out and turned over to the supervisor for appropriate handling.

When working on outgoing parcel post, don't overload the sacks. When a sack is nearly filled, put in the proper label and "drop" it. Slide labels used to dispatch parcel post, circulars or ordinary paper mail, are stamped to show the station and date.

When dropping sacks, if you find that a sack is too heavy, take time to open it, and take out enough parcels so that the sack will not be over 80 pounds. If you do not do this, a brother employee, handling the sack in subsequent operations, may be hurt by lifting it. Be considerate of the next fellow who will have to handle the sack.

Separating Parcel Post

Use discretion and judgement in separating parcel post. In many instances you can toss a parcel into a bag without damaging it. Heavier

S1800

parcels should be <u>placed</u> in the bag. Do not play basketball with the parcels and throw them 15 or 20 feet just to see if the parcel will land in the right sack. You can separate rapidly without giving the parcels a "beating up" before they are dispatched. Any parcel not too large to go into a bag should be sacked unless it is very heavy, or clearly marked as an "outside" piece.

Outside pieces include wooden boxes, iron castings, certain liquids, motion picture film if <u>inflammable</u>, articles bearing the caution notice, "This Side Up," canes, umbrellas, and perishable articles such as eggs, fruit, meat, and cut flowers.

If a large parcel fills up a sack, label it is a "direct". If you have a number of parcels for the same city, make up a direct sack.

If you misthrow a parcel, take time to retrieve it and put it into the right sack. If you do not do this, the piece will have to be re-handled several times, and it will be delayed as well, because of the error. The separation on outgoing parcel post must be <u>one hundred percent correct</u>.

Verifying Empty Sacks and Pouches

Sacks and pouches must be verified when they are emptied and before using. Verify each sack as you hang it on the rack.

When you shake out a sack, take a good look inside the sack to be sure that there is no letter or small parcel sticking to the bottom of the bag. Verification of empty sacks and pouches is everyone's responsibility.

Lifting

The use of the proper method in lifting will prevent back strain and hernia. It is to your advantage to know and observe the following rules:

1. Before lifting a sack or other heavy object, decide the best way to grasp it.

2. Place your feet close to the object or sack to be lifted.

3. Get a good balance; this means feet fairly wide apart (8 to 12 inches).

4. Bend your knees and keep your back straight.

5. Keep the load close to your body.

6. Lift with your arm and leg muscles.

7. DO NOT lift with your back muscles.

8. If a sack is too heavy, do not try to lift it alone.

In team lifting, cooperate with your partner.

THE CORRECT WAY TO LIFT

KEEP YOUR BACK STRAIGHT

Incoming Mails Section

Incoming mail is mail for delivery in <u>Manhattan</u>. Incoming mails received from local collections and from out-of-town points are processed in the terminal stations and distributed in the incoming sections to the proper delivery stations.

"UP-MAIL"

When incoming mail is received at the delivery station it is called "up-mail" and is thereafter separated in accordance with the station carrier route scheme to the appropriate carrier delivery routes. After the mail has been distributed on the "up-mail" cases, it is "skinned" out by clerks or carriers and boxed-up on the carrier sorting cases. "Up-papers" are similarly separated. First-class "slugs" and daily newspapers are boxed-up on a "slug" case.

Incoming Parcel Post

Incoming parcel post is handled similarly to incoming letter mail. When received from local collections and from out-of-town offices, it is separated and dispatched to the various delivery stations. When the parcel post is received at the delivery station, a separation is made into sacks or "tubs" to the station parcel post routes.

Each parcel post route has a separation of twenty (or more) sacks. When a "tub" is pushed over to the parcel post route racks, the parcels are distributed into the sacks, which are numbered consecutively. Direct sacks are made up for larger firms. "Outsides" are held out and the sack number put on the piece with chalk or crayon.

Special delivery pieces, first class, registered, C.O.D., custom duty and shortpaid pieces are picked out and turned over to the appropriate sections for proper handling.

Ordinarily, parcels smaller than shoe box size should be delivered by the foot carriers, and larger and heavier parcels should be delivered by the parcel post carriers. Don't overload the sacks. When a bag is nearly filled, the sack number should be placed on the label and the sack "dropped."

Delivering The Mail

A vital trust has been placed in you. The mail is in your custody — safeguard it at all times.

1. Do not throw away or destroy any piece of mail, no matter how unimportant it may look to you.

2. Keep your mail bag in your possession at all times; do not leave it on steps or in vestibules, or on a cart unless it is within your view.

3. Stick to your "route." Do not enter any building or place of business except while making deliveries.

4. When not actually delivering mail, keep your mail bag closed and buckled. This guards against loss or theft, and acts as protection to the mail in bad weather.

5. Use special care in handling large cards, calendars, photographs. Do not fold them. Do not box these pieces in the route case with letter mail.

6. Always verify the street against the street addresses on your mail.

7. Do not "scan" mail while walking or while driving a motor vehicle. This unsafe practice has resulted in serious accidents to carriers and has been a cause of motor vehicle collisions.

The districts covered by delivery stations are divided into carrier routes, each of which covers a specified area. Business districts get three delivery trips daily and residential districts get one delivery trip daily. A supplementary business trip is made in the afternoon on some routes to firms located on residential routes.

Carrier route desks are labelled to cover all numbers on streets and avenues served by the route, including buildings, apartment houses, stores, residences, etc.

When delivering mail to persons known to be living with or sharing apartments with regular tenants, furnish them with a POD Notice 11 requesting that they place their names on the mail receptacle.

Delivering employees must carry a supply of Form 3575, change of address forms, with them.

When entering a forwarding order in the route removal book, make the entry on a Form 3982 card at the same time. Make use of Form 3982 cards to avoid delivering any mail that should be forwarded.

Mail matter opened by mistake should be so endorsed by the patron who opened the piece in error, and returned to the post office for proper treatment.

Do not place mail into a mail receptacle that has been damaged or is out of order. Report any condition that might result in damage or loss of government "Arrow" locks in apartment house mail receptacles. If an open mail receptacle makes the Arrow lock accessible, report this condition to the Superintendent of Building and your Superintendent. Do not put mail into any of the boxes.

Carrier Signal Bells

"Four bells" is the signal for the carriers to pick up registered mail. "Three bells" is the signal for the carriers to pick up "postage due" mail. "Two bells" is the signal for the final sweep, at which time, also, all misboxes not previously returned for redistribution should be placed on the end-case. "One bell" is the signal to pick up mail in the end-case and leave the office on the trip.

Beats

"Beats" are pieces undeliverable as addressed. On residential routes first-class "beats" must be "marked up" prior to leaving the office. On business routes all "beats" must be marked up prior to leaving on the second trip.

Safeguarding Your Keys

Everyone given a letter box key must attach it securely to his clothing by means of the safety chain. You will be held strictly accountable for the safekeeping and proper use of the key, and must not permit it to be examined or handled by any person not authorized to do so. In the event that you lose or break your key, report it at once to your supervisor.

"Tapping" Collection Boxes and Cooperative Mailing Racks

Collection trips are made daily including Saturdays, Sundays and Holidays. When "tapping collection boxes" (collecting mail from mail boxes), insert your hand above the opening in order not to overlook any mail which may be lodged in the top of the box. Metered mail, permit mail and mail separated by the public into dual collection boxes and cooperative mailing racks must be kept separate from other mixed collection mail.

When making foot or "mounted" (truck) collections, take the collection route schedule board with you. This schedule indicates the order in which collections are to be made from the street letter boxes, collection chutes, finance stations, etc., and this order of collections must be strictly adhered to. The collection schedule should be taken with you at all times. Do not skip any stops on your collection route schedule. A box must never be collected ahead of the time indicated on the board schedule. Follow instructions given to you by your supervisor when you have a "swamp."

Report irregularities such as locks out of order, **keys broken,** boxes damaged, collection bulletins missing, collection bulletins incorrect or unserviceable, etc., to your supervisor.

Withdrawal of Mail

When making collections do not return a letter to a patron after it has been put in the collection box. The patron should be courteously advised to call at the station and request withdrawal of the letter from the supervisor in charge.

Money, damaged mail, wallets, billfolds, etc., found in collection mails must be returned to the station with other mails. Receipt of such items is reported and they are forwarded to the Inquiry Section, General Post Office.

Delivery Of Special Service Mail

1. A legible signature must be obtained for Numbered Insured, C.O.D., Certified or Registered mail before it is surrendered. Don't waste time — state that you need the proper signature, be courteous and businesslike, and be on your way.

2. Any responsible individual in a family or firm can sign for the addressee (person to whom mail is addressed), except in cases where delivery is restricted to "addressee only."

3. If you are delivering a C.O.D. piece, make certain that the correct amount of money is collected by you.

4. If money is owed (postage-due mail), be sure to collect the right amount.

5. You will be shown the correct way of using the forms on which signatures are obtained for the delivered mail.

6. These forms must be returned by you to the station.

7. The addressee has the privilege to refuse any piece of mail. **Be courteous.** Do not argue. Mark the mail "refused," and show the date, the time, and your name, button or badge number on the back of mail. Return this mail to the station at the completion of your route.

Special Delivery Mail

1. When you are given a "run" or batch of special delivery mail, make sure that it is set up in proper delivery sequence.

2. Make sure that each "special" has a legible "backstamp" (postmark).

3. Always put the "run" of "specials" into a mail bag.

4. Proceed without delay to the first indicated address of your "run". Carfare will be provided when necessary.

5. Deliver directly to the apartment or place of address, regardless of floor.

6. If there is no response to <u>several</u> rings of the door bell or knocks on the door, and the circumstances indicate that the occupants are only temporarily absent, place the article in the mail receptacle (letter box or door slot) and leave Special Delivery notice Form 3955, properly completed, on the door knob or under the door. Make sure the letter box is securely closed after delivery is made.

If the article is undeliverable, properly complete Form 3955 and place it on the doorknob or under the door. Return the special delivery article to your station at the end of your "run".

7. If the "special" is a parcel which cannot be delivered, and it is too large to fit into the mailbox, return it to the station. Form 3955 it to be placed under the door or on the doorknob advising where and when the mail can be obtained.

8. Signatures are not necessary for ordinary specials, but are required for Certified, Numbered Insured, C.O.D. and Registered mail.

9. If a "special" is undeliverable, write the reason for non-delivery, the time you tried to make delivery, the date, your name and button or badge number clearly on the back of the letter. For a parcel write same on face of wrapper.

10. Return to your station within the prescribed time.

Accountability For Registered And Other Special Service Mail

Delivering employees are charged with and sign for the number of registered pieces on their route, part of the route, or special delivery run. These registered pieces must be accounted for upon return from the trip by presenting either a receipt on Form 3849 or by returning the registered pieces to the office with appropriate notations as to the reasons the pieces were undeliverable on that trip.

When a registered or insured piece is endorsed "Return Receipt Requested," signature must be obtained on the return receipt (Form 3811) as well as on the registered or insured receipt. After the return receipt is turned in, it is postmarked and forwarded to the sender.

Registered pieces endorsed "Deliver to Addressee Only" or "Return Receipt Requested Showing Address Where Delivered" are called restricted pieces. The terms are self-explanatory and you must comply with these instructions in making delivery. A piece endorsed "Deliver to Addressee Only" cannot be delivered to anyone but the addressee.

When the piece is endorsed, "Return Receipt Requested Showing Address Where Delivered," this information must be shown on the receipt and on the return card. The word "Personal" on a letter does not restrict delivery.

Accountability on C.O.D.'s, postage due money, customs collect pieces and certified mail is similar to the accountability for registered articles. When accounting for C.O.D.'s, obtain and keep for yourself a copy of receipt Form 3821 for 90 days.

Receipts must be obtained on all numbered insured matter delivered. Care must be exercised in obtaining receipts, and signatures must be legible. (Receipts are not required on insured articles endorsed "Insured" without a number).

Great care must be taken to keep these types of mail under your protection and direct observation at all times until given to the addressee upon receipt of proper signature.

Delivery of Parcel Post

One complete parcel post delivery trip is made daily, except Sundays and holidays, on all parcel post routes.

Delivery of all parcel post, including all registered, C.O.D., numbered insured, or customs duty mail, as well as special delivery mail, must be made to the office or apartment door of the addressee without regard to the floor upon which the office or apartment is located. However, employees are not required to walk up more than six flights. Parcel post must not be left on porches or steps, in hallways, or in vestibules.

When delivering parcel post, examine all parcels carefully for the insured endorsement. Receipt must be obtained on all insured parcels, except those endorsed "Insured" without a number. Insured receipts for parcels must be completed by entering the date of delivery, your name and badge or button number, and must be turned in daily prior to completion of your tour of duty.

Delivery employees are prohibited from operating elevators or lifts other than self-service elevators in office, factory and loft buildings while making deliveries.

Customs Duty Parcels

When working on a parcel post truck be sure to collect the fees on customs duty parcels. If delivery cannot be effected, the parcel shall be endorsed with the reason for non-delivery, the time offered for delivery, your initials, and badge or button number. It is necessary to leave a call notice, Form 3570, for undeliverable customs duty pieces.

Bad Condition Parcels

When a parcel is received at a delivery office in bad order or in a damaged condition it should be endorsed, "Received in bad condition at........(station and city)....." unless a similar endorsement had been placed previously on the parcel in transit. Delivering employees should see to it that this endorsement appears on damaged parcels included for delivery.

Precanceled Stamps On Returned Parcels

When delivering parcels with precanceled stamps which are being returned to the sender, these parcels must not be delivered until the stamps have been defaced with an indelible pencil.

POSTAL TERMS IN COMMON USE GLOSSARY

This is some of the language you're likely to see on your examination. You may not need to know all the words in this carefully prepared glossary, but if even a few appear, you'll be that much ahead of your competitors. Perhaps the greater benefit from this list is the frame of mind it can create for you. Without reading a lot of technical text you'll steep yourself in just the right atmosphere for high test marks.

This list does not contain all the terms in use in the Postal Service. The effort, rather, has been to define briefly and accurately the more commonly used postal terms.

Backstamp

This expression is used when referring to the postmark impression placed on the back of registered mail, special delivery mail or missent mail, by the receiving post office or station. The postmark impression shows the name of the office, date, and hour of arrival.

Beats

Beats are pieces of mail undeliverable as addressed. When a patron moves he should file a change of address card, Form 3575. When the removal card or a post card or letter notifying of a change of address is received at the delivery station, it is postmarked and given to the carrier on the route serving the address affected. The carrier enters the removal order in his route removal book. Mail for the addressee is thereafter forwarded in accordance with the patron's instructions.

Beats include mail for which there is no forwarding order, such as "removed and left no address", "not at address given", etc. The beats are held aside and marked up after the carrier has finished his box-up.

Box Up (Or Case) Mail

To distribute letters into mail case separations.

Bums

Sacks or pouches containing a supply of verified and folded empty mail bags are called "bums"

S1800

Call

An announcement over the loud speaker system, or otherwise, indicating which separation to remove from the case to be placed on a cleated belt under the case.

Callers

Some patrons, for personal or business reasons, must have their mail early in the morning before the carrier would get to that particular address in regular course. Under these circumstances these patrons make arrangements with the station superintendent to call for their mail at 8 A.M. or shortly thereafter. These patrons are known as callers.

Call Notice

A call notice is a printed form left by a delivering employee, when the piece is undeliverable, notifying the patron to call at the post office for the piece of mail. If the delivering employee receives no response at the address given, he should leave a call notice.

If the piece is special delivery, the #3955 form should be used for the call notice. If the piece is registered, numbered insured, or certified, the #3849 form should be used. If the piece is C.O.D., the #3860 form should be used. If the piece is ordinary or postage due, the #3570 form should be used as a call notice.

Chute

A chute is a flat glass-front tube with slots, installed in high buildings for the receipt of letters that drop through the chute into a collection box on the street floor. Collectors pick up this collection mail when making their rounds of the street letter boxes.

Cleated Belt

The conveyor belt under "Mail-Flo" system cases, upon which letters are properly placed in answer to calls.

Collector

A collector is an employee assigned to take mail from street and chute collection boxes and bring it to the post office for processing and dispatch. Removing mail from a collection box is also referred to as "tapping" a collection box.

Cull (Or Culling)

To pick out certain types of mail from the bulk of the mail in order to give it different handling.

Dead Letter (Or Nixie)

A dead letter is an undeliverable letter with an incomplete or inaccurate address which cannot be returned to the sender because the return address was omitted.

Direct

A direct is a bundle made up of several letters or circulars, or a pouch containing several bundles of letters, or a sack containing several pieces of paper or parcel mail, - all for one city or station, and so labeled.

Dis Mail

Dis means "for distribution." If several post offices receive their mail through one post office, for example through Louisville, Ky., the mail for such offices may be made up in packages and labeled, "Louisville, Ky. Dis."

Dress The Rack (Or Hang The Rack)

The expression "dress the rack" means to hang empty sacks on a distributing or "shultz" rack.

Drop

A drop is a slot or opening into which patrons deposit mail in a post office or station for distribution and dispatch. The word "drop" is also used where there is a delivery by a carrier of a large quantity of mail for one building or firm.

Dump Out (or Shake Out)

To remove mail from sacks or pouches by opening the sack or pouch and turning it upside down so that the mail will fall out onto a conveyor, table or floor, as required.

End

Bundles of mail for delivery on a part of a carrier's route are called an "end".

End Case

The final mails for delivery including throwbacks, etc., are put on a designated case during the final few minutes prior to the carrier's scheduled leaving time. After the carriers have tied out their mail, and as they are leaving the office to begin their deliveries, they stop at this designated case and pick up any final pieces for their respective routes.

The case is usually on the end of a row of "up-mail" cases for convenience. As a result the case used for this purpose has come to be known as the "end case."

Facing Slip

A facing slip is a label attached to a package of letters or circulars bearing the name of the station or zip code number, city, state or other point for which the mail is intended. The name of the station distributing the mail, the tour number of which it is tied out and the date are also included on the facing slip.

Finance Station

A finance station is a small postal station manned by postal employees and providing window service to the public. There are no carriers at a finance station, and no delivery of mail is made from these stations.

Window service at finance stations includes acceptance of registered pieces, sale of stamps, money orders, and in most instances the acceptance of parcel post.

Flats

Flat pieces of first or third-class mail, too large for a letter case, that must be distributed into a special case.

Forwarding Order

A forwarding order is a request in writing or on a card form #3575 filed with the station, to send the patron's mail to an address other than that to which originally addressed.

Franked Mail

Franked mail is mail posted under the franking privilege of sending mail free of postage. Such matter must bear the word "free" and, in the case of an individual, the signature, either written or a facsimile, of the person entitled to the use of the frank, together with his official designation, if any.

The privilege of franking has been extended by authority of Congress to cover letters, documents, seeds, etc., mailed by members of Congress and other officers of the government, and to mail-matter of former Presidents of the United States and their widows.

Fraud Order

A fraud order is the term used to describe instructions from the Postmaster General for postmasters to return to senders all mail addressed to an addressee who, upon evidence satisfactory to the Postmaster General, has used the mails for purposes forbidden by law.

Free Matter

Free matter is matter sent through the mails free of postage, such as under the franking privilege, official matter, etc.

Gurney

A low hamper or tub.

H. P. O.

This is the abbreviation for Highway Post Office.

Hard

Mail without a good address.

Hit In

"Hit In" means to clock in or record your time on your time card through the use of the time clock. "Hit out" means to end your time by means of the time recorder.

Jacket

A heavy special envelope used for the enclosing of several registered letters.

Loose Pack

The placing of untied letters or flats into a small (number 3 or 4) sack in a uniform and tightly secure manner so that the mail will not be scattered in transit.

L. A. Lock

The mail lock used to lock closed pouches and for other purposes. The key to open these locks is called an L. A. Key.

Mail-Flo System

A mechanical system of conveying mail from one required operation to another on conveyor belts and rollers.

Mark-Up

A mark-up is a beat that has been endorsed in accordance with a forwarding order, or has been endorsed for return to sender.

Minimum Fee

Fee paid on an insured parcel ($10 or less) which does not receive an insured number.

Missent

Missent mail is mail erroneously sent to an office or station other than to which addressed.

Metered Mail

Metered mail is matter on which the required postage is printed by a postage meter approved for the purpose by the Post Office Department. Metered mail may be of any class and is entitled to all the privileges and subject to all the conditions applying to matter mailed with stamps affixed.

Office Time

Office time is the time a carrier spends in the office routing mail and performing other office duties.

Official Matter

Official matter is official mail carried free of postage, other than franked matter or reading matter for the blind.

Offs

Missent or misboxed mail for which there is no separation box on the case being worked. This mail must be taken to another case for distribution.

Ordinary

Mail other than airmail, registered, insured, C.O.D., special delivery, special handling or certified, is referred to as ordinary.

Outside

A parcel too large, bulky, heavy, inflammable or fragile to be placed in a sack, is handled separately and called an "outside".

Papers

Magazines and other periodicals, published less frequently than weekly, which do not get the preferential treatment accorded to "newspapers" (dailies and weeklies).

Penalty Mail

Official mail sent without prepayment of postage, bearing a printed clause citing the penalty for private use.

Permit Imprint Matter

Permit Imprint Matter refers to matter of any class mailed without adhesive or meter stamps, but with an authorized printed form of postage upon the mail. Permit Imprint mailings are brought to the post office and mailed upon meeting the requirements of the regulations with regard to preparation for mailing and payment of postage.

Philatelics

Pertaining to stamps, stamped envelopes, etc., sold for systematic collection and study; i.e. stamp collecting.

Plug

A plug is the all-purpose dating stamp used for parcels which are insured or C.O.D., for money orders, and for certain bills and receipts used in special services.

Postage Due

A postage due piece is a piece of mail upon which there is an amount due from the addressee because the postage was not fully prepaid by the sender.

Postmark

A postmark is the impression placed on a letter or other piece of mail by a canceling machine or handstamp, to show office of origin or receipt, date, and the part of the day of receipt or dispatch.

Pouch

A locked mail bag, used principally in dispatching first-class mail.

Precanceled Stamps

Precanceled stamps are canceled by printing the name of the post office across the face of the stamps before they are sold to large mailers. This eliminates the canceling operation at time of mailing. Precanceled stamps may not be used on first-class matter unless specifically authorized. A Post Office permit is necessary for the use of such stamps.

Reading Card

A plastic card inserted in a bracket on a Mail-Flo tray to direct the tray through electronic devices to its destination.

Residue Case (or Route Case)

The mail case for distributing mail for small offices which do not appear on the primary or secondary cases.

Roller Canceler

A roller canceler is a type of stamp canceler used on first, second, third or fourth-class matter which cannot be cancelled by machine.

Rotary Lock

A rotary lock is a special brass lock for pouches containing registered mail. Such a lock registers the next higher number with each successive turn of the key.

Route

A route is a course laid out for the delivery or collection of mail.

Route Card

A route card is a card on file in the station showing the order in which the carrier route is served. In the case of a collection, it shows the order in which the boxes are tapped.

R. P. O.

R. P. O. is the abbreviation for Railway Post Office.

Run

This term is usually applied to a number of specials set up for delivery on one trip for a particular area.

Sacks

Used in transporting mail matter other than that of the first class. They come in various sizes and are numbered 0, 1, 2, 3, and 4. The smaller the number, the larger the sack.

Separation

A box, or pigeonhole, on a distribution case.

Short Paid

Short paid matter refers to insufficiently prepaid mail.

Skin Out

Skin-out means to "sweep" or withdraw mail from a separation case.

Slugs

A slug is a first-class piece either too bulky or too large to be postmarked on a canceling machine. It must be postmarked with a handstamp.

Swamp

A swamp occurs when collection mails are abnormally heavy and the collector cannot complete his route because his satchel is filled to capacity. Upon his return to the station or designated collection area he reports this condition to his supervisor or designated employee, who will make arrangements for the mail to be collected from the remaining collection boxes on the route.

Sweep

Sweep means to "skin out" or withdraw mail from a distribution case.

Swing Room

The swing room is the room where employees have their lunch, or spend their off-the-clock time immediately before or after their tours of duty.

Tie-Out

Tie-out is the expression used when tying bundles of letters or circulars for delivery or dispatch.

Throwbacks

Undeliverable mail that has been processed by carriers is brought to a "throw-back" case, where the carrier places the mail in the proper separation for further handling by clerks.

Tracer

The term tracer refers to the Form 1510 used to locate lost or undeliverable mail matter.

Transfer Office

Transfer offices are located at principal Railroad stations (for example Pennsylvania R.R. Station, Grand Central R.R. Station, etc.) where essential space on trains for the mails must be procured by transfer clerks.

Trip

A trip is one complete serving of a carrier route. To make a trip means to serve the patrons on a carrier route.

Tub

A tub is a piece of equipment for the separation of bulk parcel post mails. This equipment is known also as a hamper, and the extra large size tubs are known as "Oregons."

PRIVILEGED MATTER AND CONFIDENTIAL MATERIAL

311.6   Mail Matter

Furnish information concerning mail or mailing permits to postal inspectors and to the sender, the addressee, or the authorized representative of either on proper identification. Do not give such information to others. See 123.51 and 312.1 regarding correction of mailing lists.

114.3   Privileged Matter

The following records, documents, and information are privileged matter, and may not be disclosed by subordinate officers or employees of the Department without authorization:

a.   Reports of postal inspectors, except in discrimination cases arising under Executive Order 11246. (See 747.423 and 857.84)

b.   Records of the postal inspection service.

c.   Names of post office box holders.

d.   Names and addresses of post office patron and former patrons, except when correcting mailing lists or when furnishing changes of address to election boards or registration commissions as provided in 123.5. Information on change of address orders may be revealed to the American Red Cross during times of natural disaster, pursuant to 114.5.

e.   Records regarding mail matter.

f.   Records regarding postal saving accounts, except as provided in 173.33.

g.   Records regarding money orders.

843.36 <u>Confidential Information</u>

.361 The presence of a postal inspector at or in the vicinity of an office other than his official station shall not be revealed to postmasters or employees of other offices nor to any other person except as required in carrying out the inspector's instructions.

.362 Inquiries by postal inspectors shall be treated in confidence, and the fact of such inquiries shall not be disclosed except to those having the need to know.

PART SIX

Final Exam

6

POST OFFICE CLERK-CARRIER

SAMPLE EXAM IV

Plan on taking this Examination after you have done the testing, probing, and concentrated study which the earlier Examinations showed to be needed. If you have availed yourself of the Pinpoint Practice provided, you should find this Exam an excellent review and summary of all that you have learned. Your score here will give you a fair statement of where you stand. Certainly, it should be higher than your previous scores. If you're not satisfied, there's still time. Go back and review your weaker subjects. Then test yourself again. If you show improvement, you may congratulate yourself on having picked up a few more points on the actual exam.

Time allowed for the entire Examination: 1½ Hours

This includes the time for filling out forms as well as for reviewing instructions and trying out practice questions. The actual test time is 11 minutes.

In constructing this Examination we tried to visualize the questions you are *likely* to face on your actual exam. We included those subjects on which they are *probably* going to test you.

Although copies of past exams are not released, we were able to piece together a fairly complete picture of the forthcoming exam.

A principal source of information was our analysis of official announcements going back several years.

Critical comparison of these announcements, particularly the sample questions, revealed the testing trend; foretold the important subjects, and those that are likely to recur.

In making up the Tests we predict for your exam, great care was exercised to prepare questions having just the difficulty level you'll encounter on your exam. Not easier; not harder, but just what you may expect.

The various subjects expected on your exam are represented by separate Tests. Each Test has just about the number of questions you may find on the actual exam. And each Test is timed accordingly.

The questions on each Test are represented exactly on the special Answer Sheet provided. Mark your answers on this sheet. It's just about the way you'll have to do it on the real exam.

Correct answers for all the questions in all the Tests of this Exam appear at the end of the Exam.

ANSWER SHEET FOR VERISIMILAR EXAMINATION IV.

TEST I. ADDRESS CHECKING

TEST II. MEMORY FOR ADDRESSES

TEST I. ADDRESS CHECKING

TIME: 6 Minutes. 95 Questions.

DIRECTIONS: This is a test of your speed and accuracy in comparing addresses. Blacken the proper space under A in the Answer Sheet if the two addresses are exactly alike in every way. Blacken D if they are not alike in every way.

1	405 Winter Rd NW	405 Winter Rd NW
2	607 S Calaveras Rd	607 S Calaveras Rd
3	8406 La Casa St	8406 La Cosa St
4	121 N Rippon St	121 N Rippon St
5	Wideman Ark	Wiseman Ark
6	Sodus NY 14551	Sodus NY 14551
7	3429 Hermosa Dr	3429 Hermoso Dr
8	3628 S Zeeland St	3268 S Zeeland St
9	1330 Cheverly Ave NE	1330 Cheverly Ave NE
10	1689 N Derwood Dr	1689 N Derwood Dr
11	3886 Sunrise Ct	3886 Sunrise Ct
12	635 La Calle Mayor	653 La Calle Mayor
13	2560 Lansford Pl	2560 Lansford St
14	4631 Central Ave	4631 Central Ave
15	Mason City Iowa 50401	Mason City Iowa 50401
16	758 Los Arboles Ave SE	758 Los Arboles Ave SW
17	3282 E Downington St	3282 E Dunnington St
18	7117 N Burlingham Ave	7117 N Burlingham Ave
19	32 Oaklawn Blvd	32 Oakland Blvd
20	1274 Manzana Rd	1274 Manzana Rd
21	4598 E Kenilworth Dr	4598 E Kenilworth Dr
22	Dayton Okla 73449	Dagton Okla 73449
23	1172 W 83rd Ave	1127 W 83rd Ave
24	6434 E Pulaski St	6434 E Pulaski Ct
25	2764 N Rutherford Pl	2764 N Rutherford Pl
26	565 Greenville Blvd SE	565 Greenview Blvd SE
27	Washington D C 20013	Washington D C 20018
28	3824 Massasoit St	3824 Massasoit St
29	22 Sagnaw Pkwy	22 Saganaw Pkwy
30	Byram Conn 10573	Byram Conn 10573
31	1928 S Fairfield Ave	1928 S Fairfield St
32	36218 Overhills Dr	36218 Overhills Dr
33	516 Avenida de Las Americas NW	516 Avenida de Las Americas NW
34	7526 Naraganset Pl SW	7526 Naraganset Pl SW
35	52626 W Ogelsby Dr	52626 W Ogelsby Dr
36	1003 Winchester Rd	1003 Westchester Rd
37	3478 W Cavanaugh Ct	3478 W Cavenaugh Ct
38	Kendall Calif 90551	Kendell Calif 90551
39	225 El Camino Blvd	225 El Camino Ave
40	7310 Via de los Pisos	7310 Via de los Pinos
41	1987 Wellington Ave SW	1987 Wellington Ave SW
42	3124 S 71st St	3142 S 71st St
43	729 Lincolnwood Blvd	729 Lincolnwood Blvd
44	1166 N Beaumont Dr	1166 S Beaumont Dr
45	3224 W Winecona Pl	3224 W Winecona Pl
46	608 La Calle Bienvenida	607 La Calle Bienvenida
47	La Molte Iowa 52045	La Molte Iowa 52045

S1137

48 ...	8625 Armitage Ave NW	8625 Armitage Ave NW
49 ...	2343 Broadview Ave	2334 Broadview Ave
50 ...	4279 Sierra Grande Ave NE	4279 Sierra Grande Dr NE
51 ...	165 32d Ave	165 32d Ave
52 ...	12742 N Deerborn St	12724 N Deerborn St
53 ...	114 Estancia Ave	141 Estancia Ave
54 ...	351 S Berwyn Rd	351 S Berwyn Pl
55 ...	7732 Avenida Manana SW	7732 Avenida Manana SW
56 ...	6337 C St SW	6337 G St SW
57 ...	57895 E Drexyl Ave	58795 E Drexyl Ave
58 ...	Altro Tex 75923	Altra Tex 75923
59 ...	3465 S Nashville St	3465 N Nashville St
60 ...	1226 Odell Blvd NW	1226 Oddell Blvd NW
61 ...	94002 Chappel Ct	94002 Chappel Ct
62 ...	512 La Vega Dr	512 La Veta Dr
63 ...	8774 W Winona Pl	8774 E Winona Pl
64 ...	6431 Ingleside St SE	6431 Ingleside St SE
65 ...	2270 N Leanington St	2270 N Leanington St
66 ...	235 Calle de Los Vecinos	235 Calle de Los Vecinos
67 ...	3987 E Westwood Ave	3987 W Westwood Ave
68 ...	Skamokawa Wash	Skamohawa Wash
69 ...	2674 E Champlain Cir	2764 E Champlain Cir
70 ...	8751 Elmhurst Blvd	8751 Elmwood Blvd
71 ...	6649 Solano Dr	6649 Solana Dr
72 ...	4423 S Escenaba St	4423 S Escenaba St
73 ...	1198 N St NW	1198 M St NW
74 ...	Sparta Ga	Sparta Va
75 ...	96753 Wrightwood Ave	96753 Wrightwood Ave
76 ...	2445 Sangamow Ave SE	2445 Sangamow Ave SE
77 ...	5117 E 67 Pl	5171 E 67 Pl
78 ...	847 Mesa Grande Pl	847 Mesa Grande Ct
79 ...	1100 Cermaken St	1100 Cermaker St
80 ...	321 Tijeras Ave NW	321 Tijeras Ave NW
81 ...	3405 Prospect St	3405 Prospect St
82 ...	6643 Burlington Pl	6643 Burlingtown Pl
83 ...	851 Esperanza Blvd	851 Esperanza Blvd
84 ...	Jenkinjones W Va	Jenkinjones W Va
85 ...	1008 Pennsylvania Ave SE	1008 Pennsylvania Ave SW
86 ...	2924 26th St N	2929 26th St N
87 ...	7115 Highland Dr	7115 Highland Dr
88 ...	Chaptico Md	Chaptica Md
89 ...	3508 Camron Mills Rd	3508 Camron Mills Rd
90 ...	67158 Capston Dr	67158 Capston Dr
91 ...	3613 S Taylor Ave	3631 S Taylor Ave
92 ...	2421 Menokin Dr	2421 Menokin Dr
93 ...	3226 M St NW	3226 N St NW
94 ...	1201 S Court House Rd	1201 S Court House Rd
95 ...	Findlay Ohio 45840	Findley Ohio 45840

END OF PART

*If you finish before the allotted time is up, work on this part only.
When time is up, proceed directly to the next part and do not
return to this part.*

PRACTICE FOR MEMORIZING ADDRESSES

MEMORIZING TIME: 5 Minutes

DIRECTIONS: This is a test of memory, speed, and accuracy in which you will be given names, numbers, and addresses to remember. They are divided into five groups, boxed and lettered A, B, C, D, E. For each question, mark the Answer Sheet to show the letter of the box in which the item belongs. If you are not sure of an answer you should guess. Try to remember the box-location of as many items as you can.

A	B	C	D	E
1700–2599 Wood	2700–3299 Wood	1300–1699 Wood	3300–3599 Wood	2600–2699 Wood
Dushore	Jeriel	Levering	Bair	Danby
8500–8699 Lang	8700–9399 Lang	9400–9499 Lang	8000–8499 Lang	9500–9999 Lang
Lott	Vanna	Ekron	Viborg	Lycan
6200–6399 James	5700–6199 James	6400–6499 James	5000–5699 James	4700–4999 James

1. Jeriel
2. Dushore
3. 2700–3299 Wood
4. 5700–6199 James
5. Bair
6. 8700–9399 Lang
7. Dushore
8. 8000–8499 Lang

ADDITIONAL MEMORIZING TIME: 3 Minutes

DIRECTIONS: Cover the lettered boxes. Answer as best you can from memory.

9. 8000–8499 Lang
10. 2700–3299 Wood
11. 8500–8699 Lang
12. 1700–2599 Wood
13. 5700–6199 James
14. Lott
15. 1700–2599 Wood
16. 8500–8699 Lang

CORRECT ANSWERS FOR THE FOREGOING QUESTIONS.

1.B	3.B	5.D	7.A	9.D	11.A	13.B	15.A
2.A	4.B	6.B	8.D	10.B	12.A	14.A	16.A

NOTE: Be sure to memorize the addresses for the Practice Test, as instructed. In the past, the addresses learned for the Practice Test have been the same addresses used for the actual test.

TEST II. MEMORY FOR ADDRESSES

TIME: 5 Minutes. 88 Questions.

DIRECTIONS: *Having committed to memory the box-locations in the previous Memorizing test, you must now mark your Answer Sheet for each question to show the letter of the box in which the item belongs. Do not turn back to the lettered boxes in the previous Memorizing test. Answer as best you can from memory.*

Correct Answers are consolidated after the last question.

1. Jeriel
2. Dushore
3. 5000–5699 James
4. 1300–1699 Wood
5. 8500–8699 Lang
6. Bair
7. 5700–6199 James
8. Levering

25. 2700–3299 Wood
26. 5700–6199 James
27. Levering
28. 9500–9999 Lang
29. 2600–2699 Wood
30. 3300–3599 Wood
31. Viborg
32. 9400–9499 Lang

49. Bair
50. 8700–9399 Lang
51. 6200–6399 James
52. 9400–9499 Lang
53. Viborg
54. 8000–8499 Lang
55. 4700–4999 James
56. Lycan

73. Dushore
74. 8000–8499 Lang
75. Bair
76. Ekron
77. 6200–6399 James
78. 3300–3599 Wood
79. 8700–9399 Lang
80. Viborg

9. Danby
10. Viborg
11. 8000–8499 Lang
12. 2700–3299 Wood
13. 9400–9499 Lang
14. 3300–3599 Wood
15. 4700–4999 James
16. 9500–9999 Lang

33. Jeriel
34. Bair
35. 8500–8699 Lang
36. 1700–2599 Wood
37. 8000–8499 Lang
38. Danby
39. Ekron
40. 4700–4999 James

57. Vanna
58. Danby
59. 5700–6199 James
60. Lott
61. 2700–3299 Wood
62. 5000–5699 James
63. 1700–2599 Wood
64. 8000–8499 Lang

81. 4700–4999 James
82. Lycan
83. 1700–2599 Wood
84. 8500–8699 Lang
85. 1300–1699 Wood
86. Jeriel
87. Danby
88. 6400–6499 James

17. Ekron
18. 1300–1699 Wood
19. Vanna
20. Lycan
21. 8700–9399 Lang
22. Dushore
23. 6200–6399 James
24. Lott

41. Dushore
42. Vanna
43. 5000–5699 James
44. Lott
45. 1300–1699 Wood
46. Levering
47. 5700–6199 James
48. 9500–9999 Lang

65. 9400–9499 Lang
66. Jeriel
67. 9500–9999 Lang
68. Dushore
69. 2600–2699 Wood
70. 8500–8699 Lang
71. Levering
72. 5000–5699 James

STOP.

If you finish before the 5 minutes are up, go back and check your answers.

END OF EXAMINATION

CORRECT ANSWERS FOR SAMPLE EXAMINATION IV

*(Please make every effort to answer the questions on your own before look-
ing at these answers. You'll make faster progress by following this rule.)*

TEST I. ADDRESS CHECKING

1.A	13.D	25.A	37.D	49.D	61.A	73.D	85.D
2.A	14.A	26.D	38.D	50.D	62.D	74.D	86.D
3.D	15.A	27.D	39.D	51.A	63.D	75.A	87.A
4.A	16.D	28.A	40.D	52.D	64.A	76.A	88.D
5.D	17.D	29.D	41.A	53.D	65.A	77.D	89.A
6.A	18.A	30.A	42.D	54.D	66.A	78.D	90.A
7.D	19.D	31.D	43.A	55.A	67.D	79.D	91.D
8.D	20.A	32.A	44.D	56.D	68.D	80.A	92.A
9.A	21.A	33.A	45.A	57.D	69.D	81.A	93.D
10.A	22.D	34.A	46.D	58.D	70.D	82.D	94.A
11.A	23.D	35.A	47.A	59.D	71.D	83.A	95.D
12.D	24.D	36.D	48.A	60.D	72.A	84.A	

TEST II. MEMORY FOR ADDRESSES

1.B	12.B	23.A	34.D	45.C	56.E	67.E	78.D
2.A	13.C	24.A	35.A	46.C	57.B	68.A	79.B
3.D	14.D	25.B	36.A	47.B	58.E	69.E	80.D
4.C	15.E	26.B	37.D	48.E	59.B	70.A	81.E
5.A	16.E	27.C	38.E	49.D	60.A	71.C	82.E
6.D	17.C	28.E	39.C	50.B	61.B	72.D	83.A
7.B	18.C	29.E	40.E	51.A	62.D	73.A	84.A
8.C	19.B	30.D	41.A	52.C	63.A	74.D	85.C
9.E	20.E	31.D	42.B	53.D	64.D	75.D	86.B
10.D	21.B	32.C	43.D	54.D	65.C	76.C	87.E
11.D	22.A	33.B	44.A	55.E	66.B	77.A	88.C

MORE ARCO BOOKS

Perhaps you've discovered that you are weak in language, verbal ability or mathematics. Why flounder and fail when help is so easily available? Brush up in the privacy of your own home with one of our review books.

At the same time, choose from our wide range of hobby and general interest books, designed to entertain and inform you in whatever area you select.

Each of the following books was created under the same expert editorial supervision that produced the excellent book you are now using. Whatever your goals or interests. . . you can learn more and score higher on tests with Arco.

CIVIL SERVICE AND TEST PREPARATION—GENERAL

Able Seaman, Deckhand, Scowman	01376-1	5.00
Accountant—Auditor	00001-5	8.00
Addiction Specialist, Senior, Supervising, Principal	03351-7	8.00
Administrative Assistant—Principal Administrative Associate	00148-8	8.00
Administrative Manager	04813-1	8.00
Air Traffic Controller, Morrison	04593-0	10.00
American Foreign Service Officer	04219-2	8.00
Apprentice, Mechanical Trades	00571-8	6.00
Arco's High School Civil Service Course, Gitlin	00702-8	6.95
Assistant Accountant	00056-2	8.00
Assistant Civil Engineer	01228-5	8.00
Assistant Station Supervisor	03736-9	6.00
Associate and Administrative Accountant	03863-2	8.00
Attorney, Assistant—Trainee	01084-3	10.00
Auto Machinist	04379-2	8.00
Auto Mechanic, Autoserviceman	00514-9	8.00
Bank Examiner—Trainee and Assistant	01642-6	5.00
Battalion and Deputy Chief, F.D.	00515-7	6.00
Beginning Office Worker	04849-2	8.00
Beverage Control Investigator	00150-X	4.00
Bookkeeper—Account Clerk	00035-X	8.00
Bridge and Tunnel Officer—Special Officer	00780-X	5.00
Building Custodian	00013-9	8.00
Bus Maintainer—Bus Mechanic	00111-9	8.00
Bus Operator	01553-5	5.00
Buyer, Assistant Buyer, Purchase Inspector	01366-4	6.00
Captain, Police Department	00184-4	10.00
Carpenter	00135-6	6.00
Case Worker	04979-0	8.00
Cashier, Housing Teller	00703-6	8.00
Cement Mason—Mason's Helper	03745-8	6.00
Chemist—Assistant Chemist	00116-X	5.00
City Planner	01364-8	6.00
Civil Engineer, Senior, Associate, & Administrative	00146-1	8.00
Civil Service Arithmetic and Vocabulary	04872-7	6.00
Teacher's Manual for Civil Service Course, Gitlin	03838-1	2.00
Claim Examiner Investigator	00149-6	8.00
Clerk New York City	00045-7	4.00
Clerk—Steno Transcriber	00838-5	6.00
College Office Assistant	00181-X	5.00
Complete Guide to U.S. Civil Service Jobs	05245-7	4.00
Construction Foreman and Supervisor—Inspector	01085-1	8.00
Consumer Affairs Inspector	01356-7	6.00
Correction Captain—Deputy Warden	01358-3	8.00
Correction Officer	00186-0	8.00
Court Officer	00519-X	8.00
Criminal Law Handbook for Law Enforcement Officers, Salottolo	02399-6	12.00
Criminal Science Handbook, Salottolo	02407-0	5.00
Detective Investigator	03738-5	8.00
Dietitian	00083-X	8.00
Draftsman, Civil and Mechanical Engineering (All Grades)	01225-0	6.00
Electrical Engineer	00137-2	10.00
Electrical Inspector	03350-9	8.00
Electrician	00084-8	8.00
Electronic Equipment Maintainer	01836-4	8.00
Employment Interviewer	00008-2	8.00
Employment Security Clerk	00700-1	6.00
Engineering Technician (All Grades)	01226-9	8.00
Exterminator Foreman—Foreman of Housing Exterminators	03740-7	6.00
File Clerk	04377-6	6.00
Fire Administration and Technology	00604-8	10.00
Firefighter, F.D. McGannon	05170-1	8.00
Firefighting Hydraulics, Bonadio	00572-6	8.00
Food Service Supervisor—School Lunch Manager	04819-0	8.00
Foreman	00191-7	8.00
Foreman of Auto Mechanics	01360-5	6.00
Gardener, Assistant Gardener	01340-0	8.00
General Entrance Series	01961-1	4.00
General Test Practice for 101 U.S. Jobs	05246-5	6.00
Guard—Patrolman	00122-4	6.00
Homestudy Course for Civil Service Jobs	01587-X	8.00
Hospital Attendant	00012-0	6.00
Hospital Care Investigator Trainee (Social Case Worker I)	01674-4	5.00
Hospital Security Officer	03866-7	6.00
Housing Assistant	00054-6	5.00
Housing Caretaker	00504-1	4.00
Housing Inspector	00055-4	5.00
Housing Manager—Assistant Housing Manager	00813-X	5.00
Housing Patrolman	00192-5	5.00
How to Pass Employment Tests, Liebers	00715-X	6.00
Internal Revenue Agent	00093-7	5.00
Investigator—Inspector	01670-1	10.00
Junior Federal Assistant	01729-5	6.00
Laboratory Aide	01121-1	8.00
Landscape Architect	01368-0	5.00
Laundry Worker	01834-8	4.00
Law and Court Stenographer	00783-4	8.00
Law Enforcement Positions	00500-9	8.00
Librarian	00060-0	10.00
Lieutenant, F.D.	00123-2	10.00
Lieutenant, P.D.	00190-9	10.00
Machinist—Machinist's Helper	04933-2	6.00
Mail Handler—U.S. Postal Service	05247-3	6.00
Maintainer's Helper, Group A and C— Transit Electrical Helper	00175-5	6.00
Maintenance Man	04349-0	6.00
Management Analyst, Assistant—Associate	03864-0	8.00
Mathematics, Simplified and Self-Taught	00567-X	5.95
Mechanical Apprentice (Maintainer's Helper B)	00176-3	5.00
Mechanical Aptitude and Spatial Relations Tests	00539-4	6.00
Mechanical Engineer—Junior, Assistant & Senior Grades	03314-2	8.00
Mortuary Caretaker	01354-0	6.00
Motor Vehicle License Examiner	00018-X	8.00
Motor Vehicle Operator	00576-9	4.00
Motorman (Subways)	00061-9	6.00
Nurse	05248-1	6.00
Office Aide	04704-6	8.00
Office Assistant GS 2-4	04275-3	8.00
Office Associate	04855-7	8.00
Office Machines Operator	00728-1	4.00
1540 Questions and Answers for Electricians	00754-0	5.00
1340 Questions and Answers for Firefighters, McGannon	00857-1	6.00
Painter	01772-4	5.00
Parking Enforcement Agent	00701-X	4.00
Patrol Inspector	04301-6	8.00
Personnel Examiner, Junior Personnel Examiner	00648-X	8.00
Plumber—Plumber's Helper	00517-3	6.00
Police Administration and Criminal Investigation	00563-3	10.00
Police Administrative Aide	02345-7	5.00
Police Officer, Murray	05130-2	6.95
Police Science Advancement	02636-7	15.00
Policewoman	00062-7	6.00
Post Office Clerk-Carrier	04846-8	6.00

Postal Inspector	00194-1	5.00
Postal Promotion Foreman—Supervisor	00538-6	6.00
Postmaster	01522-5	5.00
Practice for Civil Service Promotion	00023-6	8.00
Practice for Clerical, Typing and Stenographic Tests	04297-4	6.00
Principal Clerk—Stenographer	01523-3	8.00
Probation and Parole Officer	04203-6	8.00
Professional and Administrative Career Examination (PACE)	04852-2	6.00
Professional Careers Test	01543-8	8.00
Public Health Sanitarian	00985-3	8.00
Railroad Clerk	00067-8	4.00
Railroad Porter	00128-3	4.00
Real Estate Assessor—Appraiser—Manager	00563-7	10.00
Resident Building Superintendent	00068-6	5.00
Road Car Inspector (T.A.)	03743-1	8.00
Sanitation Foreman (Foreman & Asst. Foreman)	01958-1	6.00
Sanitation Man	00025-2	4.00
School Crossing Guard	00611-0	4.00
Senior Clerical Series	01173-4	8.00
Senior Clerk—Stenographer	01797-X	9.00
Senior File Clerk	00124-0	8.00
Senior and Supervising Parking Enforcement Agent	03737-7	6.00
Senior Typist	03870-5	6.00
Sergeant, P.D.	00026-0	10.00
Shop Clerk	03684-2	6.00
Social Supervisor	04190-0	8.00
Staff Attendant	LR 01739-2	6.50
Staff Positions: Senior Administrative Associate and Assistant	03490-4	6.00
State Trooper	05234-1	8.00
Stenographer—Typist (Practical Preparation)	00147-X	6.00
Stenographer—U.S. Government Positions GS 2-7	04388-1	6.00
Storekeeper—Stockman (Senior Storekeeper)	01691-4	8.00
Structural Apprentice	00177-1	5.00
Structure Maintainer Trainee, Groups A to E	03683-4	6.00
Supervising Clerk (Income Maintenance)	02879-3	5.00

Supervising Clerk—Stenographer	04309-1	6.00
Supervision Course	01590-X	8.00
Surface Line Dispatcher	00140-2	6.00
Tabulating Machine Operator (IBM)	00781-8	4.00
Taking Tests and Scoring High, Honig	01347-8	4.00
Telephone Maintainer: New York City Transit Authority	03742-3	5.00
Test Your Vocational Aptitude, Asta & Bernbach	03606-0	6.00
Towerman (Municipal Subway System)	00157-7	5.00
Trackman (Municipal Subways)	00075-9	5.00
Track Foreman: New York City Transit Authority	03739-3	6.00
Traffic Control Agent	03421-1	5.00
Train Dispatcher	00158-3	5.00
Transit Patrolman	00092-9	5.00
Transit Sergeant—Lieutenant	00161-5	4.00
Treasury Enforcement Agent	00131-3	8.00
U.S. Postal Service Motor Vehicle Operator	04426-8	8.00
U.S. Professional Mid-Level Positions Grades GS-9 Through GS-12	02036-9	6.00
U.S. Summer Jobs	02480-1	4.00
Ventilation and Drainage Maintainer: New York City Transit Authority	03741-5	6.00
Vocabulary Builder and Guide to Verbal Tests	00535-1	5.95
Vocabulary, Spelling and Grammar	00077-5	5.00
Welder	01374-5	8.00
X-Ray Technician (See Radiologic Technology Exam Review)	03833-0	8.00

MILITARY EXAMINATION SERIES

Practice for Air Force Placement Tests	04270-2	6.00
Practice for Army Classification and Placement (ASVAB)	03845-4	8.00
Practice for the Armed Forces Tests	05303-8	6.00
Practice for Navy Placement Tests	04560-4	6.00
Practice for Officer Candidate Tests	01304-4	6.00
Tests for Women in the Armed Forces	03821-7	6.00
U.S. Service Academies	01544-6	6.00

HIGH SCHOOL AND COLLEGE PREPARATION

American College Testing Program	05151-5	6.95
Arco Arithmetic Q & A Review	02351-1	5.00
Arco's Handbook of Job and Career Opportunities	04328-8	3.95
Basic Grammar Guide: Beginning Practice for Competency and Proficiency Exams, Pastva	05250-3	4.95
Basic Grammar Guide: Intermediate Practice for Competency and Proficiency Exams, Pastva	05273-2	4.95
Basic Grammar Guide: Advanced Practice for Competency and Proficiency Exams, Pastva	05294-5	4.95
Better Business English, Classen	04287-7	2.95
California High School Proficiency Examination	04412-8	6.00
Catholic High School Entrance Examinations	04844-1	6.00
The College Board's Examination, McDonough & Hansen	02623-5	6.00
College By Mail, Jensen	02592-1	4.00
CLEP: The Five General Examinations	05143-4	6.95
College, Yes or No?, Shanahan	04911-1	6.95
The Easy Way to Better Grades, Froe & Froe	03352-5	2.95
Elements of Debate, Klopf & McCroskey	01901-8	5.00
Encyclopedia of English, Zeiger	00655-X	3.95
English Grammar: 1,000 Steps	02012-1	6.00
English Grammar and Usage for Test-Takers	04014-9	6.00
The Florida Literacy Test, Morrison	04669-4	4.95
The Freshman's Handbook, Osgood	05309-7	2.95
Good English with Ease, revised edition, Beckoff	03911-6	6.00
Graph, Chart and Table Interpretation for Test-Takers	04817-4	8.00
Guide to Financial Aids for Students in Arts and Sciences for Graduate and Professional Study, Searles & Scott	02496-8	3.95

High School Entrance Examinations, Robinson	05155-8	6.50
High School Entrance Examinations—Special Public and Private High Schools	04861-1	5.00
How to Enjoy Calculus, Pine	04951-0	4.95
How to Obtain Money for College, Lever	03932-9	5.00
How to Prepare Your College Application, Kussin & Kussin	01310-9	2.00
How to Use a Pocket Calculator, Mullish	04072-6	4.95
How to Write Reports, Papers, Theses, Articles, Riebel	02391-0	6.00
Letter-Perfect: The Accurate Secretary, Gilson	04038-6	8.00
Mastering General Mathematics, McDonough	03732-6	5.00
Matematicas: Repaso Para El Examen de Equivalencia de la Escuela Superior en Espanol (Mathematics: Review for the Spanish High School Equivalency Test), Acosta & Calvo	04821-2	5.00
Mathematics Workbook for the SAT, Saunders	04820-4	6.00
National Career Directory	04510-8	5.95
New York State Regents Scholarship	00400-2	5.00
Organization and Outlining, Peirce	02425-9	4.95
Page-A-Day™ Study Guide for Competency-Based Tests, Bennett & Chang	05284-8	4.95
Page-A-Day™ S.A.T. Study Guide, Bennett & Chang	05196-5	4.95
The Parent—Student College Planning Guide, Shanahan	04996-0	6.95
Preliminary Scholastic Aptitude Tests—National Merit Scholarship Qualifying Test (PSAT-NMSQT), Steinberg	04980-4	6.00
Practice for Scholastic Aptitude Tests	04303-2	1.50
Regents Competency Tests, Forbes & DeBease	04815-8	6.95

Scholastic Aptitude Tests 04920-0 6.95
Scoring High On College Entrance Tests 01858-5 5.00
Scoring High On Reading Tests 00731-1 5.00
Student's Career Guide to a Future in the Allied
   Health Professions, Ilk 04921-9 6.95
Test of Standard Written English (TSWE),
   Arco Editorial Board 04748-8 3.95
Total Math Review for the GMAT, GRE and Other Graduate
   School Admission Tests, Frieder 04981-2 8.00
Triple Your Reading Speed, Cutler 02083-0 5.00
Typing for Everyone, Levine 04975-8 6.95
Verbal Workbook for the SAT,
   Freedman & Haller 04853-0 6.00

GED PREPARATION

Basic Mathematics, Castellano & Seitz 05126-4 5.00
Basic Skills in Writing, Kindilien 05264-3 4.95
Comprehensive Math Review for the High School
   Equivalency Diploma Test, McDonough 03420-3 4.00
New High School Equivalency Diploma Tests 04451-9 5.95
Preliminary Arithmetic for the High School Equivalency
   Diploma Test 02165-9 5.00
Preliminary Practice for the High School Equivalency
   Diploma Test 01441-5 6.00
Preparation for the Spanish High School Equivalency
   Diploma (Preparacion Para El Examen De Equivalencia
   De La Escuela Superior—En Espanol),
   Lanzano, Abreu, Ringel, Banks & Sagrista 05095-0 6.95
Step-By-Step Guide to Correct English, Pulaski 03402-5 3.95

General Education Development Series

Correctness and Effectiveness of Expression (English HSEDT),
   Castellano, Guercio & Seitz 03688-5 4.00
General Mathematical Ability (Mathematics HSEDT),
   Castellano, Guercio & Seitz 03689-3 6.00
Reading Interpretation in Social Sciences, Natural Sciences,
   and Literature (Reading HSEDT), Castellano,
   Guercio & Seitz 03690-7 5.00
Teacher's Manual for GED Series, Castellano
   Guercio, & Seitz 03692-3 2.50

COLLEGE BOARD ACHIEVEMENT TESTS/CBAT

American History and Social Studies Achievement Test—
   Second Edition 04337-7 5.95
Biology Achievement Test—Second Edition,
   Solomon & Spector 04094-7 3.95
Chemistry Achievement Test 04101-3 3.95
English Composition Achievement Test 04338-5 5.95
German Achievement Test, Greiner 01698-1 1.45
Mathematics: Level I Achievement Test, Bramson 05319-4 3.00
CBAT Mathematics Level II, Bramson 04284-2 4.95
Spanish Achievement Test, Jassey 01741-4 1.45

ARCO COLLEGE OUTLINES

American History to 1877 . . . . 04726-7 3.95
American History from 1877 . . . . 04730-5 3.95
World History Part I 04729-1 3.95
World History Part II 04731-3 3.95

ARCO SCHOLARSHIP EXAMINATION SERIES

AP

Advanced Placement Music, Seligson-Ross 04743-7 4.95

AP/CBAT

Advanced Placement and College Board
   Achievement Tests in Physics (B-C),
   Arco Editorial Board 04493-4 6.95

AP/CLEP

Advanced Placement and College Level Examinations in
   American History, Woloch 03804-7 5.95
Advanced Placement and College Level Examinations in
   Biology, Arco Editorial Board 04415-2 5.95
Advanced Placement and College Level Examinations in
   Chemistry 04484-5 4.95
Advanced Placement and College Level Examinations in
   English—Analysis and Interpretation of Literature . . 04406-3 4.95

AP/CLEP/CBAT

Advanced Placement, College Level Examinations and
   College Board Achievement Tests In European
   History 04407-1 5.95

CLEP

College Level Examination in Composition and Freshman
   English 03798-9 4.95

College Level Examination Program 04150-1 6.00

College Level Examination Program:
   The General Examination in the Humanities 04727-5 6.95

College Level Examinations in Mathematics: College
   Algebra, College Algebra-Trigonometry,
   Trigonometry 04339-3 5.95

MEDICINE

MEDICAL REVIEW BOOKS

Basic Dental Sciences Review, DeMarco 03396-7 10.00
Basic Science Nursing Review, Cheatham,
   Fitzsimmons, Lessner, King, Lafferty,
   DePace & Blumenstein 05133-7 8.00
Biochemistry Review, Silverman 04359-8 12.00
Clinical Dental Sciences Review, DeMarco 03383-5 10.00
Comprehensive Medical Boards Examination Review,
   second revised edition, Horemis 01595-0 8.00
Dental Assistants Examination Review, Hirsch 03902-7 9.00
Dental Hygiene Examination Review, Armstrong 04283-4 10.00

Endocrinology Review, Hsu 04228-1 12.00
General Pathology Review, Lewis & Kerwin 04774-7 10.00
Histology and Embryology Review, Amenta 03831-4 8.00
Human Anatomy Review, Montgomery & Singleton 03368-1 8.00
Human Physiology Examination Review, Shepard 04826-3 12.00
Internal Medicine Review, Pieroni 03881-0 11.00
Medical Assistants Examination Review, second edition,
   Clement 04854-9 10.00
Medical Examinations: A Preparation Guide, Bhardwaj . . 03944-2 9.00
Medical Technology Examination Review, Hossaini 04365-2 10.00
Microbiology and Immunology Review, Second edition,
   Rothfield, Ward & Tilton 04882-4 10.00

Neuroscience and Clinical Neurology Review, Goldblatt . 03370-3 10.00
Nuclear Medicine Technology
    Examination Review, Spies 04724-0 12.00
Obstretrics and Gynecology Review, Second edition,
    Vontver 03450-5 9.00
Patient Management Problems:
    Obstetrics and Gynecology, DeCherney 04364-4 8.00
Patient Management Problems:
    Pediatrics, Howell & Simon 04780-1 10.00
Patient Management Problems: Surgery, Rosenberg 04654-6 8.00
Pediatrics Review, Second edition, Lorin 03375-4 8.00
Pharmacology Review, Ellis 04108-0 10.00
Pharmacy Review, Second edition, Singer 04878-6 12.00
Physical Medicine and Rehabilitation
    Review, Schuchmann 04723-2 15.00
Physician's Assistant Examination Review,
    Aschenbrener 04026-2 12.00
Psychiatry Examination Review—Second Edition,
    Easson 03395-9 8.00
Psychiatry: Patient Management Review, Easson 04058-0 8.00
Public Health and Preventive Medicine Review 04690-2 9.00
Pulmonary Disease Review, Hall 04008-4 12.00
Radiologic Technology Examination Review,
    Naidech & Damon 03833-0 8.00
Specialty Board Review: Anatomic Pathology,
    Gravanis & Johnson 03858-6 14.00
Specialty Board Review: Anesthesiology, Beach 04112-9 14.00
Specialty Board Review: Family Practice,
    Bhardwaj & Yen 03943-4 12.00
Specialty Board Review: General Surgery,
    Rob & Hinshaw 03494-7 12.00
Specialty Board Review: Internal Medicine, Pieroni 04818-2 14.00
Specialty Board Review: Obstetrics and
    Gynecology, Williams 03477-7 14.00
Specialty Board Review: Psychiatry, Atkins 03471-8 12.00
Surgery Review, Kountz et al 03880-2 8.00
Systemic Pathology Review, Lewis & Kerwin 04930-8 12.00

MEDIBOOKS

Fundamentals of Radiation Therapy, Lowry 03462-9 7.50
Midwifery, Hallum 03460-2 5.50
Pathology, Mayers 04774-7 6.00

Principles of Intensive Care, Emery, Yates & Moorhead . 03461-0 6.00

MEDICAL TEXTBOOKS AND MANUALS

The Basis of Clinical Diagnosis, Parkins & Pegrum 03660-5 12.95
Differential Diagnosis in Gynecology,
    Vontver & Gamette 04129-3 12.00
Differential Diagnosis in Neurology, Smith 04033-5 14.00
Differential Diagnosis in Obstetrics, Williams
    & Joseph 04161-7 10.00
Differential Diagnosis in Disorders of the Eye,
    Kupfer & Kaiser-Kupfer 04315-6 10.00
Differential Diagnosis in Otolaryngology, Lee 04017-2 14.00
Differntial Diagnosis of Renal and Electrolyte Disorders,
    Klahr 04063-7 14.00
The Effective Scutboy, Harrell & Firestein 05159-0 7.50
Emergency Medicine, Hocutt .04983-9 12.00
Hospital-Based Education, Linton & Truelove 04776-3 10.00
Modern Medicine, Read et al .04124-2 14.75
Psychiatry: A Concise Textbook for Primary
    Care Practitioners, Kraft et al 03924-8 12.00
Simplified Mathematics for Nurses,
    McElroy, Carr & Carr 04197-8 5.00

NURSING REVIEW BOOKS

Arco's Comprehensive State Board
    Examination Review for Nurses, Carter 04925-1 8.95
Child Health Nursing Review, Second edition, Porter . . .04825-5 7.00
Fundamentals of Nursing Review, Carter 04512-4 6.00
Maternal Health Nursing Review, Second edition,
    Sagebeer 04822-0 6.00
Medical-Surgical Nursing Examination Review,
    Second edition, Horemis & Matamors 02511-5 6.00
Medical-Surgical Nursing Review, Second edition,
    Hazzard 04823-9 6.00
Nursing Comprehensive Examination Review,
    second revised edition, Horemis 02499-2 6.00
Nursing Exam Review in Basic Sciences,
    Horemis & Matamors 02946-3 4.00
Practical Nursing Review, Second edition, Redempta . . .04827-1 7.50
Practice Tests for the L.P.N., Crow & Lounsbury 05189-2 7.50
Psychiatric/Mental Health Nursing Review,
    Second Edition, Rodgers & McGovern 04824-7 6.00

PROFESSIONAL CAREER EXAM SERIES

Action Guide for Executive Job Seekers and Employers,
    Uris 01787-2 3.95
Air Traffic Controller, Morrison 04593-0 10.00
The Anatomy of Arson, French . . . . LR 04423-3 12.50
Arson: A Handbook of Detection and
    Investigation, Battle & Weston . . . . LR 04532-9 9.95
Automobile Mechanic Certification Tests, Sharp 03809-8 6.00
Bar Exams 01124-6 5.00
Careers for the Community College Graduate,
    Chernow & Chernow 05091-8 5.95
Certificate In Data Processing
    Examination, Morrison 04922-7 12.00
The C.P.A. Exam: Accounting by the "Parallel Point"
    Method, Lipscomb . . . . LR 01103-3 25.00
Computer Programmer Analyst Trainee, Luftig 05310-0 8.00
Computers and Automation, Brown 01745-7 5.95
Computers and Data Processing Examinations:
    CDP/CCP/CLEP 04670-8 10.00
Dental Admission Test, Eighth ed.,
    Arco Editorial Board 05313-5 6.00
Graduate Management Admission Test 04914-6 6.95
Graduate Record Examination Aptitude Test 04910-3 6.95

Health Insurance Agent, Snouffer 04307-5 8.00
Health Profession Careers In Medicine's
    New Technology, Nassif 04436-5 5.95
How a Computer System Works, Brown & Workman . . .03424-6 5.95
How to Become a Successful Model—Second Edition,
    Krem 04508-6 2.95
How to Get into Medical and Dental School, revised
    edition, Shugar, Shugar, Bauman & Bauman 05112-4 6.95
How to Make Money in Music, Harris & Farrar 04089-0 5.95
How to Remember Anything, Markoff, Dubin & Carcel . .03929-9 5.00
How to Write Successful Business Letters,
    Riebel 02290-6 5.00
The Installation and Servicing of Domestic
    Oil Burners, Mitchell & Mitchell 00437-1 10.00
Instrument Pilot Examination, Morrison 04592-2 9.95
Law School Admission Test, Candrilli & Slawsky 05153-1 6.95
Life Insurance Agent, Snouffer 04306-7 8.00
Medicine's New Technology, Nassif . . . . LR 04443-8 9.95
Miller Analogies Test 04990-1 5.00
Modern Police Service Encyclopedia, Salottolo 02389-9 8.00
National Career Directory, Gale & Gale 04510-8 5.95
The New Medical College Admission Test 04551-5 6.95